The Book of
EXECUTIONS

The Book of
EXECUTIONS

James Bland

WARNER BOOKS

A *Warner* Book

First published in the United Kingdom
in 1993 by Warner

A CIP catalogue record for this book is
available from the British Library

ISBN 0 7515 0365 7

Typeset by Solidus (Bristol) Limited
Printed and bound in Great Britain by
Clays Ltd, St Ives plc

Warner
A division of
Little, Brown and Company (UK) Limited
165 Great Dover Street
London SE1 4YA

Contents

Preface

This is a collection of stories, anecdotes and facts about the death penalty from many countries. Its contents include detailed accounts of many dramatic cases, some so strange as to be almost beyond belief. They have been assembled without any framework of theory and without any discussion of the pros and cons of capital punishment.

There are ghastly scenes, with desperate struggles for survival and horrifying accidents. Bizarre customs are described, amazing ironies recounted. There are also brief sketches of the lives of a number of executioners, including some of the strangest on record.

In writing this book, my sole purpose has been to present a personal selection of cases in a concise and factual manner. I have not been tempted to emulate either the frivolity of Geoffrey Abbott's *Lords of the Scaffold* (Robert Hale, 1991) or the sneeringly moralistic tone of Brian Bailey's *Hangmen of England* (W.H. Allen, 1989). Indeed, I find both attitudes quite distasteful.

The Book of Executions will, I hope, appeal to all readers who are interested in crime and punishment, particularly those with a penchant for curious facts. Some, no doubt, will find it odd that I should write at length about the death penalty without declaring myself for or against it. But perhaps they will find the book absorbing just the same.

As far as I am concerned, the design of the book is such

that my views would be out of place in it, and I do not want to give them gratuitously. Should I, at some stage, feel impelled to make them known, then I hope I will be able to find a more suitable way to do so.

For the benefit of other researchers, I have given a list of sources for each chapter, except where I have drawn upon information used in one of my other books – either *The Common Hangman* (Ian Henry Publications, 1984) or *Crime Strange But True* (Futura Publications, 1991). Both of these give full details of contemporary sources, so there is no need for me to list them again.

J.B.

1

Some Facts

The death penalty around the world

Well over a hundred countries retain the death penalty, some using it for a wide range of crimes while others never actually use it at all. The main forms of execution in force today are shooting, hanging, beheading, stoning, electrocution, the gas chamber and death by lethal injection. The crime most commonly punishable by death is murder.

China has many capital offences and has carried out a great many executions in recent years. A major nationwide campaign to reduce the country's crime rate began in 1983, with the shooting of thousands of criminals, many of whom were paraded at mass rallies before being put to death: some estimates of the number of executions between 1983 and 1987 have been as high as 30,000. In 1990, China admitted executing 700 people in one year, but Amnesty International, the London-based human rights group, said it believed the true figure to be much higher.

The Soviet Union reintroduced the death penalty in 1950, having abolished it three years earlier. In January 1991, it published statistics showing that its use of this form of punishment was far greater than had previously been thought. Soviet courts, it revealed, had sentenced 770 people to death in 1985 (twenty were pardoned); 526 in 1986 (forty-one pardoned); 344 in 1987 (forty-seven pardoned); 271 in

1988 (seventy-two pardoned), and 276 in 1989 (twenty-three pardoned). The Soviet Justice Ministry said that most of these death sentences were passed for premeditated murder or rape.

A few months after these figures were published, Anatoli Kononov, a member of the Russian Parliament's Human Rights Committee, claimed that the USSR had executed over 21,000 people between 1962 and 1989, and was still passing more death sentences than any other country. The claim was made in an article in the *Nezavisimaya Gazeta* newspaper in September 1991.

Other countries known to have carried out large numbers of executions in recent years include **Iran**, **Iraq**, **South Africa** and **Nigeria**. According to Amnesty International's 1989 report, *When the State Kills*, Iran executed at least 743 people between the beginning of 1985 and the middle of 1988, during which period China's total was at least 500, South Africa's was at least 537, and Nigeria's at least 439. During the same three and a half years, Amnesty received reports from Iraq of hundreds of executions a year, but was unable to obtain precise figures and could not always ascertain whether the victims had been convicted of capital offences or executed extrajudicially.

A more recent report from Amnesty, in December 1990, accused **Iran** of executing 5000 people in the previous three years, saying that the Iranian Government was 'apparently intoxicated with the death penalty'. Many of these executions were for drug-trafficking offences, with 1100 alleged traffickers being executed during one six-month period in 1989, said Amnesty. The state-run Tehran Radio dismissed the report as unfounded.

Since 1979, executions been carried out in public in at least eighteen countries: **Cameroon**, **China**, **Gabon**, **Iran**,

Iraq, Kuwait, Liberia, Libya, Mauritania, Nigeria, Pakistan, Saudi Arabia, Somalia, Sudan, Syria, Uganda, the United Arab Emirates and the Yemen Arab Republic.

Known mass executions include one instance of forty-five prisoners shot by police officers outside the city of Zhengzhou, in China, on 23 September 1983. Watched by crowds of spectators, the condemned were all tied to numbered wooden stakes to be executed together, each having his own executioner. They were shot in the head at close range, as is customary in China.

Some executions in Libya have been televised, including those of a number of people hanged at Tripoli University in 1984. One of the prisoners, a student named al-Sadeq Al-Shuwayhdi, was shown pleading for mercy before a crowd in a sports stadium before being put to death on a makeshift scaffold. Nine other executions – three shootings and six hangings – were televised in 1987. The condemned had all been accused of politically-motivated crimes.

Gabon, which rarely uses the death penalty, televised a triple execution in December 1982. The condemned, who were all convicted murderers, were shot by firing squad on Libreville beach. A crowd of several thousand people attended the executions.

In July 1986, it was reported that prisoners sentenced to die by firing squad in Nigeria's central Niger State were being executed in a cruel and protracted manner. By order of the State's Military Governor, repeated volleys were being used, the first fired at the prisoners' ankles, with subsequent ones directed progressively higher, at five-minute intervals, until they died. A state official was quoted as saying that the aim of this prolongation of suffering was to make the condemned pay dearly for his crime and deter other criminals.

In January 1985, Mahmoud Mohamed Taha, the seventy-six-year-old leader of a moderate religious group called the Republican Brothers, was hanged before a large crowd in the courtyard of Khartoum's Kober Prison, for opposing the imposition of Islamic law in **Sudan**. After being forced to watch the proceedings, four supporters who had been condemned with him repented – apparently in accordance with Taha's own wishes – and were spared. Taha's execution was carried out in defiance of a law prohibiting the execution of anyone over the age of seventy.

Executions in Sudan ceased following the overthrow of President Numeiri in April 1985, but death sentences continued to be imposed. In October 1987, hangings were resumed and in August 1990 two men, Hamid Suliman and Arguci Turgawi Gareeb, were reported to have been crucified in western Sudan for armed robbery. They had both been convicted six years earlier.

Executions in the **Yemen Arab Republic** are carried out in public, by beheading with a sword or by shooting by a firing squad (except for certain sexual offenders, who are put to death by stoning). In cases of aggravated robbery, the culprit may be crucified after death for up to three days.

Stoning is prescribed by law for certain offences in a number of countries, though not all of them carry out executions of this type. In those that do, the procedure seems to vary. Generally, the condemned is partially buried in the ground, either up to his neck or up to his waist, and then pelted with stones until he dies. In **Iran** the Islamic

Penal Code states that the stones used 'should not be too large so that the person dies on being hit by one or two of them' and not so small 'that they could not be defined as stones'.

In one case of stoning reported from Iran, two women were put to death on a piece of waste ground. No partial burial took place on this occasion: an eye-witness account states only that the condemned were led to their execution wearing white and with sacks over their heads. As they lay on the ground after being stoned, says the witness, Revolutionary Guards 'smashed their heads in with a shovel to make sure that they were dead'.

In a Pakistani case in 1983, a middle-aged woman and her son, aged about twenty-two, were stoned near Peshawar for killing two relatives – a man and his son – who had come to stay with them. Hundreds of people took part in the execution, but even so the offenders were still alive after being stoned for three-quarters of an hour, and were then shot dead. It was the first such execution for murder in **Pakistan**, where the use of stoning had previously been confined to cases of rape and adultery.

The United States has five different methods of execution. These include the electric chair, the gas chamber and death by lethal injection, none of which are used in any other country. The other two methods are hanging and the firing squad.

The Philippines had electrocution prior to abolishing capital punishment in 1987, and it was by this means that the last execution was carried out there in 1976. Of the 528 prisoners under sentence of death in the Republic in April 1987, 378 had been condemned by military tribunals during the rule of the deposed President Ferdinand Marcos.

Executions in **Pakistan** were halted when Benazir Bhutto
became Prime Minister in December 1988, and over 2000
death sentences were commuted. However, the use of
capital punishment was resumed after Miss Bhutto's party
lost power, a triple murderer named Muhammad Riaz
being the first to suffer. Riaz, who had killed his wife and
both of her parents, was hanged in Karachi in April 1992.

In Rwanda, in July 1987, President Juvénal Habyarimana
commuted 537 death sentences to life imprisonment. All of
them had already been confirmed on appeal.

In **Iran**, **Saudi Arabia** and other countries where Islamic
law is in force, the fate of a person convicted of murder is
decided by the relatives of the victim, who may demand his
execution, accept a financial settlement instead of it, or
waive their right to either.

• In August 1983, a Saudi man was beheaded in Jeddah
  for a murder committed seventeen years earlier. The
  victim's sons had been very young at the time the crime
  was committed, and had had to wait until they reached
  the age of eighteen before being allowed to decide
  whether the culprit should be executed. On reaching
  their majority, they agreed that he should.

• In Tehran, in December the same year, a murderer was
  reprieved at the last minute, when the mother of his
  victim decided to forgive him. The hangman's rope was
  already round his neck when she asked for the execution
  to be halted.

Mahmoud Mohamed Taha was not the oldest person to
suffer the death penalty in recent years: Fyodor Fedorenko,
who was executed in the **Soviet Union** in 1987, was
seventy-eight. Fedorenko was sentenced for war crimes

committed during the Second World War. He had been arrested following deportation from the United States.

In **Yugoslavia**, in May 1986, Andrija Artukovic, aged eighty-six, was sentenced to death, also for war crimes. In his case, the sentence was not carried out, in view of the prisoner's poor state of health. Artukovic died in a prison hospital in 1988.

Some countries execute offenders for crimes committed under the age of eighteen, notably the **United States**, **Iran**, **Iraq** and **Pakistan**. **Bangladesh** and **Barbados** have also been known to execute young people in recent years. In the case of the United States, these juvenile offenders have usually spent several years on Death Row before their sentences are carried out.

- Burma has a minimum age of seven – or twelve in the case of persons of 'immature understanding' – below which the death penalty may not be imposed, but it is not known whether child offenders are ever executed there.

- Five young people aged between fifteen and seventeen were among thirty-one Kurds executed by firing squad in Iraq in November and December 1987. Shortly afterwards, eight others, aged between fourteen and seventeen, were reported to have been executed in Abu Ghraib Prison.

Several mentally ill prisoners have been executed in the **United States** in recent years, as have some who were mentally retarded. The practice of executing the mentally ill was ruled to be constitutional by the US Supreme Court in 1989. Some US states even stipulate that a Death Row prisoner found to be insane must be given psychiatric treatment until he has recovered his sanity, and so become fit for his sentence to be carried out.

Most countries which have the death penalty have laws preventing the execution of pregnant women. In some, the culprit is exempt; in others, her execution is postponed until after her delivery. In one particular case, the **Yemen Arab Republic**, a woman may not be executed while pregnant or within two years after giving birth, and only then if there are others who are able to take over the support of her child. In two other countries, **Mongolia** and **Guatemala**, women are exempt from the death penalty altogether.

Nigeria has so many Death Row inmates that executions are sometimes carried out in order to reduce overcrowding. Fifty-five prisoners in Anambra State were reported to have been executed for this reason in November 1984, as were twelve Benin City prisoners in January 1988. One condemned man in Nigeria, Nasiru Bello, who had been sentenced for armed robbery, was executed in 1981, before his appeal could be heard. Five years later, the Supreme Court ruled that his constitutional right to an appeal had been infringed.

Hangings in **Malawi** take place at Zomba Central Prison. Usually, several prisoners are hanged the same day, the executions being performed by a visiting hangman from South Africa.

In **Taiwan**, in March 1983, Hua Ting-kuo was acquitted of the murder of his mother. It was the thirteenth time the case had been before the courts in nine years. He had been sentenced to death on each of the twelve previous occasions.

A prisoner shot by firing squad in Taiwan in 1988 was found to be still alive over an hour after the first volleys had been fired.

In **Indonesia**, in 1987, two men were executed after spending twenty-five years under sentence of death. They had been condemned for the murder of a young woman.

In **Czechoslovakia**, in April 1983, two men were hanged for the murder of a bank employee during the course of a robbery in 1979. They had initially been jailed for twenty-five years, but an appeal from the state was upheld and they were sentenced to death.

A nylon rope was used at **Zaire**'s Luzumu Prison in March 1981, when seventeen prisoners were hanged for murder and armed robbery. Those who did not die immediately were shot by guards.

In **Trinidad and Tobago**, Lalchan Nanan spent eleven years on Death Row because the jury at his murder trial in 1977 mistakenly believed that a majority verdict was sufficient to convict him. Although this mistake came to light the day after the trial ended, the Court of Appeal upheld his conviction in June 1979 and an appeal to the Judicial Committee of the Privy Council in England was denied in July 1986. Nanan was, however, released on humanitarian grounds in October 1988.

The death penalty in Britain

The earliest known executions to be carried out in Britain took place in the fifth century BC. At that time, it was customary for the condemned to be drowned in quagmires. We do not know for what offences this punishment was inflicted.

Hanging was first used in England in Anglo-Saxon times. By the early eleventh century it had become the usual mode of execution in this country, though beheading, burning, drowning, stoning and casting from rocks were also used. The monarch had the sole right to choose the form of execution that an offender should undergo.

William the Conqueror abolished the death penalty (though he used it against those who conspired against him), replacing it with punishments like blinding and castration. It was, however, restored during the reign of Henry I (1100–35), and thereafter used increasingly for some centuries.

The frequency of executions reached its peak in Tudor times, with an estimated 72,000 in the reign of Henry VIII (1509–47). But the number of capital offences went on rising until the early nineteenth century.

At the accession of William and Mary in 1689, there were about fifty crimes which were punishable by death. By 1822, however, there was an unknown number, well over 200 and perhaps as high as 350.

Notable capital statutes of the late seventeenth and early eighteenth centuries include:

- an Act of 1698 which made it a capital offence to steal from a shop to the value of five shillings;

- an Act of 1713 which made it a capital offence to steal from a dwelling-house to the value of forty shillings; and

- the Waltham Black Act of 1723, under which 'wicked and evil-disposed persons going armed in disguise' could be hanged for hunting deer, poaching fish or any one of a great many other crimes.

Of all these capital offences, there were only about twenty-five for which the death penalty was actually carried out, and even this figure includes some for which it was *rarely* carried out. According to Sir Samuel Romilly, a reformer of the time:

- Of 1872 persons committed to Newgate Prison between 1803 and 1810, on a capital charge of stealing from a dwelling-house, only one was hanged.

Many offenders escaped the death penalty because juries were unwilling to bring in verdicts which allowed them to be hanged for minor offences; there were also, by this time, a great many reprieves. But the number of people executed for crimes other than murder was still considerable.

- In 1820, forty-six people in all were hanged for forging

Bank of England notes, some of which were afterwards found to be genuine.

During Sir Robert Peel's first tenure of office as Home Secretary (1822–7), a major reform of our criminal law was undertaken and the number of capital offences was greatly reduced. Further reforms took place between 1832 and 1841, abolishing the death penalty for many more crimes. Finally, in 1861, it was restricted to four crimes only (apart from wartime military offences): murder, treason, piracy with violence and arson in a royal dockyard.

In 1820, Lord Eldon, an opponent of any relaxation of the harsh laws then in force, spoke in the House of Lords against a Bill to abolish the death penalty for cutting down trees. While conceding that death was undoubtedly a 'hardship' for cutting down a single tree, he said that if the Bill were passed, 'a person might root up or cut down whole acres or plantations ... without being subject to capital punishment'.

In 1868, public executions were abolished. Thereafter, condemned persons were hanged in the prisons in which they had been confined. During the early years of 'private' executions, newspaper reporters were sometimes allowed to watch the proceedings.

In 1908, the death penalty was abolished for persons under the age of sixteen.

Under the Infanticide Act of 1922, a woman who killed her new-born child could be convicted of infanticide rather

than murder if it appeared that she was mentally un-
balanced at the time the crime was committed as a result
of giving birth. In such cases the death sentence could not
be passed.

In 1933, the death penalty was abolished for capital
offences committed by persons under the age of eighteen.

In 1957, it was further restricted. The Homicide Act of that
year specified five categories of murder for which capital
punishment was to remain in force, the rest to be punishable by life imprisonment. The five categories were:

• murder in the course or furtherance of theft;

• murder by shooting or by causing an explosion;

• murder in the course or for the purpose of resisting,
avoiding or preventing a lawful arrest, or effecting or
assisting an escape or rescue from legal custody;

• murder of a police officer in the execution of his duty,
or of a person assisting him; and

• murder by a prisoner of a prison officer in the execution
of his duty, or of a person assisting him.

In addition to these five categories of murder, the Act
retained the death penalty for persons who committed a
second murder on a different occasion from the first.

In 1965, the death penalty for murder was effectively ended, though it was not formally abolished until
December 1969. Many attempts have since been made to
restore it, but all have been defeated.

Hanging remains on the statute book for treason, piracy
with violence and arson in a royal dockyard, however, and
for this reason the gallows at Wandsworth Prison, south-

west London, are kept in working order.

The death penalty may also be imposed for wartime military offences, such as mutiny, incitement to mutiny, serious misconduct in action or communicating with the enemy, but in such cases the mode of execution is usually shooting.

The last executions in Britain took place on 13 August 1964, when Peter Anthony Allen, aged twenty-one, was hanged at Walton Prison, Liverpool, and John Robson Walby (alias Gwynne Owen Evans), aged twenty-four, was hanged at Strangeways Prison, Manchester. They had been jointly convicted of the murder of John West, a van driver from Workington, Cumberland, in the furtherance of theft.

The death penalty in America

Most executions carried out in America in colonial times were by hanging, though other methods, such as burning, were also used. Sometimes hanging was followed by gibbeting, as in England up to the early nineteenth century.

- On 1 March 1622, a thief named Daniell Frank was hanged in Virginia for stealing a calf and other goods belonging to Sir George Yeardley. He thus became the earliest known person to be executed in America, though there had probably been others before him. The first settlers had arrived there in 1607.

- On 30 September 1630, the first execution for murder took place. The condemned man, John Billington, was hanged in Plymouth, Massachusetts, for killing another settler with a blunderbuss. Billington, who had arrived in America on the *Mayflower*, was forty years old. He left a wife and two children.

- In 1638, Dorothy Talby, the first known woman to be executed in America, was hanged in Massachusetts Bay Colony for the murder of her three-year-old daughter. It was believed that she had earlier tried to kill her husband and that she had also attempted to commit suicide. Her daughter was named Difficulty.

- In 1692, in Salem, Massachusetts, nineteen people were hanged for witchcraft. One other person was charged with the same crime and, on refusing to plead, was pressed to death (see page 103). It was one of America's greatest ever miscarriages of justice.

- In 1701, Esther Rodgers, of Ipswich, Massachusetts, was executed for the murder of her illegitimate child. She was the only woman in American history to be hanged and gibbeted.

- In 1741, an alleged conspiracy to burn down New York City and kill its inhabitants led to the execution of twenty-nine black and four white people. Eleven of the blacks were burnt at the stake; the other eighteen were hanged, as were the four whites (two men and two women). Many others were convicted in connection with this affair, but their sentences were all commuted.

- On 20 December 1786, Hannah Ocuish, a 'half-breed Indian girl' aged twelve years and nine months, was hanged in New London, Connecticut. The youngest person ever to be executed in America, she had been condemned for the murder of a girl of six named Eunice Bolles, whom she had beaten to death after luring her into a wood two or three miles out of the town. The motive for the crime was revenge, a dispute having arisen between the two girls in a strawberry field some days previously.

- In 1825, America's last execution by burning took place in the county of Abbeville, South Carolina. The condemned was a slave named Negro Jack, who had been convicted of rape and murder before an inferior court consisting of 'the magistrates and five freeholders'. It was as a result of this case that the state, in 1833, repealed all laws allowing such sentences to be imposed.

• In 1834, Pennsylvania abolished public executions, closely followed by New Jersey, New York State and Massachusetts (all of which adopted similar laws in 1835). The last public execution of all took place in Missouri in 1937, after which that state began using the gas chamber. Nowadays all executions are carried out in state prisons.

• In 1847, Michigan abolished the death penalty for all crimes except treason. Rhode Island abolished it completely in 1852; Wisconsin in 1853. There had been no executions in Michigan since 1830.

In Salt Lake City, Utah, in 1859, Thomas N. Ferguson, aged twenty-seven, made a speech of very great length – somewhere between four and eight hours, according to the various reports – before being executed for the murder of his employer. The crime had been committed under the influence of drink.

• On 2 December 1859, John Brown, the famous anti-slavery crusader, was hanged for treason in Charlestown, West Virginia, following an abortive rebellion. With a small band of supporters, he had seized the Federal Arsenal at Harper's Ferry, intending to lead the slaves in the area to freedom. But no slaves joined him, and after two days of fighting, he surrendered to a force of marines commanded by Colonel Robert E. Lee.

• On 26 December 1862, America's biggest mass execution took place, with thirty-eight Sioux Indians being hanged near Mankato, Minnesota, for their part in the slaughter of hundreds of men, women and children.

Their death warrant was signed by Abraham Lincoln.

- On 6 August 1890, William Kemmler, a drunken pedlar who had killed his mistress with a hatchet, was executed in the electric chair at Auburn State Prison, New York. It was the first time that this method of execution was used, and witnesses found it harrowing to watch. The state, however, was satisfied that it was more humane than hanging, and saw no reason to abandon it.

- On 11 December 1917, a mass hanging of thirteen black soldiers of the United States Army took place at Fort Sam Houston, San Antonio, Texas. They had been tried by court-martial for mutiny, following a race riot in which seventeen white and two black people were killed. In later courts-martial, another sixteen of those involved in the outrage were sentenced to death and over fifty to life imprisonment.

- On 8 February 1924, the gas chamber was used for the first time. The condemned was a Chinese gunman named Gee Jon, who had murdered a member of a rival tong. Gee's execution, in Carson City, Nevada, seemed painless enough to most observers, but some newspapers were scathing about it – one claiming that there was 'a terror in this thing that even Edgar Allan Poe could not equal'. Lethal gas remained Nevada's official mode of execution, however, and by 1960 had been adopted by eleven other states.

- In 1967, the death penalty was suspended nationwide while the US Supreme Court investigated its constitutional validity.

- In 1972, the Supreme Court ruled that all existing laws which permitted the use of capital punishment were in violation of the Constitution, because they allowed it to be used in an inconsistent and arbitrary manner. States wishing to restore the death penalty had therefore to rewrite their laws, and all persons then under sentence of death were automatically spared.

- In 1976, the death penalty was reinstated in a new ruling by the Supreme Court. By this time, six hundred people had been sentenced to death under new state laws brought in as a result of the 1972 ruling.

- On 17 January 1977, Gary Gilmore was shot by a firing squad in the state of Utah (see pp. 187–8), becoming the first person to be executed in the United States for ten years.

- On 7 December 1982, in Huntsville, Texas, Charlie Brooks, a forty-year-old murderer, became the first person to die by lethal injection. Brooks had been sentenced to death for his part in the murder of a second-hand car salesman in Fort Worth six years earlier. A convert to Islam, he remained calm throughout his final ordeal, and his execution was carried out without incident. It seemed from this case that the lethal injection was a great improvement on all other methods of execution. More recently, however, its use has sometimes been attended by serious mishaps (see pp. 231–5).

- On 22 May 1992, Robert Black became the 176th person in the United States (and the fiftieth in Texas) to be executed since the ending of the moratorium in 1976. By that time, there were over 2500 prisoners on Death Row nationwide.

- Thirty-six states currently have the death penalty, seven of them offering alternative methods of execution. The lethal injection is available in twenty-two states, the electric chair in eleven, the gas chamber in six, the firing squad in two and hanging in two.

- The states which do not have the death penalty are Alaska, Hawaii, Iowa, Kansas, Maine, Massachusetts, Michigan, Minnesota, New York, North Dakota, Rhode Island, Vermont, West Virginia and Wisconsin.

Between 1900 and 1985, at least 350 innocent people were convicted of capital offences in the United States, according to a study published by Hugo Adam Bedau of Tufts University and Michael L. Radelet of the University of Florida. Of these, twenty-three were executed and others came close to being executed before their lives were spared. More recent cases in which miscarriages of justice are believed to have occurred include those of Edward Earl Johnson, executed in Mississippi on 20 May 1987 and Willie Jasper Darden, executed in Florida on 15 March 1988.

In January 1993, the US Supreme Court decided by six votes to three that new evidence of innocence was not necessarily sufficient reason to halt an execution. It was only in a 'truly extraordinary' case, where the new evidence was conclusive, that judges were empowered to do this, the court ruled.

Abolition or non-use of the death penalty

The world's first abolitionist ruler appears to have been the Buddhist King Amandagamani of Lanka (**Sri Lanka**), who outlawed the use of the death penalty in the first century AD. Several of his successors followed the same policy.

The Emperor Saga eliminated it from Japanese law in 818 AD, and it was not reintroduced in **Japan** for the next three centuries.

Today over forty per cent of countries have either abolished the death penalty or given up using it. The countries most worthy of note in this respect are as follows:

- **Andorra** has had only one execution this century. That was in 1943, when a man was shot by firing squad for the murder of his two brothers.

- **Anguilla**'s last execution took place in the 1820s.

- **Belgium** has carried out only one execution for a non-military offence since 1863: that was in March 1918, when a soldier was guillotined for the murder of a pregnant woman. Its last executions for military offences took place between November 1944 and August 1950, when about 242 people were shot by firing squad for crimes committed during the Second World War.

- **Brazil**'s last execution took place in 1855. The victim, who had been convicted of murder, was later found to have been innocent.

- **Cape Verde** has had no executions since 1835, when two leaders of a peasant revolt were hanged.

- **Columbia**'s last executions took place in 1909, when two men were shot by firing squad for attempting to assassinate President Rafael Reyes.

- **Costa Rica**'s last executions were of two men shot for treason in 1878.

- **Denmark**'s last execution for a peacetime offence was in 1892. Its last executions for wartime offences took place after the Second World War, when forty-six people were shot for crimes committed during the German Occupation.

- **Ecuador** abolished the death penalty in 1906, having begun to restrict its use fifty-five years earlier. From 1878 it had been in force only as a punishment for parricide.

- **Finland**'s last execution for a peacetime offence took place in 1826. Its last executions for war crimes took place between 1939 and 1944, when 500 people were shot.

- **Iceland** has not had an execution since 1830, when two offenders were beheaded for murder.

- **Israel**'s only execution since its foundation in 1948 has been that of the German war criminal, Adolf Eichmann, who was hanged in 1962 for genocide.

- **Liechtenstein**'s last execution, by beheading, took place in 1785.

- **Monaco**'s last execution was carried out by guillotine in 1847.

- **The Netherlands** carried out its last execution for a peacetime offence in 1860. Its last executions for wartime offences were carried out after the Second World War, when thirty-nine people were put to death for crimes committed during the German Occupation.

- **Norway**'s last execution for a peacetime offence was by beheading, in 1876. Its last executions for wartime offences took place after the Second World War, when thirty-seven people were put to death for treason and other crimes connected with the German Occupation.

- **Panama** has not had a single execution since it came into existence as an independent nation in 1903.

- **Portugal**'s last execution for a non-military offence was in 1846. Its last execution for a military crime was in 1849.

- **San Marino**'s last known execution took place in 1468. The death penalty was abolished there in 1848, re-introduced for certain offences during the 1850s, then abolished again a few years later without having been used.

- **Sweden**'s last execution was carried out in 1910.

- **Uruguay** abolished the death penalty in 1907. Its last execution had taken place at the end of the nineteenth century.

- **Venezuela** abolished the death penalty in 1863.

Surinam carried out its first execution for over fifty years on 13 March 1982. The victim, Sergeant Major Wilfred Hawker, was shot by firing squad under an emergency decree introduced two days earlier, for attempting to overthrow the country's military government. The decree was rescinded ten days later.

2

Some Hangings

A surgeon for
Jack Sheppard

Jack Sheppard was the most famous criminal of his time. His career as a robber was short, and the crime for which he was hanged was quite unremarkable. But his exploits as a jailbreaker were spectacular and have rarely, if ever, been surpassed. His execution at Tyburn, near the present-day Marble Arch, attracted the largest crowd for over fifty years.

Sheppard was a thin little man, just five feet four inches in height, but with enormous strength and an amazing skill at picking locks. Born in Spitalfields in 1702, he turned to theft at the age of twenty-one, while serving an apprenticeship as a carpenter; and after confining himself to pilfering for a while, he began housebreaking. Before long, he was arrested.

Committed for one night to St Giles's Roundhouse in Soho, Sheppard broke out through the roof and climbed down into a churchyard at the back of the prison, using a sheet and a blanket tied together. The street outside was full of excited people, one of whom had raised the alarm after being struck by a falling tile. Sheppard, however, mingled with them – and made his escape.

A few weeks later, on being arrested again, he was sent to the New Prison in Clerkenwell. This time his mistress, Elizabeth Lyon – a corpulent thief and prostitute known as 'Edgworth Bess' – was committed with him. And as they were regarded as man and wife, they were put into a cell together, Sheppard in fetters. But after they had been there for a few days, Sheppard filed through his chains and made a large hole in the window, using tools which had been smuggled in to him by friends. He then used a makeshift rope to lower Bess into the yard of the Clerkenwell Bridewell next door before climbing down himself.

Their last obstacle to freedom was a twenty-two-foot wall, but Sheppard was undaunted by it. Using gimlets to make footholds, he scaled one of its massive wooden gates, then hauled Bess up after him. He then attached his rope of blankets and petticoats to a spike, and he and Bess slid down it into the street.

It was an incredible feat, which naturally won Sheppard the admiration of his fellow thieves. But after another two months at liberty, he was recaptured again, and committed to Newgate Prison.

Appearing for trial at the Old Bailey Sessions in August 1724, he faced three charges, one of them concerning a burglary in the Strand on the night of 12 July, when he and an accomplice had stolen goods to the value of about fifty pounds. It was on this charge that he was sentenced to death, the other two resulting in acquittals for lack of evidence.

On being taken from the courthouse after hearing his sentence, Jack Sheppard was placed in Newgate's Condemned Hold. This was a dark ground-floor cell adjoining the Lodge, an entrance hall from which visitors could see and speak to the occupants of the Hold over a heavy door with spikes along the top of it. He remained there for the next two and a half weeks, fettered again – as were all of the condemned – but by no means in despair.

Given some tools by another prisoner, he began surreptitiously filing one of the spikes, and gradually weakened it. On 31 August, when Edgworth Bess and an associate named Poll Maggot came to see him, he snapped it off and wriggled out through the gap, unnoticed by a group of turnkeys who were drinking at the other end of the Lodge. Wearing a nightgown which reached to his ankles – and hid his fetters – he calmly walked out into the street, accompanied by one of the women. A hackney coach was waiting for them nearby, and Sheppard was able to get well away from Newgate before his absence was discovered.

This third escape, four days before he was due to be hanged, caused much public excitement. But only a week and a half later, on 10 September, Sheppard was retaken by a party of turnkeys during a search of Finchley Common. Back in the Condemned Hold, manacled, fettered and chained to the floor, he received many visitors, as was usual for such a famous prisoner. Later, he was moved to a third-floor cell known as the Castle, which was one of the strongest in the prison.

On the evening of 15 October, the young robber made his fourth and last escape: one of the greatest jailbreaks of all time. First he freed himself from his handcuffs, probably with the use of a nail; then he picked the padlock securing his fetters to a staple in the floor. That left the fetters themselves intact, but he found a weak link in the chain and managed to break it at that point.

Taking off his boots and stockings, he tied the broken pieces of chain round his legs to prevent them from dragging along the ground. He then made a large hole in the chimney-breast by scratching mortar from the brickwork, and was thus able to remove an iron bar blocking his way and climb up to the next floor. There, using the iron bar, Sheppard smashed his way into an empty room above his own cell. The door to this was locked, but it took him only a few minutes to break it open, working in complete darkness. He then made his way up to the roof, breaking open five more doors in the process.

When he finally reached the open air, he could find no way down except by lowering himself over twenty feet to the roof of one of the houses below. He therefore had to return to his cell and get his blanket to use as a rope. He then climbed down to the roof of the house, made his way across other roofs and climbed through an open window into an attic. Although the house was occupied, he rested in the attic for two hours and then managed to go downstairs and out through the front door without being discovered. That was about midnight, and it was not until eight o'clock in the morning that he was found to be missing from his cell.

As news of this latest escape spread, crowds of visitors flocked to Newgate to marvel at Sheppard's handiwork, all of them paying fees for the privilege of being admitted. But again Sheppard was not free for long, for on 31 October he was apprehended at a gin-shop in Drury Lane.

On arrival back at Newgate, he was lodged in yet another cell until 11 November, when he was put back into the Condemned Hold. He was now weighed down with an even heavier lot of irons than before – it was said that there were 300 pounds of them in all – and again chained to the floor of the cell. A constant watch was kept on him, day and night.

But large numbers of people were still allowed in to see him, each paying an entrance fee as before. Among these visitors was Daniel Defoe, author of *Robinson Crusoe* and *Moll Flanders* and chief contributor to John Applebee's *Original Weekly Journal*. It is Defoe who is believed to have written a first-person account of Sheppard's life which Applebee published as a pamphlet.

With his execution fixed for 16 November, Sheppard implored persons of influence to intercede with the King on his behalf, to try to get him pardoned. But no one apparently did so, and no pardon came for him. He was also unable to see any way in which he could make a fresh escape from Newgate. However, he never gave up hope of saving himself by one means or another, as the events of his execution day show.

On that fatal morning, as he was being prepared for the procession to the gallows, Sheppard had an unpleasant surprise. It was customary at this time for the condemned to have his handcuffs and fetters taken off, and his arms bound to his sides with rope. Sheppard, however, had only his fetters removed, and on learning that he was to be taken to the place of execution in handcuffs, he protested vehemently.

At this, he was searched and a sharp knife was found in the lining of his waistcoat. It was positioned in such a way that had there been no departure from custom, he could have used it to cut the rope which bound him. He afterwards told his jailers that he had intended throwing himself from the hanging cart at a certain point along the route and disappearing among the crowds. He said he was sure he would have succeeded in getting away but for the handcuffs.

He was probably right. The streets that day were thronged with people who admired or pitied him, and had he tried to escape he would almost certainly have been aided. But with his plan foiled he made no such attempt, relying instead upon an even more desperate scheme to save his life.

The gallows at Tyburn, called the Triple Tree, was a huge triangular construction, with enough room for eight people to hang from each of its three cross-beams. Many multiple executions were carried out there, the condemned being hanged in batches from the back of the cart. On this occasion, however, there was only Sheppard himself to suffer, as three other condemned had been hanged five days earlier.

Standing beneath one of the beams, Sheppard was questioned about his crimes by the Under-Sheriff. He confessed that he was guilty not only of the one for which he had been sentenced, but also of the two others for which he had been tried. When the deputy Ordinary of Newgate (the chaplain attending him) had finished his ministrations, the Under-Sheriff gave the signal for the execution to be carried out – and the hangman went to work.

Being of slight build, the prisoner struggled for some minutes after the cart had been driven off. This often happened, and friends of the condemned were sometimes allowed to pull his legs in order to terminate his suffering. But in this case, nobody tried to do so.

When the movements of his limbs finally stopped, about a quarter of an hour after he had been 'turned off', a soldier sprang from among the crowd, pushed his way through the ring of constables guarding the gallows and cut him down. A large number of other men immediately rushed forward, seized the hanged man and carried him off on their shoulders. The constables made no attempt to stop them.

A few of the men concerned were friends of Sheppard's, acting in accordance with his own wishes. He had asked them to try to revive him in the event of his being hanged, by putting him to bed in hot blankets and letting his blood. A room had therefore been rented nearby, and a surgeon waited there for the body to be brought to him. But in trying to get possession of it, Sheppard's friends found themselves unexpectedly opposed by other sympathizers, who suspected that they were trying to take it for anatomization (dissection), a practice much feared and hated at that time.

An outbreak of disorder ensued, in the course of which a hearse provided by John Applebee for Sheppard's funeral was smashed to pieces. The hanged man, who had actually shown signs of life after being cut down from the gallows, was pulled this way and that – and so denied any chance of being resuscitated. His friends soon had to accept that their opponents had unwittingly finished the hangman's work for him.

Before long, Sheppard's body fell into the hands of a group of men who carried it off to a tavern in Covent Garden. A mob followed, wanting to make sure that it was decently buried, and a rumour that it had been stolen sparked off a riot. This eventually subsided when troops arrived on the scene.

That night the body was buried in the churchyard of St Martin-in-the-Fields, at the expense of some unknown gentleman – possibly Applebee – after being taken there under a strong military escort.

Jonathan Wild, the thief-taker who numbered Sheppard among his many victims, was himself the head of a criminal empire and a large-scale receiver of stolen goods, which he specialized in selling back to their rightful owners. In 1725, he was convicted on a capital charge concerning the sale of a quantity of stolen lace, under an Act of Parliament designed to bring this practice to an end. And on 24 May of that year, in company with two other offenders, he was hanged at Tyburn.

His execution was attended by an even greater crowd than Sheppard's – not because he was a popular criminal, but because he was hated. Many of the spectators gave shouts of joy as the cart moved through the streets, and some pelted him with stones.

After being cut down from the gallows, Wild's body was taken away in a coach and horses paid for by his wife. It was buried in St Pancras Churchyard during the early hours of the following morning – only to be dug up and anatomized a few days later.

No mercy from the
Edinburgh mob

For much of the eighteenth century, Edinburgh's usual place of execution was a site at the east end of the Grassmarket. A huge block of sandstone, with a hole in the middle, stood there permanently, providing a socket for a portable gallows whenever occasion demanded. It was there, on 14 April 1736, that a well-known criminal named Andrew Wilson was hanged, sparking off a sequence of events that shocked the whole country.

Wilson was a smuggler who, with two other men, had been convicted of robbing a custom-house at Pittenweem, in Fife. His companions had both been condemned to death with him, but one's sentence had afterwards been commuted to transportation and the other, with Wilson's help, had managed to escape.

After that, Wilson himself was so popular among the lower classes that it was feared that an attempt might be made to rescue him.

On the day of his execution, the Grassmarket was in a state of tension. The City Guard, commanded by Captain John Porteous, had, by order of the magistrates, been called out in force – and a party of Welsh Fusiliers had been drawn up nearby, in readiness to assist them in the event of a riot breaking out. But Porteous, a cruel, arrogant and

much-hated man, was determined to show that his own
soldiers could keep order without the help of these regular
troops.

The condemned man, with his wrists in manacles, was
marched from the Edinburgh Tolbooth (the city prison) to
the gallows, where the Guard took up positions to hold
back the dense crowd. This made a rescue virtually
impossible, and Wilson's many admirers watched helplessly as he stood on a ladder with the rope round his neck,
waiting to be turned off. When he had finally been hanged,
the two magistrates who were officially in attendance
withdrew – as was customary – to a tavern overlooking the
scene.

Porteous and his soldiers remained at the place of
execution, guarding the hanging corpse, while the hangman, John Dalgleish, waited for a signal from the magistrates to cut it down. This was usually given about half an
hour after the hanging had taken place, but on this
occasion, after twenty-four minutes, Dalgleish saw a
window opening and mistakenly assumed that that was it.
As he was about to cut the dead man down, however, some
of the spectators began to pelt him with stones.

With his nose bleeding, he abandoned the task, descended to the foot of the Gallows Stone (as that great block
of sandstone was called) and took cover behind the
soldiers. No further attempt was made to cut the body
down at this stage, as the magistrates, on being consulted,
gave orders for it to be left hanging for another quarter of
an hour.

But the crowd had by this time become disorderly, and
while some threw stones or dirt at the soldiers, others cut
the body down themselves and carried it off. With tempers
rising, Porteous allegedly fired at the rioters and ordered
his men to do likewise – with the result that three people
were killed outright and others were wounded, some of

them fatally. During a second incident, as they were returning to the Guard House, some of the soldiers again opened fire – also on Porteous's orders, it was afterwards alleged – killing three more people and wounding several others.

With an outraged populace clamouring for justice, Porteous was arrested and committed to the Tolbooth. The Town Council dismissed him from his post and cut off his pay, but later voted him an aliment of 1s 6d a day after he petitioned them for subsistence, declaring that he was starving. After three months in prison, he appeared before the High Court of Justiciary, charged with murder.

Pleading not guilty, he denied having fired on the crowd or ordering his men to do so, and the evidence given against him was confused and contradictory. Of the fifteen members of the jury, only eight were in favour of a verdict of guilty, while the other seven were all against it. The outcome, however, was the same as if the verdict had been unanimous: Porteous was sentenced to death.

But while the lower orders of the city were overjoyed at the prospect of seeing him hanged, many people of power and influence were dismayed by the verdict, regarding the prisoner's acts merely as excesses resulting from his zeal for duty. Intercessions were therefore made on his behalf, and on 26 August – two weeks before he was due to be hanged – Porteous was granted a reprieve by Queen Caroline, acting as Regent while her husband was on a visit to Hanover. It was confidently expected that this would be followed by a commutation of sentence when the King returned to England.

The reprieve arrived in Edinburgh on 2 September, and Lord Milton, the Justice-Clerk, wrote to the Duke of Newcastle, Secretary of State for Scotland, acknowledging its receipt. 'This act of Her Majesty's Royal mercy, and as it points to further, meets with almost a general approbation, especially among those of the higher rank and greatest distinction,' he commented. 'And the few who grumble are only of the meaner sort, or such as either have confined ways of thinking, or such as seem determined to complain whatever happens.'

Clearly, he had no idea how the news of Porteous's reprieve had really been received outside his own circle of friends and acquaintances – and no inkling of the trouble which was already afoot as a result of it. Moreover, his ill-founded complacency appears to have been shared by most other members of his class, despite rumours throughout the city that an organized riot had been planned for 8 September – the day on which Porteous was to have been hanged – to enable the Edinburgh mob to take the law into its own hands.

But such an outrage *had* been planned – evidently in some detail – though by whom we do not know. It was to take place on the night of 7 September, rather than the following day, the conspirators having deliberately spread a false rumour about the timing in order to give themselves the element of surprise. And that night, as it happened, there were only a few members of the City Guard on duty, none of whom had been supplied with ammunition. The city magistrates could see no need for any special precautions to be taken!

Between nine and ten o'clock, however, a large body of men armed with staves and cudgels assembled in the suburb of Portsburgh, to the west of the city, and forced the burgh drummer to beat a call to arms. Calling on the populace to join them and avenge the shedding of innocent blood, they then entered the city by the West Port – rough-handling two officials in the process – and nailed up the gates behind them.

With that part of their plan accomplished, and with others joining them all the time, the excited and noisy band set about securing each of the other four entrances to the city: two on the east side and two on the south. After that, they attacked the Guard House, turned out its startled occupants – including some minor offenders they found in the cells – and carried off all the firelocks and Lochaber axes they could lay their hands on. They then broke into a shop, stole some ammunition, and loaded their guns.

By now they were four to five thousand strong – and the city was in their hands. Surrounding the Tolbooth, they began battering one of its outer doors with sledge-hammers, but an hour later it was still intact. They therefore gave up trying to break it down and set fire to it instead. Before long the door had been burnt down and the mob burst into the prison.

Porteous, dressed in his nightgown, cap and breeches, was dragged out into the street, begging for mercy. The mob carried him to the Grassmarket, punching and beating him all the way, then broke into a shop to get a coil of rope and tied one end of it round his neck. At this, Porteous again begged for mercy – but again to no avail. The rioters were determined to hang him.

The usual gallows, being portable, was not kept at the place of execution, but a dyer's pole, about fifteen feet high and of a similar shape, stood nearby. The mob threw the free end of the rope across it and hauled their terrified captive up by his neck. But it seems that he was not just left hanging, for a contemporary account tells us that he was repeatedly let down alive and then pulled up again. He was also struck with an axe as he struggled to loosen the halter.

Eventually, though, his tormentors had to accept that the object of their hatred could be made to suffer no more. They then fastened the rope to the dyer's pole and dispersed in an orderly fashion. Porteous's dead body went on hanging where they had left it until early the following morning.

With the outrage over, extensive inquiries were made with a view to bringing those responsible to justice. But only two men were ever tried in connection with it – neither of them people who had played an important part in the disturbance – and both were acquitted. No member of the 'cool, resolute gang' which had actually led the riot was ever identified.

During a lengthy investigation of the affair before the House of Lords, the city magistrates, headed by the Lord Provost, were shown to have been negligent in failing to take measures to protect Porteous from the rioters. Because of this, the City Corporation was fined £2000, and the Provost was disqualified from holding office as a magistrate anywhere in the United Kingdom. The £2000 was paid to Porteous's widow.

Second time
at the gallows

One cold morning in November 1717, three condemned men were taken to Tyburn to be hanged, only to find that there was nobody to carry out their sentences. All had therefore to be reprieved, and all were afterwards given conditional pardons. But one of them, a burglar named John Meff, was destined to ride in the cart a second time four years later: a twist of fate which makes his particular case all the more remarkable.

Meff, alias Murth, alias Mason, a weaver by trade, was about thirty-five years old when he first fell foul of the law, but had evidently been involved in many burglaries by this time. The crime which led to his arrest took place on 17 September that year, when he and an accomplice, John Wood (another of the three), broke into the house of John Westerbane, a Stepney ropemaker, during the hours of darkness. Both were armed with pistols and hangers (short swords), and put up a desperate fight when discovered by two of the victim's workmen.

Meff managed to escape after shooting one of the workmen in the chest, but Wood was apprehended and confessed his part in what had happened. Some days later, Meff was himself arrested in Shoreditch, and he, too, made a confession, saying that he was sorry for what he had done. Among his possessions was found a pocket book containing information about robberies which he had committed during the course of the previous year.

At the Old Bailey the following month the two culprits appeared for trial, Wood admitting the offence at the ropemaker's house and Meff denying it. After a short trial, Meff – whose name is recorded in the printed *Sessions Papers* as 'John Murth alias Mason' – was found guilty, so both men left the court under sentence of death. They remained in Newgate's Condemned Hold, together with other capital offenders, for the next three weeks.

On 6 November, they were placed in the hanging cart with a thief named Hugh Oakley and the procession to Tyburn began. Despite the cold weather, the streets were lined with spectators, as was often the case on hanging days. There was, at first, no reason for anyone to think that the condemned men might return from the gallows alive; nor would they have done but for a misfortune which befell the hangman, William Marvell.

Instead of riding at the front of the cart with the driver, as he usually did, Marvell had gone on ahead of the procession on foot. On reaching Holborn, however, he was confronted by three bailiffs, who arrested him for debt and started to carry him off to prison. He eventually persuaded them to release him, but was then recognized by an unruly mob, who set upon him without any apparent cause and beat him unmercifully. By the time they had finished with him he was in no fit state to hang anybody.

The procession, in the meantime, had passed him by and gone on to Tyburn, where the Under-Sheriff tried to find somebody to officiate in Marvell's place. A bricklayer showed a willingness to do so, but the mob turned on him and forced him to give up the idea – after which nobody else *dared* to volunteer. It was one of the few occasions on which the crowds actually succeeded in preventing an execution from being carried out.

After the three condemned had been kept waiting at the gallows for two hours, the Under-Sheriff reluctantly accepted that the hangings would have to be postponed. The prisoners were therefore taken back to Newgate, where, after further confusion and delay, they were put back into the Condemned Hold.

In view of what had happened, their sentences were initially respited and then commuted to seven-year terms of transportation. They were then kept in prison until places could be found for them aboard a transportation vessel, but eventually set out for America, where their sentences were to be served.

During the course of the journey, their ship was captured by pirates, but – contrary to a statement attributed to Meff in the published accounts of his case – it was retaken shortly afterwards.

The three men arrived in Charleston, South Carolina, on 20 March 1719 (as is proved by a landing certificate in the Corporation of London Record Office), and were presumably sold to some planter in the normal way, to work without wages until their terms expired. But two years later, Meff returned to England by some unknown means and resumed his life of crime.

Towards the end of April 1721, he was arrested for a robbery near London. The offence was found to have been committed during the period covered by an Act of Grace (a general pardon), so he could not be tried for it. However, his past was discovered, and he was indicted for returning from transportation without lawful cause: another of the eighteenth century's many capital offences.

Early in July, while he was still awaiting trial, Meff and another prisoner named Cornish – a bricklayer serving a short sentence for stealing lead – broke out of Newgate and escaped over the roofs of nearby houses. Cornish remained at large until 12 August; Meff until two days after that. Meff's recapture led to the discovery of a great quantity of stolen linen at his lodgings.

At the Old Bailey Sessions beginning on 30 August, he appeared for trial on the charge on which he had earlier been indicted, his name being this time recorded in the printed proceedings as 'John Merthe alias Meffe, alias Mason'. The record of his conviction and sentence four years previously was read out, then witnesses were called to identify him as the offender in question. He was found guilty and again sentenced to death.

Two weeks later, on 11 September 1721, he was taken from the Condemned Hold, in company with three men convicted of highway robbery, and conveyed to Tyburn for the second time. No obstruction of the course of justice took place on this occasion: all four prisoners were hanged without incident. Meff's body was afterwards taken to Stepney, where he was buried two days later.

There is another noteworthy feature of this strange case. That is the fate of William Marvell, the hangman.

As a result of his failure to hang Meff, Wood and Oakley in November 1717, he was dismissed from his post, and so had to find some other means of earning his living. Although a blacksmith by trade, his reputation as a former 'finisher of the law' seriously reduced his opportunities for finding work, and he eventually turned to theft.

In October 1719, he was convicted at the Old Bailey of stealing ten silk handkerchiefs from a haberdasher's shop in Coleman Street, the jury undervaluing the goods in order to bring him in guilty only of a non-capital offence.

Sentenced to transportation (probably for seven or

fourteen years), he left England aboard a ship bound for Maryland later the same month, and was never heard of again.

When hanging was not
the end

Survival of the gallows, in the days when death normally resulted from strangulation, was by no means an impossibility. It is known to have occurred in quite a number of well-attested cases, and may well have happened on other occasions of which we are unaware. Here are brief accounts of four famous cases, in each of which the condemned survived without any scheming on anybody's part. Deliberate attempts to thwart the execution of justice, like that of Jack Sheppard, seem to have been generally unsuccessful.

Anne Greene

Anne Greene, a domestic servant aged about twenty-two, was hanged in the Castle Yard, Oxford, on 14 December 1650, for allegedly murdering her illegitimate child. In her 'dying speech' to the spectators, she said she was innocent of the crime for which she was about to suffer and made certain allegations against the family of her former master, Sir Thomas Read, of the village of Dunstew. When she was ready, she was turned off the ladder and left to swing from the overhead beam.

To prevent her from suffering unnecessarily, friends and sympathizers began swinging on her body. They then started to lift her up and pull her down with a jerk, until the Under-Sheriff stopped them, for fear that the rope would break. It is also known that a soldier struck her several times with the butt of his musket. So when she was cut down, after hanging for at least fifteen minutes – and probably nearer to half an hour – nobody could have suspected that she was still alive.

But on being taken to the home of a local apothecary, where physicians from Oxford University had arranged to use her body as a subject for anatomization, the supposedly dead woman – with part of the rope still round her neck – was seen to be breathing. This alarmed friends who were, for some unknown reason, present, and one of them immediately stepped into the coffin and began stamping on her breasts and stomach. However, she was still showing signs of life shortly afterwards, when the first two physicians arrived on the scene.

William Petty and Thomas Willis had come early to prepare for the dissection. But when they saw that there was a chance of their 'subject' being revived, they poured spirits down her throat and set about rubbing parts of her body. A little later, they let some of her blood and put her into a well-heated bed. Having thus started the process of resuscitation, they stayed to attend her throughout the day, letting out more of her blood and administering, among other things, suppositories and sweet drinks, while another woman lay in bed with her to ensure that she was kept warm. Occasionally, Anne opened her eyes for a moment or coughed, but for several hours she was unable to speak. Late that night, however, her powers of speech suddenly began to return.

For several days she remained in bed at the home of the apothecary, complaining of pains in her throat, neck, breasts, side and stomach, and a deadness in the tip of her tongue, as though she had bitten it. But she was visited regularly by those who had saved her, and cared for by others in their absence, so that five days after she had been hanged, Petty was able to record that her symptoms had all decreased and that she was now able to get up.

Anne's recovery was accepted as miraculous by the city magistrates, who granted her a reprieve in the expectation that a pardon would follow. Many people who visited her out of curiosity also marvelled at this manifestation of 'the just Providence of God', declaring that it was proof that she was innocent of the crime for which she had been sentenced. A collection taken on her behalf – to which the physicians themselves contributed – raised many pounds.

Her former master, Sir Thomas Read, who had also been her prosecutor (and whose grandson had been responsible for her pregnancy), had in the meantime died. He is recorded as having choked to death at his own table 'almost as soon as the probability of her reviving could be well confirmed to him'. Some, no doubt, saw this as further proof that the hand of God had been at work on her behalf.

In her petition praying for a commutation of sentence (in William Petty's handwriting), Anne again denied having killed her child, claiming that the 'victim' of her alleged crime had been an imperfectly formed foetus miscarried about the eighteenth week of her pregnancy. It appears from the evidence of a midwife and other women who had examined it that this was indeed true, and that the petitioner may not have even realized that she was pregnant until the miscarriage occurred. She was therefore given an unconditional pardon.

Within a month of her attempted execution, Anne was fully recovered from its effects and went to stay with

friends in her native village of Steeple Barton, in the same
county. She later married and had three children, but is
believed to have died in 1659, at the age of about thirty-
one. The cause of her death is unknown.

John Smith

John Smith, a housebreaker aged about forty-three, was
hanged at Tyburn on 12 December 1705 – some accounts
state erroneously that it was on 24 December – but cut
down and resuscitated on the late arrival of a reprieve. He
was afterwards granted an unconditional pardon, and so
became a familiar figure in the London underworld. In
view of his experience at the gallows – which could hardly
be called salutary – he was commonly known by his
nickname, 'Half-Hanged' Smith.

A native of Malton, near York, he was a packer by trade,
but had given up working as a journeyman to go to sea. It
is known that he served aboard a man-of-war at the Battle
of Vigo Bay in 1702, and that he was discharged from the
service when his ship returned to London. He then enlisted
as a soldier in the Second Regiment of Foot Guards, in
which he remained until late in 1705, when he was arrested
for breaking into a shop and stealing a quantity of gloves
and stockings.

Though he was not a known offender at this time, it
soon became clear that Smith was a professional criminal,
guilty of many other offences, and when he was tried at
the Old Bailey Sessions House, one of his accomplices
told the court that he and the prisoner had been thieving
together for six or seven years. Arraigned on four separate
capital charges, Smith was convicted on two of them and
sentenced to death. A week later, he was hanged from the

Triple Tree, the hangman pulling his legs to curtail his suffering.

His reprieve arrived unexpectedly a short while afterwards (about fifteen minutes after he had been 'turned off', according to most reliable accounts, though one states that it was only seven), and after being cut down, he was carried to a nearby public house, where his blood was let and he was put into a warm bed. By such means, he was quickly revived – a matter which caused great public excitement – and later that day he was well enough to be taken back to Newgate.

His free pardon was almost certainly granted in return for disclosures about other offenders, for we know from one contemporary source (the diary of Narcissus Luttrell) that by 3 March 1706 he had accused about 350 'pickpockets, house breakers, &c., who gott to be soldiers in the guards, the better to hide their roguery'. These were all drawn out when the regiments were mustered, and shipped off to serve in Spain.

What became of Smith during the nine years following his release we do not know, except that for part of that time he kept a public house in Southwark. But eventually he returned to crime, and on the morning of 28 January 1715, he was apprehended in a turning off Fenchurch Street, after breaking into a nearby warehouse.

He was clearly guilty, for he had been arrested by two watchmen while running from the premises, and a lock which he had wrenched from the door was found in his possession, together with burglary tools. But the warehouse was part of a dwelling house, and although the warehouseman appeared as prosecutor when Smith was brought to trial, the indictment on which he was tried charged him with burglary rather than housebreaking. Because of this mistake, the jury brought in a special verdict, referring the case to a panel of judges.

That was in April 1715, and it was not until 10 November the following year that the judges announced a predictable decision in Smith's favour. By this time, a second indictment, charging him in the name of the householder, could not be proceeded with, as the householder had died in the meantime. Smith had therefore to be set free.

Three and a half years later he was apprehended after leaving a cellar in Mincing Lane about three o'clock in the morning, and charged with stealing a padlock from the cellar door. A newspaper reporting his committal reminded its readers that the prisoner had once been hanged at Tyburn, and commented that 'it looks as if he was not born to be drowned'. But the padlock had not been found on him, and when Smith appeared for trial, the jury acquitted him.

A year and a half after that, on 12 September 1721, he was arrested after leaving a warehouse – also in Mincing Lane – during the early morning, and found to have picklock keys and a tinder-box in his possession. This time he was charged only with a misdemeanour, and, on being tried, was convicted. He was given a sentence of three years' imprisonment.

From the reports of this fairly minor case it is clear that, sixteen years after he had been cut down from the Triple Tree, 'Half-Hanged' Smith was still a well-known character. It was undoubtedly his legend which, three years later, inspired Jack Sheppard's last desperate scheme, and it is interesting to reflect that Smith, having completed his sentence, may have been among the crowds at Sheppard's execution.

If so, it had little effect upon him, for his own criminal practices continued to the end. At the Old Bailey Sessions of 17–18 May 1727, under his alias of John Wilson, he was indicted for stealing a padlock in circumstances similar to those of 1720. In this case, however, the padlock was recovered, and the prisoner was found guilty. He was sentenced to transportation, probably for seven years.

Smith was now sixty-five years of age and suffering from poor sight. But his petition praying for a mitigation of sentence was rejected and the following month, with a large number of other convicts, he was placed aboard a transportation ship bound for North America. We do not know whether he survived the journey.

Margaret Dickson

Margaret Dickson was a native of Musselburgh, a small town six miles to the east of Edinburgh. A young married woman, separated from her husband, she left her two children in Musselburgh early in 1723, and set out to visit two aunts living in Newcastle. But on arriving in the village of Maxwell Heugh, about thirty-seven miles south-east of her home town, she took up an offer of work at the home of a local family named Bell, and remained there for almost a year.

On the morning of 9 December, a member of the Bell family found a child's body in the River Tweed, not far from the house, and a search was begun for any woman in the district who had recently given birth in secret. Margaret admitted that the child was hers, claiming that it had been born dead, but as she had concealed her pregnancy and not called for help when she went into labour, her story was not believed. She was accused of murder and committed to prison, to await her trial.

There was no real evidence to justify the charge, but when she appeared before the High Court of Justiciary in July 1724, the prosecution contended that a woman who was so unnatural as to throw her child into a river early in the morning 'will easily be presumed to have murdered him'. The jury agreed with this, and the prisoner was convicted. She was sentenced to death.

For the next four weeks she lay in the Tolbooth, reconciling herself to the prospect of being hanged. While she still denied that she was guilty of murder, she accepted that her sentence was just, no doubt feeling that the child had died as a result of the clandestine manner in which she had given birth. But she also blamed her employer's son William for her pregnancy, claiming that he had forced himself upon her one night while she was asleep.

On the afternoon of Wednesday, 2 September, Margaret was hanged in the Grassmarket, after calling upon the crowds to take warning from her untimely end. She was left hanging for the usual half an hour, during which time her legs were pulled by the hangman, and then cut down and given to a group of her friends for burial.

Her friends nailed her into a coffin, put the coffin on to a cart and set out for Musselburgh, where she was to be buried in the Inveresk parish churchyard. As they left the city, the coffin was damaged in a struggle with some surgeons' apprentices, who wanted the hanged woman's body for dissection. But her friends managed to fight them off and continued on their way.

Reaching a village called Peppermill, they stopped for refreshment, and while they were there two joiners, looking at the coffin out of curiosity, heard a noise coming from inside it. They told Margaret's friends about this, and when the coffin was opened, the limbs of the 'corpse' were seen to move. The friends, with great excitement, then opened one of Margaret's veins, and soon she began to show further signs of life.

She was still alive on arrival in Musselburgh, where the local magistrates ordered that she should remain overnight. Restoratives were used and a minister prayed over her, but she was quite unaware of her surroundings. The following morning, she was taken to the home of her brother, where, within a day or two, she started to make a steady improvement.

The news of her survival spread far and wide, and many people came to visit her. On the Sunday after she had been hanged, she was well enough to go to church, but her appearance there attracted such a large crowd that there were fears for her safety. The following Wednesday, she spent the day in fasting and prayer, and said that she would do the same thing every Wednesday for the rest of her life, out of gratitude for her deliverance.

No attempt was made to hang her again, as it was considered that, under Scottish law, the sentence of the court had already been carried out. The following month, it was reported that she and her husband had remarried, their first marriage having been dissolved by Margaret's abortive execution.

What became of her after that is not known for certain. Various accounts state that she lived for many years longer, had several other children and sold salt through the streets of Edinburgh. But, while this may well be true, there seems to be no way of confirming it. So perhaps it is not true at all.

William Duell

William Duell, an illiterate youth of seventeen, was hanged at Tyburn with four other prisoners on 24 November 1740, following his conviction for rape at the Old Bailey the previous month. His apparently lifeless body was afterwards taken to be dissected at Surgeons' Hall, in Monkwell Street, where it was found that he was still breathing. He was therefore bled by one of the surgeons, and began to recover.

On being informed that he was still alive, the two
Sheriffs and their officers hurried to the scene. It was their
intention to take the resuscitated youth back to the gallows,
to 'complete his execution', but Surgeons' Hall had by this
time become the centre of much excitement and a threatening mob prevented them from doing so. Duell was
therefore kept in the Hall for the rest of the day, and then,
about midnight, taken back to Newgate.

There he was given some warm broth and his condition
improved further. The next day his recovery was the main
subject of conversation in London and various accounts of
it were published, some claiming that after being turned off
he had had wonderful glimpses of the 'other world'. But,
in fact, he had no recollection of his ordeal at all – as his
many visitors were undoubtedly disappointed to learn.

There was, of course, much speculation about the reason
for his survival. Some thought that he had not been hanged
for long enough; some that the rope had not been placed
correctly; some that the prisoner was too light. But,
according to one of the Sheriffs, Duell had been in a 'high
raging fever' ever since his committal to Newgate, and
was, for the most part, delirious. He therefore had 'no
impressions of fear on him', and his blood,

> circulating with violent heat and quickness, might be the
> reason why it was the longer before it could be stopped
> by the suffocation.

This, the Sheriff added, also accounted for Duell's am-
nesia.

Whatever the reason for it, his recovery was no less
astonishing than any of the other cases recounted here. But,
from Duell's point of view, the outcome of the affair was
far from happy. Though no attempt was made to hang him
afresh, he was not given a free pardon: only a commuted

sentence of transportation for life. He left England, bound
for Maryland, in April the following year, and nothing
more was ever heard of him.

Hanged with deference

On 5 May 1760, a peer of the realm was hanged at Tyburn after being convicted of murder before the House of Lords. Earl Ferrers, whose family seat was at Staunton Harold, near Ashby-de-la-Zouch, in Leicestershire, was a dissipated and brutal man, who had killed his steward, John Johnson, in a fit of madness. At his trial, he pleaded not guilty by reason of insanity, but conducted his defence with such skill that he did not seem mad at all. He was thus found guilty and sentenced to death.

Under an Act of Parliament of 1752, all persons convicted of murder were to be hanged two days after receiving sentence – or three, if one of the days was a Sunday – and their bodies were afterwards to be anatomized or gibbeted. In Ferrers's case, the execution was respited for two weeks, in consideration of his rank, but the direction that he should be anatomized was left unchanged. In spite of this impending horror, however, the condemned man, who was imprisoned in the Tower of London, was treated with the deference normally afforded to persons of his station.

Though Tyburn was still London's main place of execution, the Triple Tree had been pulled down the previous year, having stood since 1571. Since then, a 'new moving gallows' had been erected there when needed, with the condemned still being hanged from the back of the cart.

But for Ferrers's execution a scaffold with a raised platform was constructed, similar to that used for the hanging of pirates at Execution Dock. The Sheriffs of London and Middlesex, who were responsible for the arrangements, obviously thought that this would be an improvement on the usual method of hanging.

On the day that he was to die, Ferrers put on his wedding clothes: a light-coloured suit embroidered with silver. Friends had provided him with a mourning coach for the procession to Tyburn, but he rejected this in favour of his own landau, drawn by six horses and attended by liveried servants. The procession left the Tower at nine o'clock in the morning, amid vast crowds of onlookers.

A large body of constables, headed by a High Constable, led the way. These were followed by a party of horse grenadiers and a party of foot soldiers. Behind these came one of the Sheriffs, a Mr Errington, in his official chariot, accompanied by his Under-Sheriff. Then came the landau, in which the other Sheriff, a French bookseller named Vaillant, rode with the condemned, as did the chaplain of the Tower. This was guarded by more horse grenadiers and foot soldiers.

Behind the landau came Sheriff Vaillant's chariot, in which his Under-Sheriff was riding; then the mourning coach and six, occupied by some of Ferrers's friends; and finally a hearse and six, in which the condemned man's body was to be taken away for dissection after the execution had been carried out.

The procession, which was undoubtedly the grandest that ever made the fatal journey to Tyburn, took two and three-quarter hours. Ferrers remained calm throughout that time, though he told Sheriff Vaillant he thought it hard that he should have to die at the place appointed for the execution of common felons. He refused to discuss religion with the chaplain and said that he would have no religious service at the gallows except the Lord's Prayer.

At Tyburn, he alighted from the landau and mounted the scaffold, which was hung with black baize. He knelt for the prayer which he had agreed to, repeated it devoutly and called on God to forgive his 'errors'. He then made a present of his watch to Sheriff Vaillant and asked to see the executioner. Thomas Turlis, the hangman of London, immediately came forward to beg his Lordship's pardon, as was customary at the execution of a nobleman, and to this Ferrers replied, 'I freely forgive you, as I do all mankind, and hope myself to be forgiven.'

He had five guineas to give Turlis, but gave it to the hangman's assistant by mistake. This caused an un-dignified dispute between the two men in which Vaillant had to intervene. He presumably settled it in Turlis's favour, for the hangman accepted the outcome without further protest.

Soon the condemned man stood on the raised platform, his arms bound with a black sash and a white cap on his head. The halter was placed round his neck, the cap pulled down over his face and, at a signal from Sheriff Vaillant – for Ferrers refused to give it himself – the platform was lowered. But the mechanism was faulty and it did not fall as far as expected, with the result that Ferrers's toes continued to touch it. He died with the hangman and his assistant pulling his legs.

His body was left hanging for over an hour, during which the Sheriffs – according to a letter written by Horace Walpole – 'fell to eating and drinking on the scaffold and helped up one of their friends to drink with them'. It was then cut down, placed in a coffin, and taken away in the hearse to Surgeons' Hall, where the remainder of the sentence was to be carried out.

'The executioners fought for the rope and the one who lost it cried,' says Walpole. 'The mob tore off the black cloth as relics but the universal crowd behaved with great decency and admiration, as well they might, for no exit was ever made with more sensible resolution and with less ostentation.'

The rope was not made of silk, as some accounts state. The Sheriffs had considered a proposal to use such a rope, but it had not been found possible to have one made in the time available. But the rope which *was* used was still of considerable value to the hangman, who could sell it by the inch in some nearby tavern. There was always a buyer for any article associated with the execution of a famous criminal.

At Surgeons' Hall, after being anatomized, Ferrers's body was put on public display, and remained so for the next three days. It was then delivered to his friends for burial.

This was the only case in which a drop was ever used at Tyburn, for it was clearly not a success. Subsequent executions there were carried out by the old horse-and-cart method, which had been in use for centuries.

The blind man

Cornelius Saunders, a thirty-three-year-old blind man, was a familiar figure to the inhabitants of Spitalfields in 1763. He made his living in and around the parish, mainly from the sale of small washing-tubs, which he made from used salmon kits. Born in Holland, he had lived in England since the age of about ten. It was believed that his blindness had been caused by an attack of smallpox shortly after he arrived here.

Saunders obtained his salmon kits from a fishwife named Mary White, with whom he had been dealing for thirteen years, and it was for this reason that he called at her home in Lamb Street on 27 May. Mary White lived with her husband Joseph and worked in partnership with another woman named Sarah Dobey. She was busy when Saunders called, and having sold him eight kits, she allowed him to go down into her cellar on his own to fetch them.

But while he was down there, the blind man found Mrs White's savings – over £40 – in a canvas bag hidden in a shoe. Evidently a simple fellow, he took the money, concealed it in one of the kits and managed to leave the premises without exciting suspicion. It was not until the following day that the theft was discovered. By the time he was apprehended, Saunders had bought himself some new clothes and a pair of silver buckles for his shoes. The rest of the stolen money was found in his possession.

Charged with the crime, Saunders appeared for trial at the Old Bailey Sessions on 6 July, pleading not guilty. The court was told of two confessions which he had made on the day of his arrest, but the prisoner denied making them. He said that Mrs White's money had been in one of the salmon kits and that he had not discovered it until after he left the house.

Convicted of a capital offence, he was sentenced to death and taken back to Newgate to share a condemned cell with eight other men. The *Ordinary's Account* of his case tells us that he daily attended chapel, but seldom spoke or made responses, as he was unaccustomed to religious services. He was in better health than most of the other condemned and, although initially resentful of his plight, he became peaceful and resigned, occupying himself in preparation for death. On 17 August, he and five of his companions were ordered for execution on the 24th.

When the hanging day arrived, there was a last-minute respite for one of the condemned. The others were made ready for their final ordeal.

There were two carts, and Saunders rode in the first. One of the men in the second cart was handcuffed and fettered after attempting to escape. The march to Tyburn took about an hour, and another half an hour was spent tying the five men up to the movable gallows, in readiness to be hanged from a single cart.

All were penitent and asked the crowds – which were very large – to join in prayers. The crowds did so, but while the prayers were in progress there was a loud crack of timber from the gallery overlooking the scene. Some of the occupants of the gallery swung to the ground and many of the other spectators drew back in alarm. There was, however, no accident, and after a brief pause the prayers were resumed.

After the Ordinary had completed his ministrations, the condemned continued praying. Their caps were drawn over their faces and the cart was driven off. Many of the people present were moved to tears, almost certainly for the blind man.

When the proceedings came to an end, and the bodies of the five hanged men were cut down from the gallows, the tears of the multitude gave way to anger. A great many people – some thousands, according to one account – made their way to Lamb Street, forced their way into Mrs White's house, and began bringing her furniture out into the street. It is not known whether any member of the family was at home at the time.

Before long, soldiers arrived at the scene to restore order. But the blind man's body, which had been carried from Tyburn, reached the house at the same time, and was placed at his prosecutrix's to urge the rioters on to further excesses. Having made a fire of all Mrs White's furniture, the mob threw stones at the soldiers, to prevent them from putting it out. By the time the crowd was dispersed, the house had almost been demolished.

The following day, Saunders's body, which the mob had left behind, was buried in Spitalfields Churchyard. The ceremony was attended by soldiers and magistrates, as a precaution against any further outrage.

The cursing octogenarian

On 4 October 1843, a feeble Scottish octogenarian who had been convicted of murder was led out to the place of execution in Stirling to expiate his crime. Sitting on a chair on the scaffold – for he was unable to stand without assistance – Allan Mair protested his innocence and cursed the witnesses who had given evidence against him.

'I have been most unjustly condemned through false swearing, and here I pray that God may send his curse upon all connected with my trial!' he said. 'I curse the witnesses with all the curses of the 109th Psalm!'

The crowds were shocked. To them, it was quite improper for a condemned man to speak like this during his last moments of life. They had no doubt expected him to confess his sins in the usual way, and call on them to take warning from his untimely end. But Allan Mair had no intention of doing any such thing.

'There is one person connected with the parish who brought in false witnesses to condemn an innocent man,' he continued. 'When in prison this person came to visit me, but I told him that it was a wonder the God of heaven did not rain down fire and brimstone upon him, as he did upon Sodom and Gomorrah.

'He it was who brought false witnesses against me – who brought Roman Catholics, who worship stocks and stones, and others to swear away my life – but God will curse and eternally damn him!'

As nobody tried to restrain him, the old man went on to make further allegations. The hangman, wearing, for some unknown reason, a black crêpe mask, stood waiting patiently nearby.

'They told me that witnesses would be got to defend me, but no one appeared and I was left to the mercy of false swearers,' said Mair. 'I wished them to allow me to get a paper drawn up of what my little house contained, so that the articles might be sold, but they would not let me. If they had, I would have got witnesses myself, and I would not have been here today.'

After going on in this manner for another minute or two, the prisoner suddenly fell silent. The hangman then came over to him and asked whether he was done.

'No, Sir, I am not done!' replied Mair, striking his knee with his clenched fist. 'I'm not done. I'll say much more if they will allow me!

'Before this multitude, in whose presence I am to be sent into eternity, there to appear before God, I declare I am innocent. And do you think I would appear before Christ with a lie in my mouth?

'I have been unjustly accused, falsely sworn against and unlawfully condemned. I say these things that the people from my parish, when they return home, may tell those who have so sworn against me what I have said regarding them, and how my curse was poured out upon them.

'The moment I am thrown into eternity may their plagues commence; may they be eternally blasted! My most fervent hope is that the Almighty God may speedily and everlastingly damn them!'

The old man, who was eighty-two or eighty-three years of age, had been convicted of beating his eighty-five-year-old 'reputed wife', Mary Fletcher, to death. In spite of this, the crowd had at first felt sorry for him, for he was bent almost double and hardly seemed capable of such a deed. But as they listened to his violent speech, their feelings of sympathy subsided, giving way to cries of horror and detestation.

When, at last, it was over, the clergyman who was with him, the Reverend Mr Leitch, offered up a prayer on his behalf. The prayer was such that everyone was moved by it, except the condemned man himself. Afterwards, when Mr Leitch bade him farewell, Mair extended his hand, saying, 'Farewell, Sir, farewell. I'll soon be in eternity!'

The hangman then went to work, putting a cap on his head and adjusting the rope round his neck. With the cap drawn over his face, the old man was asked to stand, so that the chair could be removed, but he replied that he could not and wept piteously. He was therefore hanged sitting down, his last words being, 'May God be—' before the bolt was withdrawn and he fell with a heavy groan.

He did not die instantly, and as his hands had not been properly pinioned, he was able to raise one of them to the back of his neck. But having grasped the rope in an attempt to save himself, he immediately let go of it and so went on hanging until he expired. The newspaper accounts of his execution state that it was some time before his struggles ended.

Hanged in black satin

On 13 November 1849, Frederick George Manning and his wife Marie – or Maria, as she called herself – were hanged together at Horsemonger Lane Jail, in Southwark, south London, for the murder of Marie's lover, Patrick O'Connor. The couple, who had been in financial difficulties, had invited O'Connor to their home in Bermondsey, and had there killed him for the sake of his money and some railway shares. Afterwards they had tried to destroy his body by burying it in quicklime.

The case naturally caused intense excitement. Frederick Manning, an unemployed railway guard, claimed that his wife was solely to blame for O'Connor's death. Marie, Swiss by birth and a former lady's maid, denied involvement, and on being convicted made a speech in which she claimed that there was no justice in Britain for a foreign subject. 'If my husband, through jealousy and a revengeful feeling against O'Connor, chose to murder him, I don't see why I should be punished for it!' she declared.

To the masses, she was an object of hatred, and on the morning that she and her husband were to die, many thousands of people gathered at the front of the prison. Their mood was one of brutal flippancy, as was often the case at well-attended executions, and Charles Dickens afterwards wrote a famous letter to *The Times* about it, stating that the horrors of the gibbet, and the crime for which the Mannings had been condemned, faded in his mind before the 'atrocious bearing, looks and language' of the assembled spectators.

Shortly before being taken out to the gallows, the condemned couple met in the prison chapel, at Manning's request. After the accusations which they had made against each other, he was anxious that she should bear him no animosity. She assured him that she did not, and leaned towards him so that he could kiss her. After receiving the sacrament, they kissed and embraced each other several times, and Manning was heard to say, 'I hope we shall meet in heaven.'

They were then taken to different parts of the chapel for the pinioning of their arms. Manning suffered this procedure patiently, but Marie almost fainted and had to be given brandy. When she recovered, she asked the prison surgeon to bind a black silk handkerchief over her eyes, and this he did. He then, at her request, put a black lace veil over her head, and this she tied under her chin. After that, her arms were pinioned without difficulty.

Soon the two prisoners were escorted out on to the prison roof, where the scaffold awaited them. Manning, wearing a black suit with his shirt collar loosened, had to be assisted by two warders. His wife, who wore a black satin gown, was led by the surgeon and, in spite of being blindfolded, walked with firm steps. She showed no further sign of agitation.

When Manning took his place under the fatal beam, William Calcraft, the hangman, pulled a white nightcap over his head, as was customary, and began putting the halter into place round his neck. When he had finished, Manning turned to his wife, who was now standing alongside him, and, whispering something, put his hand out in her direction. With the help of one of the warders, she took it, and so took leave of him for the last time before submitting herself to Calcraft.

When she, too, was ready, the scaffold was cleared of all its occupants except the condemned, the chaplain and the hangman. The chaplain then gave Marie a final opportunity to confess her guilt – as her husband had already done, after a fashion – but she declined to do so. The chaplain therefore withdrew, and a moment later the drop fell.

It seemed at first that both prisoners died quickly, almost without a struggle. But when their bodies were cut down, after hanging for about an hour, Marie's features were found to be frightfully distorted, showing that she had suffered acutely. Calcraft, on leaving the prison, was heard to say that he 'did not much like hanging a man and his wife'.

Tradition has it that Marie's gown caused black satin to become unfashionable, but this appears not to be true. At the Great Crystal Palace Exhibition less than two years later, seven manufacturers, including one British firm, all won awards for garments of this material. And other evidence, collected from periodicals of the time, suggests that the demand for black satin was unaffected by the execution.

It is, however, worthy of note that Dickens later used Marie as his model for Hortense, the murderous French-woman, in *Bleak House*.

Shocking mishaps
at the gallows

In Lifford, County Donegal, in 1831, two brothers, James and Alexander Stewart, were hanged at the front of the local jail, on a drop erected about forty feet above the ground. James Stewart died easily, without a struggle, but Alexander's rope broke and he fell to the pavement below.

It seemed at first that he had been killed by the fall, but on being taken back into the jail he was found to be still alive. Within twenty minutes he had recovered well enough to be hanged again, and walked back out on to the drop more firmly than before.

This time, however, the working of the drop was obstructed by his brother's body, which was still hanging. Alexander thus fell without a jerk and died slowly from strangulation – a spectacle that was observed by a crowd of 12,000 people.

Four months later, Patrick Stewart, a third brother, was hanged at the same jail. By an amazing coincidence, the rope broke on this occasion as well, and the condemned man fell to the ground, cutting his head or neck on the steps leading up to the jail door, so that he bled profusely. He was nonetheless hanged again, this time with a shorter length of rope than before, and died almost immediately.

On 11 January 1806, a cow thief named Patrick Connor was hanged above the entrance to Dublin's New Prison, but the rope broke and he fell on to a railing below the scaffold. Badly bruised and cut, he was escorted back to the drop and hanged again, this time without any mishap.

In New York, in 1837, the execution of a murderer named Cadiche was badly bungled, the hangman allowing the condemned so much rope that he fell to the ground and broke his collarbone. The accident caused astonishment and indignation among the spectators, and the executioner was vilified for his lack of skill. But the officers in charge of the execution had no intention of postponing it, and a second attempt to carry it out was only averted by the discovery that Cadiche was already dead.

At a multiple execution in Ilchester in 1785, three of the six condemned had to be hanged a second time, their halters having slipped from their necks at the first attempt. The three who did *not* have to face the ordeal again included Thomas Woodham, the Gloucester hangman (see p. 132).

John Kimmarly, a convicted murderer, survived three attempts to hang him, the rope breaking each time. At the fourth attempt, the rope finally held and he went on hanging until he was dead.

The execution took place on St Michael's Hill, Bristol, on 4 May 1739, and it was reported that the condemned man used each interval to make an address to the spectators, 'forgiving and begging forgiveness of all men'.

A burglar who was hanged with him died without incident.

At an execution in Crawfordsville, Indiana, on 16 October 1886, the rope broke twice. The condemned man, John Coffey, landed heavily the first time and lost consciousness, with blood spurting from his ears. But he was

---

When Martin Clench and James Mackley were hanged at Newgate Prison on 5 June 1797, the platform gave way unexpectedly and the executioner, his assistant and two clergymen fell through the trap with the condemned. One of the clergymen was badly hurt.

---

immediately carried back on to the scaffold to be hanged again.

As the rope was being adjusted for the second attempt, he suddenly regained consciousness and begged to have the cap taken off, so that he could make another speech, but this was not permitted. When the rope broke for the second time, he was caught before he reached the ground.

At the third attempt, the prisoner was slowly strangled, dying in twelve minutes. A newspaper report of the affair states that the spectators 'were nearly overcome with horror'.

For the execution of Robert Johnston, which took place in Edinburgh's Lawnmarket on 30 December 1818, a small collapsible platform was used. But the rope was too long, and when the platform was lowered the prisoner's toes were still touching it. This infuriated the crowds, and the officials in attendance were driven from the scaffold by a shower of stones.

Some of the spectators then climbed on to the scaffold themselves, cut down the prisoner and removed the ropes from his arms and neck. Before long, they were carrying him off towards the High Street, while others stoned the police, manhandled the executioner or tried unsuccessfully to demolish the scaffold.

Johnston, a twenty-two-year-old robber, was retaken in

Advocates Close and carried into the nearby police office, where a surgeon attended him. Unable to speak, he was kept there until order was restored, then taken out to be hanged again.

At the place of execution, the Lord Provost exhorted the crowds to behave peacefully, explaining that the magistrates had a painful duty imposed upon them and that they had to fulfil it, whatever the circumstances. But the second hanging was bungled in the same way as the first, and the prisoner had to be lifted up so that the rope could be shortened with a few turns round the hook above him. This led to further shouts of protest from the spectators, but no further outrages were committed, as the place was now guarded by soldiers.

The following morning, the hangman, John Simpson, was dismissed from office.

An extraordinary incident occurred at Newgate Prison in 1814, when a robber named John Ashton was hanged. Ashton, who appeared to be insane, kicked and danced on the scaffold before a large crowd of spectators, exclaiming repeatedly, 'I'm Lord Wellington!' When the platform on which he stood fell from under him, he rebounded from the rope, landed back on the scaffold and started dancing again, apparently unhurt. 'What do ye think of me?' he cried. 'Am I not Lord Wellington now?' The hangman had to climb back on to the scaffold and push him off.

Forty-two years after Ashton's execution, a murderer named William Bousfield, who had killed his wife and three children, was hanged at the same prison. He was ill and weak, and had actually tried to kill himself by burning his face on the fire in his cell. His condition, in fact, was so bad that he had to be carried to the scaffold and hanged sitting on a chair.

Calcraft, the hangman, was nervous and agitated, having received a letter warning him that he would be shot on the scaffold. Because of this, he hurriedly drew the bolt operating the drop, and left the scene without waiting to see the result.

After hanging motionless for a second or two, the condemned man, with a tremendous effort, raised himself up to the level of the drop, got both of his feet on to it and began trying to raise his hands to the rope. At this, there were shrieks of horror from the crowd and one of the turnkeys, rushing on to the scaffold, pushed his feet away.

But Bousfield's desperate struggle continued, and Calcraft had to be brought back to finish his work. Four times the condemned man succeeded in getting his feet on to the drop, and four times they were pushed off. Even then, the hangman had to swing on Bousfield's body in order to hold his legs down until he finally died.

The shocking spectacle naturally caused an outcry, with opponents of the death penalty intensifying their demands for reform. Calcraft, however, was officially cleared of blame, in view of the circumstances in which the execution had been carried out.

Of the various devices used for hanging in America, the strangest was undoubtedly one which jerked the condemned upwards. This technique was developed in the hope that it would prove to be more efficient than other methods of hanging, and appears to have been used quite widely during the latter part of the nineteenth century. But it could be bungled, with ghastly results, as we see from a case which occurred in New York in 1884.

Alexander Jefferson, a black double murderer, was hanged at Raymond Street Jail, Brooklyn, in the presence of a small group of reporters. To carry out the execution, the hangman cut a rope which held two heavy weights in place; these then fell on to a mattress behind a partition, and the prisoner was pulled five feet into the air, with a jolt intended to break his neck. When his body fell back limp, it seemed that he was dead, but suddenly he began to writhe in agony. Soon his knees were drawn up almost to his chin, and he kicked and moaned in a piteous manner.

'The Sheriff was bewildered,' says a newspaper account. 'His face turned pale and his eyes filled with tears. The hangman was called from his pen to witness his clumsy work. He looked at his struggling victim, but said he could do nothing for him.'

Before long, Jefferson began freeing his hands and clutching the noose desperately. Unable to loosen it, he pulled the black cap from his head and reached out imploringly towards all who were there. But nobody went to his aid, and the hanged man's struggles continued for several minutes longer. The Sheriff, the hangman and the reporters all watched helplessly until death overtook him and the terrible spectacle came to an end.

Far more gruesome from the spectators' point of view, but not nearly so painful from his own, was the execution of Thomas H. Ketchum, in Clayton, New Mexico, seventeen years later. Ketchum, commonly called 'Black Jack', was a notorious outlaw from Wyoming who had been captured during an attempted train robbery. His hanging, in April 1901, took place in public, on a scaffold with a trapdoor, and was attended by a large crowd.

A handsome, good-humoured man, Ketchum went to the gallows with a display of bravado which his audience loved. He shook hands with everyone on the scaffold, joked with the hangman and even helped to adjust the noose round his own neck. 'I'll be in hell before you start breakfast!' he said to the witnesses.

But there were a number of delays, and before long he

began to get nervous. 'Let her go, boys!' he said impatiently. The call went unheeded. A little later, when they were finally ready, he shook hands all round for the second time. 'Let her go, boys!' he said again.

At last the Sheriff cut the rope holding the trapdoor and 'Black Jack' fell to his death. But he did not die in the manner intended, for the drop which he had been given was too long for a man of his weight. Because of this, he was decapitated by the rope. Grotesquely, his headless body landed feet first on the ground, stood upright for a moment, then swayed and fell, with blood spurting from it. His severed head, still in the black cap which had been pulled down over it, rolled to one side.

A photographer who was present recorded the event in a sequence of shots taken immediately before and after the hanging. These were apparently printed for sale to the public, for many copies are still in existence. If so, we may be sure that he did well out of it.

At the execution of John Holloway, Owen Haggerty and Elizabeth Godfrey, who were hanged at Newgate on 23 February 1807, the pressure of the crowds was so great that a fierce struggle broke out. In the panic which ensued, thirty people were trampled to death and fifteen others were injured.

The men they could not hang

In Sydney, in 1803, Joseph Samuel was sentenced to death for breaking into a house and stealing a writing-desk containing money and other articles of value. Three attempts were made to hang him, but each time the rope broke or unravelled. His sentence was afterwards commuted.

Samuel had originally been given seven years' transportation for larceny at the Old Bailey in 1795, when he was fourteen years old, but had not arrived in Australia until 1801, by which time his term had almost expired. At the gallows he caused a sensation by accusing Isaac Simmons, a former convict constable, of a brutal murder for which he (Simmons) had already been tried and acquitted.

Samuel is known to have absconded from public labour in 1805. He is believed to have died in a tempest in April 1806, after putting out to sea in an open boat with seven other escaped convicts.

In 1885, John Lee, a servant convicted of murdering his employer, endured three attempts to hang him at Exeter Prison, the trapdoors failing to open at each attempt. His sentence was commuted to life imprisonment and like Samuel, he became known as 'the man they could not hang'.

Lee was released after serving over twenty years in prison and later married, but eventually abandoned his wife and two children and disappeared into oblivion. He is believed to have died in the United States, at the age of sixty-eight, in 1933.

In 1894, Will Purvis, the son of a Mississippi farmer, survived an attempt to hang him in Columbia, Marion County, for a murder which he had not committed. After a number of appeals had been dismissed, a new date was set for his execution, in December 1895, but friends and sympathizers broke into the jail where he was being held and rescued him. He gave himself up when a new State Governor offered him a commutation of sentence, and in 1898 was pardoned and set free in response to public pressure.

The case was resurrected in 1917, when Joe Beard, aged sixty, made a deathbed confession, proving Purvis innocent of the crime for which he had been sentenced. Purvis was subsequently paid $5000 compensation 'for services rendered the State in the State Penitentiary for an erroneous conviction'. At his death in 1938, he had outlived every member of the jury which had found him guilty forty-five years earlier.

When a soldier named Hales was hanged in Jersey in 1807, the hangman, by suspending himself on the condemned man's body, caused the rope to slip so far that the prisoner's feet touched the ground. He then tried to strangle him by pulling him sideways, and when this caused it to slip even further, he suddenly climbed on to the prisoner's shoulders.

The spectators watched in shocked disbelief as Hales suddenly stood upright with the hangman still on his shoulders and loosened the halter with his fingers. But when the Sheriff called for another rope to be prepared, the crowd intervened and persuaded him to postpone the execution. The case was afterwards referred to the King and, as no subsequent reports were published in connection with the affair, it is likely that the prisoner's sentence was commuted.

In Tallinn, Estonia, in 1942, an unsuccessful attempt was made to hang Ronald Seth, an agent of the Special Operations Executive who had fallen into German hands.

Seth later described in one of his many books how he was taken out to a public scaffold and stood swaying in the cold, with the noose round his neck. When the lever was pulled, the trap fell only a few inches, the machinery having been sabotaged by students the night before. The execution was therefore postponed, but no fresh attempt was ever made to carry it out.

Also during the Second World War, Sim Kessel, a prisoner in Auschwitz concentration camp, was hanged for trying to escape. In his case, the rope broke, but again no second attempt was made. Kessel, like Seth, lived to write about his experiences.

The thirty-eight Indians

The mass hanging of Sioux Indians at Mankato, Minnesota, in December 1862, followed the suppression of a spontaneous uprising four months earlier. A great many Indians had taken part in the revolt, and hundreds of white settlers – men, women and children – had been brutally murdered before order was restored by a force of cavalry.

In all, 303 of the Indians who were taken prisoner were sentenced to death by a military court. Most of them were spared by President Lincoln, who confirmed the sentences only of those who had 'wantonly and wickedly' killed civilians. Even so, thirty-eight prisoners were ordered for execution, and a huge scaffold was erected so that they could all be hanged together.

Those who were to die spent their last few days in a different building from the other prisoners, chained in pairs and with the chains fastened to the floor. Resigned to their fate, they made no complaint about their treatment and showed little emotion of any sort.

On the morning of their execution, they adorned themselves with paint, beads and feathers, and distributed keepsakes among friends who came to see them. Every now and then they started up a tribal death-wail, which white observers found quite unearthly. When their chains had been cut off, their hands were bound and white caps were placed on their heads, ready to be pulled down at the last minute. A priest entered their cell for the second time that morning, and after addressing them at length, offered up prayers on their behalf. The Provost Marshal, Captain Redfield, then came to summon them and they immediately got to their feet and fell in behind him.

He led them out through files of soldiers to the place of execution, the Indians wailing in unison all the way. The scaffold, which was twenty-four feet square, had crossbeams on all four sides, each of them long enough to provide space for ten offenders to be hanged together. When they reached it, the condemned rushed up the steps after Redfield, as though each was determined not to be left behind. On the scaffold, they kept up their lament as they moved into position of their own accord. The halters were placed round their necks, the white caps pulled down over their faces. At this point, the conduct of the condemned became even stranger still.

'All joined in shouting and singing, as it appeared to those who were ignorant of the language,' the *St Paul Pioneer* reported two days later. 'Their bodies swayed to and fro and their every limb seemed to be keeping time. The drop trembled and shook as if all were dancing.'

Although they were bound, they were so close together that many of them were able to grasp the hands of those beside them. As many as three or four in a row were hand in hand, swaying together with the rise and fall of their voices. One old man, however, reached out on both sides, but could find no hand to grasp. His struggles were painful to behold.

When all was ready, a drumbeat sounded, then another – both of them almost drowned by the voices of the condemned – and the drop fell with a crash. The crowds gave a loud cheer but then fell silent, watching the swinging bodies.

One of the ropes had broken, but it seemed that the

victim of this mishap was already dead. His body, which had fallen with a heavy thud, was nonetheless hanged again without delay.

The *Pioneer's* report tells us that at first none of the Indians struggled, their only movements being 'the natural vibrations occasioned by the fall'. But after hanging for a short while, several of them drew up their legs once or twice, and there was some movement of their arms. One was still breathing after ten minutes, at which point his rope was adjusted. He then expired.

'It is unnecessary to speak of the awful sight of thirty-eight human beings suspended in the air,' the report commented. 'Imagination will readily supply what we refrain from describing.'

After the bodies had hung for about half an hour, army physicians examined them and reported them all dead. They were left hanging for a little longer, however, until a number of mule teams arrived on the scene. They were then cut down and placed in the wagons without ceremony, to be taken off for burial in one large grave.

Having witnessed their departure, the crowds began to disperse, evidently satisfied that justice had been done.

More of the roast

The first notable execution to be carried out at California's San Quentin Prison was that of William Henry Theodore Durrant, who was hanged there on the morning of 7 January 1898. Durrant, aged twenty-seven, was a former medical student and Baptist Sunday-school official who had killed two young women in San Francisco's sensational 'Demon in the Belfry' murder case of 1895. His execution caused much excitement, and a large crowd of 'unofficial witnesses' came to watch the proceedings. They were all allowed into the prison after leaving their guns outside.

San Quentin's gallows stood in a large whitewashed room on the top floor of an old industrial building. It had been constructed just a few years earlier, after the legislature decided that executions should be conducted in state prisons rather than in the county jails where they had previously taken place. The mechanism was operated from a booth on a corner of the platform, where three guards, unseen by the witnesses, sat at a long, narrow table, each with a cord in front of him. At a signal from the hangman, all three cords were cut, and the trap fell – with only the hangman himself knowing which guard had released it.

While awaiting execution, Theodore Durrant had sometimes been cheerful and confident, but at other times nervous and on the point of breaking down. On his last morning, in a holding cell adjoining the execution chamber, he was in a good humour and had a big breakfast. 'The man who had but three hours to live ate heartily of beefsteak and potatoes, eggs and ham, tea and toast, consuming all that they gave him and appearing to relish it,' a *San Francisco Chronicle* report informs us.

The condemned man denied to the end that he was the killer of the two women. A convert to Catholicism, he was heard to say in a loud voice to the priest who heard his confession, 'No, I will not confess the murders, because I am not guilty!' And from the gallows, as he stood with the noose round his neck, he spoke to the crowd at length, accusing the newspapers of persecuting and hounding him to his grave.

When the trap fell, his neck was broken, but eleven minutes elapsed before he was declared dead. This, however, did not prevent the Warden, William E. Hale, from expressing himself satisfied with the way in which the hanging had been carried out.

'It was the most successful execution that has ever taken place in this institution,' he declared. 'There was not a hitch. The spectators all conducted themselves properly and even Durrant seemed to want to do everything he could to make the affair successful. I have never before seen a condemned man meet his fate so calmly and with less apparent fear. I do not think he ever once harboured a thought of suicide, and for the past week I believe he was without hope!'

The body was cut down and placed in an official coffin, but had afterwards to be transferred to a less formal one which the dead man's parents had provided. When this was carried into the reception room where the bereaved couple were waiting, the black cap was taken off, revealing a face which was itself almost black. Both parents kissed it and wept, Mrs Durrant exclaiming, 'My boy! My boy! They have murdered you!'

She seemed at that moment to be on the verge of hysteria, and others who were present turned away in sympathy. But within a short time the couple were sitting down together, chatting pleasantly, and Mrs Durrant was smiling. A convict named Wilson, who had the job of looking after the room, then asked her if she would like a cup of tea. 'Thank you, I would,' she replied.

Wilson went off to the kitchen and brought back a large tray containing not just tea but a considerable quantity of food as well. This he set down on a table three feet from their son's coffin – and Mr and Mrs Durrant immediately began eating it. It was not long before Mrs Durrant was heard to say, 'Papa, I'll take some more of that roast.'

It seems that they ate almost as voraciously as their son had eaten his breakfast, for a journalist who observed them claimed afterwards that he had been shocked and disgusted by what he saw.

Later that day, the couple returned to San Francisco, taking the body with them. The coffin was carried into the front parlour of their cottage and opened – to remain thus until arrangements could be made for its cremation. For although their son had expressed a wish to be buried, Mrs Durrant insisted that he be cremated, so that she and her husband could have an urn of ashes that would be 'forever a comfort' to them.

But no crematorium in the city would accept the body, so they had to start looking further afield. Because of this, it went on lying in their home for five days, with Mrs Durrant talking to it for hours on end. However, the Pasadena Crematory eventually agreed to take it, and the cremation took place there on 13 January.

A hanging in Japan

Tokichi Ishii, the central figure of one of Japan's strangest murder cases, was a professional criminal from Nagoya, in south-east Honshu. Brought up in poverty, he had had little education and turned to crime at an early age. He committed many thefts and burglaries, sometimes wandering from place to place in the guise of a pedlar, but was rarely at liberty for long. From the age of nineteen onwards, most of his life was spent in prison.

On the night of 29 April 1915, Ishii arrived on foot in the Tokyo suburb of Suzugamori, and sat down to rest in front of a teahouse that was closed. As he sat there, his attention was attracted by a geisha passing nearby, and he suddenly found himself possessed by an ungovernable passion. Pausing only to make sure that there was nobody else about, he rose to his feet and took hold of her roughly.

Alarmed for her own safety, the woman, whose name was Oharu, screamed and began calling for help. To silence her, Ishii took the towel that hung at his belt, twisted it round her neck and went on tightening it until her struggles ceased. He then released her and, finding that she was dead, took her purse and a small book from one of the sleeves of her kimono. With these, he fled from the scene of the crime.

Though a bitter and violent man, Ishii had never killed anyone before. But the crime did not trouble him unduly and the following month, in Yokohama, he strangled a married couple in the course of burgling their house. About the end of July, a party of policemen in Toyohashi tried to arrest him on suspicion, and in making his escape, Ishii wounded one of them with a sword. In another such incident, in Okazaki, he wounded a policeman with a knife.

The geisha's lover, a man named Komori, had in the meantime been accused of her murder. He confessed to the crime but later denied it, claiming that his confession had been extracted by torture. He had, however, been seen in Oharu's company not long before she was killed, and it was known that they had quarrelled. On being brought to trial, he was therefore convicted and sentenced to death.

On the evening of 8 December, Tokichi Ishii and an accomplice named Sekiguchi were arrested on suspicion, following an attempted burglary in Tokyo. Ishii was confident that they would be released, as there was no real evidence against them, but while waiting in a police cell he heard several other men talking about Komori and Oharu's murder. On learning that an innocent man was to be hanged for his own crime, Ishii confessed that he was the real culprit.

The confession caused a sensation. Komori was released from prison on parole and Ishii was put on trial for the geisha's murder. But no evidence could be found to corroborate his account of the crime and, to his own amazement, Ishii was acquitted.

By this time, however, he was a different man and the court's verdict was not to his liking. A convert to Christianity, he was now haunted by his own wrongdoings and determined to expiate them. He therefore protested at his acquittal, insisting that he was guilty.

Under Japanese law, the Public Procurator can appeal against the court's judgment, and in this case he decided to do so. The case was accordingly reopened in the Appeal Court, and this time evidence was produced to bear out the prisoner's confession – including that of a woman to whom he had shown the book taken from Oharu's body. The lower court's verdict was thus reversed and Ishii sentenced to death.

With the proceedings dragging on for many months, this remarkable case had attracted a great deal of publicity. Ishii had become the centre of much attention and many people went to see him in his cell in Tokyo Prison. Two missionaries whose teachings had brought about his own conversion, both of them women, visited him regularly.

Ishii did not regret having brought the death sentence on himself, and did not expect or hope for mercy. 'It was God's own judgment and I am satisfied,' he told Caroline Macdonald (one of the missionaries) the morning after the sentence had been passed.

He did not know when he would be hanged, for in Japan the condemned are not told beforehand. He nonetheless began writing his life story, striving to ensure that it was completed as quickly as possible. It was not until several months after he had finished it that the day finally arrived.

Throughout the time that he lay under sentence of death, Tokichi Ishii showed neither dread nor impatience. 'I wish everyone to know that I spend my days in happiness because of the love of God which passes our power to measure,' he wrote towards the end. 'Christ's love really does mean that there is eternal salvation for even the most abandoned, if he repents and believes.'

His faith never left him.

He was eventually hanged, at the age of forty-seven, on 17 August 1918: over two and a half years after making the confession which had saved Komori's life. The prison's Buddhist chaplain, who was with him on the scaffold, said that Ishii's conduct inspired respect among all who were present.

He died with fortitude, declaring that his soul was returning to the City of God.

A double hanging
inside the Arctic Circle

The first Eskimos to be hanged under Canadian law were two hunters from the sealing grounds of Kent Peninsula, at the eastern end of Coronation Gulf, Northwest Territories. Tatamagama and his nephew Aligoomiak were members of the Cogmollock tribe which, in the early 1920s, had a reputation for lawlessness and bloodshed. Between them, they killed several fellow Eskimos and two white men, one of whom was a corporal in the Royal Canadian Mounted Police.

The first killings occurred as a result of Tatamagama and his friend Pugnana becoming involved in a dispute with another of their tribe named Hanak. There was, as always, a shortage of women among the Cogmollocks, due to their practice of killing unwanted female children, and Tatamagama and Pugnana objected to Hanak having not just a wife but several other women as well. In a violent showdown among the igloos, a friend of Hanak's and an innocent bystander were shot; Hanak himself was shot and then stabbed as he lay dying, and his wife was stabbed to death as she tried to run from the scene.

Pugnana afterwards took Kupak, the most attractive of Hanak's women, as his wife, and the couple settled down together. But Tatamagama, who had wanted the same woman himself, gained nothing from the conflict and was left feeling secretly jealous. Eventually, his thoughts turned to murder again, and he enlisted the help of his eighteen-year-old nephew for a plan to kill Pugnana.

A few days later, Tatamagama and Aligoomiak went out with their intended victim in search of caribou. They walked through the snow for some time without seeing any, but then a herd on a wind-swept ridge came into view. Tatamagama and Pugnana both aimed their rifles and fired, then started to run in that direction. As they did so, Aligoomiak, who had deliberately fallen behind, fired at Pugnana and killed him outright.

Leaving the dead man's body to be eaten by wolves, the two murderers returned to their village and claimed that Pugnana had been shot by accident. Tatamagama then took Pugnana's wife, nine-month-old daughter and igloo for himself, apparently without encountering any resistance from Kupak. Not long afterwards, he persuaded Aligoomiak to kill the child for him, as her cries kept disturbing his sleep.

When news of these crimes reached the Royal Canadian Mounted Police headquarters at Herschel Island, off the northern coast of the Yukon mainland, two police officers were sent to arrest the culprits. Travelling by sea and by land through hundreds of miles of snow and ice, they reached the Cogmollock village on Kent Peninsula in December 1921, and secured the arrest of both men by means of bribery. They then began the long and arduous journey back, taking their prisoners with them.

The prisoners were not closely guarded, as neither seemed likely to give any trouble, and before long they began to assist their captors by carrying out routine tasks. But on 2 April 1922, Aligoomiak escaped from a police barracks at Tree River, at the western end of Coronation Gulf, having shot and killed Corporal William Doak. He afterwards killed a white trader named Otto Binder, but was recaptured later the same day.

On arrival at Herschel Island, four and a half months later, the thickset Tatamagama and his slim and youthful nephew were put into cells to await trial, but were allowed out every day for exercise. Gradually, their liberty was increased, with Tatamagama becoming the RCMP's official seal-hunter and Aligoomiak a servant to the wife of the officer in charge. Soon, in their free time, they were being allowed to wander around the island at will, retiring to the guardroom at whatever time suited them.

But in July 1923, a judicial party arrived from Edmonton, 2000 miles away, to conduct the trial of the two Eskimos for murder. It consisted of a judge, a clerk of the court and lawyers for both prosecution and defence, all travelling together under a Mounted Police escort. A hangman named Brown was also included in the party.

Before long, Tatamagama and Aligoomiak were put on trial in a makeshift courtroom, in a building belonging to the RCMP. The evidence against both men proved overwhelming, and on being convicted they were sentenced to death. The judicial party afterwards set out on their journey back to Edmonton, leaving the hangman behind.

While awaiting execution, the two Eskimos continued to move freely about the island, sometimes carrying rifles in search of seal, but without making any further attempt to escape. Brown was for some time engaged in constructing a scaffold in a large warehouse, and Aligoomiak, who had taken a liking to him, often called in to watch him at work. It was even rumoured that he and 'Neck-tie Bill' had got into the habit of playing poker together on the scaffold platform.

The death sentences aroused indignation in various parts of Canada, with many people taking the view that it was not yet time for uncivilized natives to be tried in the same manner as white men. But the Dominion Government did not accept this and on reviewing the case decided that the law should be left to take its course. The two condemned men were accordingly hanged on 1 February 1924, Tatamagama going to his death without protest and Aligoomiak saying he had always known that the Mounted Police disliked the Eskimos.

3

Monstrosities
and Curiosities

A horrible way to avoid the gallows

Peine forte et dure, or pressing to death, was a form of judicial torture used in England between the fifteenth and eighteenth centuries against persons who, on arraignment for felony, refused to plead to the charges against them. There were quite a number of such cases, for conviction for a capital offence in those days entailed forfeiture of goods to the Crown, while 'standing mute' enabled the accused to avoid being tried at all. But the ordeal of 'the press' was far worse than hanging and few could withstand it for long.

Wearing just a cloth to cover his loins, the defiant prisoner would be spreadeagled on the floor of a prison room or dungeon, with his arms and legs stretched taut and tied securely. A frame would then be placed on his chest, and this would be loaded with heavy weights of iron or stone – as much as he could bear 'and more'. The sentence of the court specified that he should continue thus, with no sustenance except bread one day and water the next, until he died.

In practice, if he expressed himself willing to stand trial, he was usually given another chance to do so, and most prisoners subjected to this treatment *did* capitulate within a short time. Some, however, did not, and so died under the weights in great agony.

One of the best-known cases in which *peine forte et dure* was used was that of George Strangeways, of Mussen, in

Dorset, who suffered at Newgate Prison at the end of February 1659. Strangeways, a Civil War veteran known to his associates as Major Strangeways, was charged with the murder of his brother-in-law, John Fussel, who had been shot dead at his lodgings in London two weeks earlier.

There had been considerable animosity between the two men, and the Major, who had himself been in London at the time of the crime, was arrested on suspicion. He eventually said that the shots which caused Fussel's death had been fired by somebody else at his instigation, but claimed that they had only been intended as a warning. He would not name the person who had fired them.

A few days later, on appearing for trial at the Old Bailey, Strangeways asked the court to give an assurance that in the event of his conviction he would be shot rather than hanged, and said that he would otherwise refuse to plead. He would thereby save his estate for his friends as well as saving himself from an ignominious death on the public gallows, he pointed out.

The court could not accede to his wishes, and the prisoner was warned of the fate which awaited him if he refused to plead. But the Major was determined to avoid the gallows at all costs, and was duly sentenced to be pressed to death.

On the morning that he was to die (the Monday after the sentence had been passed on him), the Major dressed all in white: 'waistcoat, stockings, drawers, and cap, over which was cast a long mourning cloak; a dress that handsomely emblemed the condition he was then in', a contemporary account, *The Unhappy Marksman* (1659), informs us.

The two Sheriffs of London and their officers arrived at the prison, and escorted him down to the dungeon. A number of the condemned man's friends were also present.

Before submitting himself to the executioner, Strangeways spent some time in prayer, assisted by the Rev Dr

> Prior to the introduction of *peine forte et dure*, prisoners who refused to plead were confined in a narrow cell and starved.

Warmsley, one of a number of clergymen who had attended him since his condemnation. He then made a short speech, declaring that he died a Christian and hoped to be gathered to the bosom of Christ. Finally, he took leave of his friends and prepared himself for the execution of his terrible sentence.

Stripped of his clothes, he lay face upwards, his arms and legs stretched towards the corners of the cell. According to *The Unhappy Marksman* his friends were permitted to lay on the weights themselves, and did so, at a prearranged signal from the prisoner, in such a way as to hasten his death. The relevant part of the account states that when Strangeways cried, 'Lord Jesus, receive my soul!' (which was the signal he had said he would give), 'those sad assistants'

> laid on at first-weight, which, finding too light for a sudden execution, many of those standing by added their burthens to disburthen him of his pain; which, notwithstanding, for the time of his continuance, as it was to him a dreadful sufferance, so was it to them a horrid spectacle, his dying groans filling the uncouth dungeon with the voice of terror.

It would seem from this that several friends laid on one lot of weights, then others laid on a second lot, but some writers have taken it to mean that some of the people present actually *stood* on the press. If they did, then *The Unhappy Marksman* could hardly have told us so less clearly.

However they did it, the prisoner's friends succeeded in crushing him to death in the space of eight to ten minutes and thereby spared him hours – perhaps days – of suffering. It must have been quite illegal for them to do this, and it has even been suggested that they may have been guilty of murder. But the Sheriffs apparently took no action to restrain them, and nobody seems to have been punished in connection with the affair.

The Major's body was afterwards exposed to public view and many visited the prison in order to see it. His friends were later allowed to take it away for burial.

Peine forte et dure continued to be used in England until the reign of George III. A famous engraving in *The Newgate Calendar* depicts the pressing of a highwayman named William Spiggot, in January 1721.

Newgate, in the early eighteenth century, had a special Press Room on the second floor, and it was there that Spiggot suffered. With weights totalling 350lbs on his chest, he remained obdurate for half an hour, but begged to be allowed to plead when a further fifty pounds was added. He was hanged shortly afterwards.

There was an alternative method of inducing prisoners to plead, normally used in the case of females: that was to tie their thumbs tightly together with whipcord. Like *peine forte et dure*, this usually resulted in the accused begging to plead, though sometimes only after considerable resistance. When a woman named Mary Andrews was subjected to this treatment in 1721, three successive cords broke before the pain reduced her to submission.

Both of these forms of torture were effectively abolished in 1772, by a new law which provided that refusal to plead was to be treated as a plea of guilty.

From 1828 onwards, the plea in such cases was registered as not guilty.

The only known case of *peine forte et dure* in America took place in Salem during the witchcraft trials of 1692. Giles Corey, a man of eighty, was one of the accused, and was pressed to death in a field next to the jail for refusing to plead. It is recorded that when the dying man's tongue was forced out of his mouth, the Sheriff pushed it back in with his walking-cane.

Women burnt for the
sake of decency

The ghastly form of execution known as hanging, drawing and quartering – it would be more accurately called drawing, hanging and quartering – was the penalty for treason in England for some centuries, having first been imposed in a case of piracy in 1241. Many people were put to death by this method in Tudor and Stuart times, when treason included religious offences, such as being a Roman Catholic priest.

The condemned in such cases were drawn along the ground on a sledge or hurdle, instead of being conveyed to the gallows in a hanging cart. After being hanged, they were cut down and disembowelled; their entrails were burnt by the executioner; they were then beheaded and their bodies were quartered. Their remains were afterwards exhibited in public places, as a warning to others.

How long the condemned were left hanging before being cut down varied a great deal. The sentence of the court invariably directed that they should be cut down from the gallows alive, and in many cases this actually happened. Dr John Story, a Catholic jurist executed in 1571, was certainly alive when he was cut down, and a contemporary account of his execution states that while the executioner was 'rifling among his bowels', the condemned man rose and dealt him a blow.

In the case of a Catholic priest named Barkworth, who

was executed in 1601, it is recorded that on being cut down, the hanged man 'stoode uprighte on his feete and strugled with the Executioners, cryinge, "Lord, Lord, Lord," and beinge holden by the strengthe of the executioners on the hurdle in dismembringe of him he cryed, "O God," and so he was quartered'.

On other occasions, however, the prisoner was not cut down until he was dead. It appears that the hangman was sometimes allowed to use his own discretion in the matter, and readily exercised it in favour of those who had given him a gratuity. In the case of John James, a religious fanatic who suffered at Tyburn in 1661, extortion was attempted, the hangman telling the prisoner that he would 'torture him exceedingly' if he did not receive five pounds. But the threat was not carried out, in spite of the condemned man's insistence that he had nothing to give. John James was hanged until he was dead.

Sentences of hanging, drawing and quartering continued to be passed in England until 1812, but by this time it had long been the custom for all offenders undergoing this method of execution to be left hanging until they were either dead or insensible. In some cases, as when Dr Archibald Cameron was executed for his part in the Jacobite Rebellion of 1745, the quartering of the body was omitted.

When a nobleman was convicted of treason, the monarch of the day invariably followed the custom of 'remitting the severities' of his sentence and leaving him to suffer death by beheading. This, apparently, could only be done because decapitation was part of the original sentence.

Women found guilty of treason were treated differently from men: instead of being hanged, drawn and quartered they were burnt at the stake. This, according to Blackstone, was for the sake of decency, as 'the natural modesty of the sex' forbade the exposure and public mangling of their bodies. But many of the women concerned suffered for coining, 'a treason of a different complexion from the rest', which was punishable only by hanging when committed by a man. Others were burnt for petty treason (the murder of their husbands).

Most of these women were actually strangled by the hangman before the flames reached them, but some were burnt alive, either deliberately or by accident. One shocking case occurred in 1685, when Elizabeth Gaunt, for sheltering a man who had been involved in a plot to kidnap Charles II two years earlier, was burnt alive at Tyburn, the favour of strangulation being denied her. Surprisingly, a barber named Fernley, who helped the same man after he had taken part in Monmouth's Rebellion, suffered only hanging.

Such cases of discrimination against women are not explained by Blackstone's remark about 'the natural modesty of the sex'. In fact, there seems to be no way of accounting for them at all. They nonetheless continued until almost the end of the eighteenth century.

The last case of burning in England was that of Christian Murphy, on 18 March 1789. Christian and her husband had both been sentenced to death for coining. Her husband was one of eight men hanged in front of Newgate Prison on the morning of her own death; she was brought out shortly afterwards and chained to a stake a few yards from the scaffold.

After a few minutes spent in prayer, she was hanged from a projecting arm at the top of the stake, and left for half an hour to ensure that she was dead. Faggots were then piled all round and over her body and set on fire.

The following year, judicial burning was abolished.

Sport with severed heads

The following is an extract from *The History of the Life of Thomas Ellwood*, published in 1714. It concerns an incident which took place in Newgate Prison while the author was a prisoner there in 1661. The hangman of London at that time was Edward Dunn, who died two years later.

When we came first into Newgate, there lay (in a little By-place like a Closet, near the Room where we were Lodged) the Quartered Bodies of three Men; who had been Executed some Days before, for a real or pretended Plot: which was the Ground, or at least Pretext, for that Storm in the City, which had caused this Imprisonment. The Names of these three Men were Philips, Tongue and Gibs: and the Reason why their Quarters lay so long there was, The Relations were all that while Petitioning to have leave to bury them: which at length with much ado was obtained for the Quarters; but not for the Heads, which were Ordered to be set up in some Parts of the City.

I saw the Heads, when they were brought up to be Boyled. The Hangman fetch'd them in a dirty Dust Basket, out of some By-Place; and setting them down amongst the Felons, he and they made Sport with them. They took them by the Hair, Flouting, Jeering and Laughing at them: and then giving them some ill Names, box'd them on the Ears and Cheeks. Which done, the Hangman put them into his

Kettle, and parboyl'd them with Bay-Salt and Cummin-Seed: that to keep them from Putrefaction, and this to keep off the Fowls from seizing on them. The whole Sight (as well that of the Bloody Quarters first, as this of the Heads afterwards) was both frightful and loathsom; and begat an abhorrence in my Nature. Which as it had rendered my confinement there by much the more uneasie: so it made our Removal from thence to Bridewell, even in that respect, the more welcome.

Execution dock

London's traditional place for the hanging of pirates and other offenders whose crimes had been committed at sea was Execution Dock, on the River Thames at Wapping. There, for some centuries, the condemned were hanged on the foreshore at low tide, the gallows being erected as occasion demanded. The executions often attracted large numbers of spectators, even in bad weather, and many watched the proceedings from craft on the river. In cases of piracy, the bodies were afterwards gibbeted in prominent positions nearby.

It is not known when the site was first used for this purpose, but it appears to have been the scene of a double hanging during the reign of Henry VI. By the last years of the sixteenth century, at any rate, it had become 'the usual place' for the execution of pirates, and it was then customary for the bodies of those who had died to be left hanging until three tides had passed over them. This custom was, however, abandoned during the course of the eighteenth century.

As at Tyburn, multiple hangings were not uncommon. Probably the largest one was that which took place on 13 November 1700, when eight carts were needed to convey the twenty-four prisoners to the gallows. A newspaper report of that execution tells us that the condemned were 'Poor Miserable Fellows, being French Men, who were taken on the Coast of Virginia by Colonel Nicholson, the Governor of that Colony'. Another states that several of them were 'in a manner dead' before they were hanged.

Traitors whose crimes had been committed at sea were also put to death at Execution Dock, but in such cases a hurdle rather than a hanging cart was used. Thomas Rounce, condemned for fighting against his King and Country on board a Spanish privateer, was drawn thus to the gallows on 19 January 1743, and hanged for about fifteen minutes. According to the *London Evening-Post*, the executioner then 'cut him down, ript up his Belly, and threw his Heart and Bowels into a Fire prepar'd for that Purpose'. Finally, he was quartered and the parts of his body placed in a coffin, in readiness to be taken for burial by his friends.

The most famous person to suffer at Execution Dock was Captain William Kidd, who was hanged on 23 May 1701, the rope breaking at the first attempt. Kidd is generally described as a notorious pirate, and had indeed been convicted of both piracy and murder. But it appears from documents discovered over two hundred years after his death that he was not a pirate at all, but merely a privateer. His name is, for some unknown reason, given as Captain John Kidd in *The Newgate Calendar*.

Other notable executions of the eighteenth century include that of John Gow and seven other pirates on 11 August 1729. Gow, like Kidd, had to be hanged twice, as a result of the rope breaking the first time. In his case, the mishap was caused by friends pulling his legs in an attempt to curtail his suffering.

James Buchanan, a Scottish mariner, was hanged on 20 December 1738, for murdering the fourth mate of an English merchant ship lying at anchor in the Canton River in China. But while he was still alive a party of his fellow sailors climbed on to the scaffold and, fighting off officials who tried to resist them, cut the prisoner down and carried him off in a boat in the direction of Deptford. Buchanan was never recaptured and all attempts to trace those who had rescued him ended in failure.

Execution Dock remained a place of execution until well into the nineteenth century. The last execution of note to be carried out there was that of Captain John Sutherland, who was hanged in 1809 for the murder of his negro servant. The last one of all appears to have been that of John Pater, who suffered, also for murder, on the morning of 1 February 1820.

EXECUTION – *John Pater*, who was convicted last Friday at the Admiralty Sessions, of murder, yesterday morning underwent the sentence of the law. As the clock struck nine he entered the cart, with his arms pinioned, a halter round his neck, and a red cap on his head. The executioner sat behind him with a drawn sword, taking hold of the halter. Mr. Deacon, a naval officer, with the Ordinary, followed in a coach, accompanied by a great body of constables. The cart moved through the City, down the Commercial-road, to Execution-dock, Wapping. Throughout the whole scene the prisoner, as on his trial, manifested the utmost indifference, and seemed hardly conscious of existence. He was above sixty years of age; the greater part of his life had been spent as a smuggler. The last offices of religion were performed by the Ordinary, and at a quarter past ten the unhappy man was launched into eternity.

The Times, 2 February 1820.

A sharp and heavy axe

James Scott, Duke of Monmouth, was one of Charles II's many illegitimate children. Born in Holland in 1649, he was publicly recognized by Charles as his son, and became one of England's most important political figures of the 1670s. However, he fell from favour at Court as a result of his involvement in various plots to have the King's brother James excluded from the throne, and was eventually forced to leave the country.

Early in 1685, Charles died, leaving no direct heir, and his brother became King of England. James II was a Roman Catholic and a believer in arbitrary rule, and his accession caused alarm among the country's Protestants. Monmouth, who was still in exile, began to make plans for a popular uprising, intending to overthrow his uncle and seize the throne himself. He was sure that he would find enough support in England to enable him to do this.

Finally, in June of that year, he landed at Lyme Regis, in Dorset, with a small band of fellow exiles, declared himself his father's lawful heir and called upon all English Protestants to join him in the name of their religion. Miners and peasants responded to the call in large numbers, willing to fight with whatever weapons came to hand, and soon he had 7000 men under arms. On 20 June, in Taunton, he was proclaimed King, and a price was put on James's head for treason.

But Monmouth failed to inspire any of the powerful Whig families on whose help he had counted, and at Sedgemoor in Somerset, on 5 July, his army was routed by royal troops. The 'Protestant Duke' was found hiding under some straw in a ditch three days later, and was taken to London and imprisoned in the Tower.

He had no trial to face, for his life had already been declared forfeit in an Act of Attainder hurried through both Houses of Parliament when the first news of his rebellion reached London. And although he was granted an interview with the King – at which he is believed to have offered to become a Catholic if James would pardon him – his pleas for mercy were contemptuously rejected. His execution was fixed for 15 July.

Monmouth was a handsome, vain and sensuous man. Though broken in spirit after the Battle of Sedgemoor, he managed to recover his composure during the short time left to him, and so was able to die with dignity.

On the morning of his execution he took leave of his wife and their six children in the Tower, and was afterwards taken out to Tower Hill, where a large crowd awaited him at the scaffold. Dressed in a grey suit and wearing a dark periwig, he was attended by four clergymen who had been sent by the King to be his 'assistants' (to 'prepare him for death').

'I shall say but very little,' he said to the spectators. 'I come to die. I die a Protestant of the Church of England.'

The clergymen were not satisfied with this, and urged him to make a 'public and particular' confession of guilt. But Monmouth declined to do so, saying merely that he died 'very penitent' and that he had said all he had to say about 'public affairs' in a paper which he had signed.

'My Lord, you must go to God in His own way,' one of the ecclesiastics persisted. 'Sir, be sure you be truly penitent and ask forgiveness of God for the many you have wronged.'

'I am sorry for everyone I have wronged,' replied Monmouth. 'I forgive everybody. I have had many enemies. I forgive them all.'

'Sir, your acknowledgment ought to be public and particular.'

'I am to die,' insisted the Duke. 'Pray, my Lord. I refer to my paper.'

'They are but a few words that we desire. We only desire an answer to this point.'

Monmouth continued to brush the question aside for as long as possible, even claiming at one point that he had a clear conscience. But he was eventually obliged to admit that he was guilty of a grave crime.

'I am sorry for invading the Kingdom, and for the blood that has been shed – and for the souls which may have been lost by my means,' he said. 'I am sorry it ever happened.'

On being asked to make his confession aloud, however, he fell silent, and so was not regarded as truly repentant. He nonetheless joined in with fervour when the four clergymen began praying, and was then invited to pray for the King. He did so reluctantly.

When the prayers were over, he spoke briefly to Jack Ketch, the executioner, who stood waiting with his axe. But afterwards, as he began getting ready to meet his end, he was again asked to go to the rail of the scaffold, this time to speak to the soldiers below 'and entreat them and the people to be loyal and obedient to the King'.

'I have said I will make no speeches,' replied Monmouth. 'I will make no speeches. I come to die.'

Before taking off his coat and periwig, he turned back to Ketch, to give him his customary gratuity. 'Here are six guineas for you,' he said. 'Pray do your business well. Do not serve me as you did my Lord Russell. I have heard you struck him three or four times.' He then said to his servant, who attended him even on the scaffold, 'Here, take these remaining guineas and give them to him if he does his work well.'

'I hope I shall,' said Ketch.

'If you strike me twice, I cannot promise you not to stir,' warned the Duke.

The four clergymen, after uttering various 'ejaculations proper at that time' (as one observer called them), began reciting part of the 51st Psalm. Monmouth lay down on the floor of the scaffold – the block being a low one – and placed his neck in position. But he was still worried about Ketch's reputation for incompetence, and suddenly raised himself on his elbow.

'Prithee, let me feel the axe,' he said.

Ketch allowed him to do so, but after touching the edge of the blade he was still not satisfied.

'I fear it is not sharp enough,' he remarked.

'It is sharp enough and heavy enough,' insisted the executioner.

Monmouth, unconvinced, put his neck back into position and the clergymen began their pious outbursts afresh:

'God accept your repentance! ... God accept your repentance! ... God accept your imperfect repentance! ... My Lord God accept your general repentance! ... God Almighty show his omnipotent mercy upon you! ... Father, into thy hands we commend his spirit.... Lord Jesus, receive his soul!'

The crowd was silent, as it had been for almost the whole time that Monmouth had been on the scaffold.

Ketch, a brutal fellow, raised his axe. Having been hangman of London for quite some years – perhaps since 1663 – he had had considerable experience of putting people to death. But the Duke's remarks about his bungling of Lord William Russell's execution two years earlier must have unnerved him, for he brought down the axe too lightly and inflicted only a gash.

Monmouth raised his head and turned to look at him, perhaps intending to speak, but lay down again without saying anything. Ketch then raised the axe and struck a second blow, but again the Duke's body moved. A third desperate attempt also failed to complete the decapitation – and at this point the executioner, now greatly agitated, suddenly threw down the axe.

'God damn me, I can do no more!' he cried. 'My heart fails me!'

There was shock and anger all round, and some of the spectators on the scaffold wanted to throw him down to the crowd, who would certainly have killed him. But the two Sheriffs made him take up the axe once more and go on with his work – which he did as clumsily as ever. After two further blows, Monmouth's head had still not been completely severed, and Ketch had to finish cutting it off with a knife.

He then picked it up and showed it half-heartedly to the crowd as the head of a traitor. But there were no shouts of glee, as were often to be heard at executions: indeed, there was much grief and indignation at the frightful manner in which Monmouth had been treated. For his own protection, Ketch had to be taken from the scene under guard.

With the execution finally accomplished, many people rushed on to the scaffold to dip handkerchiefs and shirts in the victim's blood. The body was put into a coffin covered with black velvet and taken back to the Tower in a hearse drawn by six horses. The head was sewn back on to it prior to interment.

Of Monmouth's supporters in the West Country, many had already been summarily executed after their defeat at the Battle of Sedgemoor. Those who survived were tried during the 'Bloody Assize', presided over by Lord Chief Justice Jeffreys.

An unknown number of them – generally believed to be over 300 – were hanged, drawn and quartered, and their dismembered bodies gibbeted along the roadsides. Many hundreds more were sentenced to transportation and sold into virtual slavery in North America or the West Indies. Lesser offenders were subjected to brutal floggings.

These savage reprisals met with the King's approval, and on his return to London the sadistic and fearsome judge was made Lord Chancellor. But three years later, James was overthrown by William of Orange, and had to flee the country. Jeffreys was then arrested and imprisoned in the Tower.

He died in custody, at the age of forty, from the effects of excessive drinking and dissolute behaviour.

Other bungled beheadings

Probably the worst-ever case of a bungled beheading in Britain was not Monmouth's but that of Margaret Pole, Countess of Salisbury, who was executed at the Tower of London in 1541. The executioner on that occasion was not the regular London hangman but a clumsy novice who, according to a contemporary source, 'hacked her head and shoulders to pieces' before his work was finished. The Countess was sixty-eight years old.

France had a similar case in 1517. The executioner, a swordsman named Fluraut, bungled his work so badly that an enraged mob chased him from the scene and burnt down a house in which he tried to take refuge. Another notable French case occurred in 1626, when the Count of Chalais was beheaded by an amateur, who only undertook the task in order to save his own life. The Count's head was not severed until the twenty-ninth stroke, and he was observed to be still alive at the twentieth.

The execution of Margaretha Vöglin, which took place in Nuremberg in 1641, was by no means as protracted as that, but it was still a shocking spectacle which could easily have caused a riot. The condemned woman, who had been sentenced for child-murder, had to sit unbound on a chair – supported, no doubt, by the executioner's assistant as she awaited the fatal blow. But when the executioner struck her with his sword, he missed her neck and cut just a small *piece of flesh from her head, knocking her off the chair in the process.*

The unfortunate culprit rose to her feet and begged to be spared for being brave. But she was not spared and had to sit down and face the ordeal again. At this point, the assistant executioner wanted to take over the execution himself, but his chief would not hear of it.

At the second attempt, the executioner, Valentin Deusser, again failed to cut off her head, though he dealt her a powerful blow which again knocked her off the chair; he then finished his work while she lay on the scaffold. Later, on his way home, he had to be rescued from a hostile mob, who would otherwise have stoned him. The following day, he was dismissed from his post on account of his 'slovenly workmanship'.

Pardoned on condition
of losing a leg

In England, in the late seventeenth century, many capital offenders managed to avoid the death penalty on conviction by pleading benefit of clergy. A prisoner who wished to avail himself of this medieval privilege would have to satisfy the court that he was literate by reading aloud the first verse of the 51st Psalm: the 'Neck Verse', as it was called.

If he did this successfully, it was accepted that he read 'like a clerk', and his life was spared. Instead of being hanged, he was branded in the left thumb: a procedure which was supposed to ensure that offenders were only afforded the privilege once.

In practice, however, benefit of clergy provided a loophole which was frequently exploited by criminals who were totally illiterate. Many of them knew the 'Neck Verse' off by heart, and could put on a convincing pretence of reading it – after the Bible had been opened at the right place for them – whenever the need arose. Others bribed the prison chaplain to whisper it to them at the appropriate time, so that they, too, could use it to escape the gallows.

As for the branding, even this could not have served its real purpose to any great extent, for some offenders are known to have been 'burnt in the hand' repeatedly. By

1700, it seems to have become generally accepted as a form of punishment in itself: an alternative to hanging where such severity seemed unwarranted.

Though the custom of reading the 'Neck Verse' was abandoned in 1705, benefit of clergy could still be claimed up to 1827. But its importance diminished during the course of the eighteenth century, as a result of the growing number of crimes which were made 'non-clergyable' capital offences from the time of William III onwards.

Besides those who claimed benefit of clergy, there were many female offenders who escaped the gallows by 'pleading their bellies'. When this happened, a panel of matrons was sworn by the court to examine the prisoner, and if they found her to be quick with child, i.e., to have reached the stage of pregnancy at which she was conscious of the child's movement, she was reprieved until after the delivery.

In general, such offenders seem not to have been hanged at all, or not until they had offended again, at any rate; *The Daily Gazetteer* of 23 December 1738 records the execution of a thief named Constantia James, who was believed to have pleaded her belly on nine previous occasions.

Many prisoners convicted of capital offences were recommended to the King's mercy by the trial judge, and these were almost invariably pardoned – most of them on condition of transportation or enlistment in the army or navy.

The pardons were usually granted in batches, the prisoners concerned having first been given leave to plead for them 'at the next general pardon' in the courts in which they had been sentenced. They pleaded on their knees and presented the court with gloves, according to custom.

The pardons remained *offers of pardon* until this had been done, although they were generally referred to as 'pardons' in advance of it. They could therefore be refused by the prisoners themselves, as happened in 1681, in the case of two Whigs condemned 'for saying that it was lawful to kill the King'. In that event, the sentence of death was not commuted.

At the Wicklow Assizes in August 1785, the evidence of a pardoned capital offender was objected to on the grounds that he was still under sentence of death, 'not having pleaded his Majesty's pardon'.

Another strange custom of which we occasionally find mention was that of a number of 'maids clothed in white' begging the life of a particular offender. One such reference is to be found in the diary of Narcissus Luttrell, who recorded in 1686:

> Edward Skelton, one of the criminalls that received sentence of death this last sessions at the Old Baily, has been beg'd of the king by 18 maids clothed in white, and since is married to one of them in the Presse yard.

In 1719, a condemned man named James Lyon was hanged in Durham while a messenger with a pardon for him travelled to Morpeth by mistake. The *Original Weekly Journal* of 29 August, reporting the execution, said that the gallows broke down and the prisoner had to be hanged from an oak tree.

Such appeals were not always successful, for in December 1700 *The London Post* reported the case of eight women in white begging the life of a highwayman to no avail.

Where they *were* successful, marriage between the offender and one of the maids was almost certainly a condition of his pardon – perhaps the only one.

There was also a practice of granting general pardons from time to time, under Acts of Grace. When John Meff, an old offender, was arrested for robbery towards the end of April 1721, his crime was found to have been committed during the period covered by such an Act, so he could not be tried for it. However, his past was discovered and he was indicted for returning from transportation instead.

Some condemned prisoners were pardoned for making disclosures or giving evidence about the crimes of others. 'Half-Hanged' John Smith, for example, gave information about a great many offenders after being cut down from Tyburn alive in 1705. In his case, the pardon was unconditional.

The Gentleman's Magazine of 1735 (p. 558) records that a counterfeiter named Joshua Dean, sentenced to death at the Old Bailey, was granted a conditional pardon for revealing a plot by other condemned prisoners to break out of jail.

Others obtained pardons by agreeing to take part in medical experiments. In 1721, for example, a number of prisoners in Newgate had their sentences commuted for their willingness to undergo a smallpox inoculation. Forty-two years later, a robber named George Chippendale was offered a pardon on condition that he submitted to the amputation of a limb, 'in order to try the efficacy of a new-invented styptic for stopping the blood-vessels'.

Chippendale had himself petitioned the King for this indulgence, and accepted it thankfully. But the condition of his pardon was later changed, as we learn from *The London Chronicle* of 24–26 May 1763:

> George Chippendale, now in Newgate, is not to have his leg amputated to make trial of a new styptic, but to be transported for life; it being thought better to try the new styptic on some hospital patients, where the limb is obliged to be taken off.

That, as far as Chippendale was concerned, was the end

of the matter. But four years later the same thing happened to John Benham, a burglar, after arrangements had been made for the experiment to be carried out on him at the Old Bailey Sessions House. As *The London Chronicle* of 23–25 June 1767 reported:

> Yesterday Mr. Pearce waited upon the Secretary of State, when he was informed that the intention of trying his styptic upon John Benham, a convict in Newgate, was entirely laid aside.
>
> We are inform'd that the cause why the publick are disappointed of being truly informed with respect to the utility of Mr. Pearce's styptic, was upon account of it having been represented to his Majesty, that it was quite improper to try the same on the above convict.

Benham, like Chippendale, was pardoned for his willingness to undergo the operation, and ordered to be transported for life.

In 1811, William Townley was hanged for burglary in Gloucester after a reprieve had been erroneously sent to the Under-Sheriff of Herefordshire. When the mistake was discovered, an attempt was made to notify the Gloucester authorities in time to halt the proceedings, but the message arrived twenty minutes after the culprit had been turned off.

A long delay
at Tyburn

On 25 August 1779, four condemned men rode in the cart to Tyburn, to be hanged from the movable gallows which had come into use twenty years earlier. Michael Brannon and Martin Gullivan, both bricklayers' labourers, had been sentenced for robbery; James Barrett, a sailor, for raping a girl of fourteen, and Thomas Ricketts, a wheelwright, for burglary. All were suitably penitent as they waited to be turned off, but twenty minutes or so after they had been tied up, a rumour spread among the spectators that one of them had been reprieved.

The proceedings were therefore interrupted, and a messenger sent to Lord Weymouth, the Secretary of State for the South, to find out whether the rumour was true. All four men were untied and left sitting in the cart for some hours, none of them knowing whether they were to be hanged or not. During that time a fresh rumour was started, that they had all been reprieved: because of this, crowds began to gather outside Newgate Prison to witness their return.

But eventually the messenger reappeared at Tyburn, badly bruised after being thrown from his horse, and informed the Sheriffs that the condemned were all to be hanged. The four men were thereupon tied up again, and *this time turned off without delay. It appears from the newspaper reports that the spectators watched mutely while the execution was carried out.*

Forerunners of the guillotine

Long before the French Revolution, a device similar to the guillotine was used for carrying out executions in the Yorkshire town of Halifax. Known as the Halifax Gibbet, this machine is described in some detail in Holinshed's *Chronicles* (1577), and is the subject of *Halifax and its Gibbet Law* (1708) by Dr Samuel Midgley. It appears to have been used for some centuries prior to 1650, though its earliest recorded use was in 1541.

The machine comprised a wooden frame, five yards in height; a sliding block with a heavy axe attached to its underside; and a lower block on which the offender had to place his neck. It was operated by means of a long rope attached to a wooden pin, and on most occasions all of the men who were near enough would take hold of the rope together, while the others reached out towards it as a token that they wished to see justice done.

If, however, the prisoner had been condemned for stealing a horse, an ox, a sheep or any other such animal, the beast itself, or another of its kind, would have the rope tied to it, and would then be driven away. It would thus be the animal which drew out the pin and so performed the execution, albeit unwittingly.

The Gibbet stood on a stone scaffold or pedestal on a site known as Gibbet Hill. In all, forty-nine people are known to have been beheaded there between 1541 and 1650, when it seems the town was obliged to bring the custom to an end. The last to suffer by this method were two thieves, Wilkinson and Mitchel, who had stolen some cloth and two colts.

Impressed by the Gibbet's efficiency, the Earl of Morton had a similar machine constructed in Edinburgh in 1565. This was known as the Maiden, and was used for the execution of some of the noblest men in Scotland, including Morton himself in 1581. Its use was discontinued in 1710, after some 120 executions had been carried out with it.

Another decapitation machine is known to have existed in Ireland during the early fourteenth century, though for how long we do not know. A woodcut in Holinshed depicts its use for the execution of Murcod Ballagh 'near to Merton' on 1 April 1307. It is clear from this that it was no different in principle from the guillotine, though it was obviously cruder in design.

Several other such machines are known to have existed in Germany, some as early as the Middle Ages. Contemporary drawings show one with a sliding blade and another with a blade which had to be forced through the neck with hammer blows. We have, however, few details of their use.

Other decapitation machines appeared elsewhere in Europe at one time or another. In Naples, in 1266, the beheading of Conrad of Swabia was carried out with one (or so it would appear from a fifteenth-century mural in the Lorch chapel in Würtemburg). And nearly four centuries later, after describing an execution of a different type in Rome, the diarist John Evelyn added: 'At Naples they use a frame, like ours at Halifax.'

A French work of the late seventeenth century describes yet another of these instruments of death. In Toulouse, says *Les Mémoires de Puységur* (1690), 'they use an axe which is between two pieces of wood, and when the head is placed on the block, the rope is released and the axe falls and separates the head from the body.' It was by this means that the Maréchal de Montmorency was executed in 1632.

And in the early eighteenth century there was a machine of the same type in Milan. An anonymous work, *Voyage historique et politique de Suisse, d'Italie, et d'Allemagne* (1736–43), gives an account of its use for the execution of Count Bozelli in 1702. It reads as follows:

> After the criminal had confessed himself, the penitents, who are for the most part of noble families, led him up on the scaffold, and, making him kneel before the block, one of the penitents held the head under the hatchet; the priest then reading the prayers as usual on such occasions, the executioner had nothing to do but cut the cord that held up the hatchet, which, descending with violence, severed the head, which the penitent still held in his hands, so that the executioner never touched it.

The author concludes by saying: 'This mode of executing is so sure that the hatchet entered the block above two inches.'

Hangmen who were hanged

In 1538, the hangman of London, a fellow named Cratwell or Gratnell, was himself hanged for robbing a booth at Bartholomew Fair. The execution, which took place in Clerkenwell, was attended by the chronicler Edward Hall, who estimated that there were 20,000 people present. Cratwell, who had been hangman since 1534, is described in Wriothesley's *Chronicle* as 'a conninge butcher in quarteringe of men'. He was the first known member of his profession to be hanged in this country.

> John Price, the old Hangman, is to be executed this Day in Bunhil-Fields; and the late Hangman, who was turned out of his Place for being arrested in going to Tyburn, by which Means the Criminals escaped being executed, is making Irons for him (he being also a Smith by Trade) to be hang'd in Chains after he is executed, at Stonebridge near Kingsland. The said Price is so far from being penitent for his Crime of the barbarous Murder, that he hath since Sentence of Condemnation been drunk for several Days successively, and committed most horrid Outrages.
>
> *The Weekly Journal or Saturday's Post*,
> 31 May 1718.

Last Saturday, John Price, the quondam Hangman, but in his Conversation with Mr. Lorrain the Ordinary of Newgate, he stil'd himself Finisher of the Law, was hang'd in Bunhill-Fields for the Murder of Elizabeth White there, which he confess'd at the Place of Execution, and afterwards he was hang'd at Stone-Bridge at Kingsland in Chains, which were made for him by William Marvel, his Successor in the Place of common Executioner.

The Weekly Journal or British Gazetteer,
7 June 1718.

A hangman with a stump leg, whose name is unknown, suffered a similar fate at Tyburn in 1556. He had been London's 'finisher of the law' for some years and, according to a diarist who recorded his execution, had 'hangyd mony a man and quartered mony, and hed (beheaded) many a nobull man and odur (other)'.

He was hanged for theft.

Alexander Cockburn was appointed hangman of Edinburgh on 1 July 1681, having previously been hangman of Stirling. On 20 January the following year, he was hanged and gibbeted for the murder of a licensed beggar named John Adamson. The man who carried out the execution was his predecessor at Stirling, whom Cockburn had himself undermined and had dismissed from office there, presumably in order to replace him.

Pascha Rose, described as a butcher in the diary of Narcissus Luttrell, was appointed hangman of London when Jack Ketch was removed from office at the beginning of 1686. In April the same year, he and another man were apprehended after breaking into a house in Stepney and stealing various articles of apparel, and on 28 May he was hanged at Tyburn. Ketch, in the meantime, had been reinstated as hangman.

John Price, a former seaman, became hangman of London in about 1714, but lost his position the following year as a result of being imprisoned for debt. He later escaped from prison and committed a brutal murder while under the influence of drink. He was hanged and gibbeted on 31 May 1718, the execution being carried out in Bunhill Fields, where the crime had taken place.

Thomas Woodham, hangman of Gloucester, was hanged at Ilchester, in Somerset, on 10 August 1785, for a highway robbery committed near the village of Batheaston. Woodham was sixty-nine years old and is known to have carried out an execution in Gloucester less than a fortnight before he was brought to trial. A newspaper reporting his own execution states that he had been tried several times before, but gives no information about what happened on any of those occasions.

Other Capital Offenders

Gregory Brandon, hangman of London, was convicted of manslaughter in 1611, but escaped the gallows by pleading benefit of clergy. Following his release, he continued as hangman until about 1639, when he was succeeded by his son Richard.

John Thrift, a later occupant of the same post, was convicted of murder in 1750, having killed a man with a hanger during an affray. He was granted a free pardon shortly afterwards and managed to retain his position until his death two years later.

Edward Dennis, yet another holder of that office, was condemned to death for demolishing a house during the Gordon Riots of 1780. He, too, was granted a free pardon and allowed to resume his duties, probably in time to hang some of his fellow rioters. He died in office in 1786.

Edward Barlow, hangman of Lancaster, was sentenced to death in 1806 for stealing a horse. The sentence was commuted to ten years' imprisonment, and 'Old Ned', as he was commonly called, remained a prisoner in Lancaster Castle until his death in 1812. However, he continued as hangman throughout the time he was in jail, serving in that capacity for thirty-one years in all. He died at the age of seventy-six.

Various authors have claimed that Derrick, the executioner of the Earl of Essex, had once been under sentence of death for rape, and that it was Essex himself who saved his life. But the only evidence ever given in support of this story is that of a contemporary ballad of no real worth, so there is probably no truth in it.

The execution of animals

At Falaise in Normandy, in 1386, a sow was executed, as though it were a human being. The animal had attacked a child, causing injuries to its face and arms which had resulted in the child's death, and had been tried and convicted by the local court. The execution, by hanging, took place in a public square, with the sow dressed in men's clothes. It was preceded by the infliction of wounds commensurate with those which its victim had suffered.

To the people of Falaise, the event was evidently of some significance, for prior to 1820 it was represented in a fresco painting on the west wall of the Church of the Holy Trinity in that town. But although unusual, it was by no means unique, for, taking Europe as a whole, we have many records of animals being tried and punished for criminal offences. And there were undoubtedly many other such cases of which no record survives.

In 1266, a pig convicted of eating a child was burnt to death at Fontenay-aux-Roses, near Paris. This was the earliest known of a large number of cases involving pigs, which in medieval times were allowed to run freely about the streets. The execution was carried out by order of the monks of Ste Geneviève.

In 1314, a bull was hanged at Moisy-le-Temple, north-east

of Paris, for fatally wounding a man on the highway after escaping from its owner's farm in the nearby village of Moisy. The judges were officers of the Count of Valois, who was afterwards declared to have no jurisdiction in Moisy. The hanging, which took place at the common gallows, was therefore an illegal act.

In 1379, Philip the Bold, Duke of Burgundy, pardoned two herds of swine which had been condemned as accomplices in the killing of a child by three sows near the town of St Marcel-le-Jeussey. The herds, which had been feeding when the attack on the child began, were alleged to have supported and shown an eagerness to take part in it. The pardon, which was granted in response to a petition from the local prior, did not apply to the three sows.

In 1474, the magistrates of Basel sentenced a cock to be burnt for 'the heinous and unnatural crime of laying an egg'. The sentence was carried out on a height outside the city, before a huge crowd of townsmen and peasants. It was later claimed that on cutting the dead cock open afterwards, the executioner found three more eggs inside it.

In 1578, a cow which had been sentenced to death in Ghent was slaughtered and its flesh sold as meat. Its head, however, was stuck on a stake near the gallows, to show that it had been convicted of a capital offence. Usually, the carcass of an executed animal was buried at whatever site was used for the interment of human offenders.

In cases of bestiality, man and beast were generally tried, condemned and executed – often by burning – together. But in a French case, in 1750, a female ass was acquitted on such a charge while the man tried with it was convicted and sentenced to death. In reaching its decision, the court was influenced by a remarkable document, signed by the principal inhabitants of the Commune of Vanvres, stating that the ass was a virtuous and well-behaved creature whose conduct had never given rise to scandal.

At Pleternica, in Slavonia, in 1864, a pig was sentenced to death for biting off the ears of a one-year-old girl. After the execution had taken place, the animal's flesh was cut into pieces and thrown to the dogs. Its owner was obliged to compensate the victim for her injuries by providing her with a dowry.

At Délémont, in Switzerland, in 1906, two robbers named Scherrer – they were father and son – committed a murder with the assistance of their fierce dog. The dog, in fact, was regarded as the chief culprit, as without its involvement the crime could not have taken place. Because of this, the dog was condemned to death, while the two men were given sentences of life imprisonment.

When an animal was condemned, it was usually the official executioner who carried out the sentence. In the Falaise case of 1386, for example, it was the 'master of high works', – i.e., the hangman – of that town who officiated. Besides his normal fee for performing this service, he is known to have received payment for one new glove.

A receipt dated 16 October 1408, and signed by the jailer of the royal prisons in Pont de Larche, shows that a pig was in his custody from 24 June to 17 July of that year, when it was hanged for killing a child. The jailer charged two deniers tournois a day for the pig's board – the same as for boarding other prisoners – but added a further charge of ten deniers tournois for a length of rope 'for the purpose of tying the said pig that it might not escape'.

How five revolutionaries died

On 1 May 1820, five men convicted of high treason were executed outside the Debtors' Door of Newgate Prison. The Cato Street Conspirators, as Arthur Thistlewood and his companions were called, had plotted to kill the entire British Cabinet, in the hope of bringing about a socialist revolution. The penalty for treason at this time was hanging followed by beheading.

The executions took place in an atmosphere of great excitement and tension, with stringent measures being taken to keep the crowds under control. The scaffold on which they were carried out was unusually large, the one normally used at Newgate having been extended to provide space for the condemned men to be decapitated after death.

Before the prisoners appeared, their coffins were carried on to the new part of the scaffold and put down on the floor side by side. Sawdust was thrown into each of them to absorb the culprits' blood, and a block with a slanted surface was placed at the head of the first. Soon the condemned began to ascend the scaffold, one at a time, and were made ready for the drop.

Undaunted to the end, Thistlewood and three of the others – Richard Tidd, James Ings and John Thomas Brunt – refused the services of the Ordinary, the first three asking not to have their caps pulled down over their eyes until the last minute. Thistlewood made a short statement to a journalist, declaring that he died 'a sincere friend to liberty'.

Ings was boisterous. Facing the crowds, who were kept well away from the scaffold, he gave three cheers, in which many of them joined him. He sang 'Give me death or liberty' in a hoarse voice, and said he was 'an enemy to all tyrants'. Tidd sucked an orange as he waited to be 'launched into eternity'; Brunt took a pinch of snuff. William Davidson, the only one of the prisoners to accept the ministrations of the chaplain, was quiet and decorous throughout the proceedings.

When the preparations were finally completed, the Ordinary began praying aloud and the executioner left the scaffold. A few seconds later, the platform fell. Four of the prisoners died quickly. Ings, the fifth, was not so lucky: the hangman's assistants had to pull his legs before his struggles ended.

The bodies were left hanging for half an hour, then lifted back on to the floor of the scaffold. Thistlewood's was cut down and placed in the first coffin, with his head over the end and his neck on the edge of the block. A masked man then mounted the scaffold and began cutting off his head with a knife.

At this, there were many exclamations of horror and reproach, but the masked man went on with his grim task until the head was severed. With one of his assistants holding up the ghastly object alongside him, the hangman then announced to the spectators on one side of the scaffold, 'This is the head of Arthur Thistlewood – a traitor!'

Though greeted with hisses and shouts of disapproval, this procedure was repeated at the front of the scaffold, and then on the other side, before the head was put into the

The executioner raised the axe, and struck at the neck with all his force. At that instant there was a burst of horror from the crowd. The executioner then took up the head, and holding it by the hair addressed the people, "Behold the head of Jeremiah Brandreth, the traitor." Hitherto the multitude had been quiet and motionless. The instant the head was exhibited, there was a tremendous shriek set up, and they ran violently in all directions, as if under the impulse of sudden phrenzy. Those that resumed their stations groaned and hooted. The javelin-men and constables were all in motion, and a few dragoons, who had been stationed at both ends of the street, drew nearer with drawn swords. But all became immediately calm. Very few of the immense multitude now remained, and these looked quietly on while the heads of Turner and Ludlam were successively exhibited in the same way. The heads and bodies were then thrown into the coffins, and all spectators dispersed.

From a report of the execution of three men hanged and beheaded for high treason in Derby.
The Times, 8 November 1817.

coffin with Thistlewood's body. The other men's heads were then all cut off in turn, each of them being shown to the crowds in a similar manner. It was not until this shocking ceremony ended that the crowds began to disperse.

The execution was the most sensational for many years, and the number of people who attended it was enormous. It was clear from their occasional cries of support and encouragement that some of them were in sympathy with the prisoners. But no outrage followed and the troops stationed at the scene or in the neighbourhood of Newgate were soon able to return to barracks.

Thistlewood and his fellows were the last offenders to be hanged and beheaded in England. There were, however, three such executions in Scotland later the same year: one in Glasgow at the end of August, the other two in Stirling shortly afterwards. In each case, the decollation was performed by a masked man who was not the hangman.

The last time a nobleman was beheaded in Britain was on 9 April 1747, when Lord Lovat was executed on Tower Hill for treason, following the Jacobite Rebellion of 1745. On that occasion, a scaffolding which overlooked the scene collapsed with nearly a thousand people on it and twelve of them were killed. Lord Lovat was eighty years of age.

The guillotine's most shocking failure

The guillotine was first used for an execution in Paris on 25 April 1792, following experiments with live sheep and human corpses: the victim was Nicolas-Jacques Pelletier, who had been sentenced to death for robbery with violence. The machine was at this time believed to be the invention of Antoine Louis, the Secretary of the Academy of Surgery, and for this reason was called the *louison* or the *louisette*. The name by which it is now known came into use shortly afterwards.

The device had been introduced by the Revolutionary Government as a method of capital punishment that was quick and painless. It could certainly be quick, for the spectators at Pelletier's execution complained that it was all over before they had time to see anything. But whether the severing of the head resulted in instant death was not so certain, for some cases seemed to suggest otherwise. So, even without taking the occasional mishap into account, one could never be sure that it was really painless.

In spite of these doubts, the guillotine remained the official mode of execution in France until the death penalty was abolished 189 years later. For much of that time – up to 1939, in fact – executions were carried out in public, though after the first few decades of the nineteenth century there were comparatively few of them. By 1870, the number had fallen so far that only one executioner was needed to serve the whole country.

This 'national' functionary was obliged to live in Paris, and to travel to any part of the country where his services were needed. He was allowed five assistants, all of whom also had to reside in the French capital.

A number of horrific incidents involving the use of the guillotine are known to have taken place, the worst of them at Albi, in the south of France, on 12 September 1831. The condemned on that occasion was a murderer named Peter Hebard, who, after five months under sentence of death, accepted the news of his impending execution calmly. He asked for a priest and made a confession of his crime.

At the appointed time he was taken from his cell and placed in the cart in which he was to be taken to the scaffold. But it was then learnt that the execution had been postponed for two hours, as the scaffold had been damaged. Hebard's removal from the prison had therefore to be delayed while a carpenter carried out the necessary repairs.

When the two hours had expired, he was driven to the place of execution, where excited crowds had to be held back by *gendarmes* with drawn swords. He ascended the scaffold with a firm step, and was bound to the *bascule* and tipped into a horizontal position under the guillotine blade. His throat was then placed in the lower semicircle of the *lunette*, the upper half of which was immediately lowered on to the back of his neck, to hold his head in position.

At this point, he should have been only a few seconds from death. But when the blade was released it slid down its grooves with a trembling motion and suddenly came to a halt before reaching the condemned man's neck. With the spectators crying out in alarm and disgust, it was raised and released again – but again it came to a sudden halt. This time, Hebard himself let out piercing cries, and some of the spectators threw stones at the executioner and his assistants.

A third attempt to carry out the sentence resulted in a slight wound to the culprit's neck, causing him to cry out in pain. The stone-throwing then started again and the executioner and his assistants, fearful for their own safety, left the scaffold and ran for cover. Hebard was thus left unattended and unable to move for some minutes, before the executioner returned to brave the missiles on his own, in yet another attempt to finish his work.

But the fourth attempt was no more successful than the third, and the crowds became more hostile than ever. After the blade had descended for the fifth time without cutting off Hebard's head, the executioner took fright and once again left the scaffold. What happened next was even more shocking still.

To the astonishment of the spectators, the wounded man, without any help, managed to get his neck free of the *lunette*. Still bound to the plank, he raised himself to his feet and began begging for help. But the crowds, though on his side, were unable to give him the assistance he wanted, so he just went on standing there, streaming with blood.

After this terrible spectacle had continued for several minutes, one of the executioner's assistants climbed on to the scaffold, grimly determined to put an end to it. Seizing the condemned man, he tried to finish the execution with a shoemaker's knife, but did not succeed even in this. Before long, he had to jump down from the scaffold and make his escape among the *gendarmes*.

With his half-severed head hanging to one side, Hebard, according to witnesses, went on breathing for another half an hour, his mouth opening and closing repeatedly, before he finally died. His corpse was afterwards left bound to the plank in an upright position for an hour and a half, until cut down and taken away under a military escort.

The spectators, of course, blamed the executioner for what had happened, and during the course of the evening a crowd surrounded his house and broke all the windows. But when the guillotine was examined it was found to have been tampered with in such a way that it was prevented from functioning normally.

One of the executioner's former assistants, who had been dismissed for misconduct, was suspected of being the person responsible.

Among other shocking incidents at executions of this type, we find one which occurred in Auxerre, in central France, in 1841. This time the victim was a man named Rouillard, who had been convicted on a number of charges of attempted murder and arson. He was sixty-four years of age.

A report of his death, published in an English newspaper, informs us that the guillotine used was faulty. The condemned man's head was not severed at the first attempt, and 'a most horrible scene ensued, the operation being renewed over and over again, by three executioners, before he was dead'.

The report concludes by stating that the crowds were furious and would have torn the executioners to pieces but for the presence of a large military force.

A third such incident – almost as bad as the first – occurred on the island of New Caledonia, in the south Pacific, sixty-five years later. An Arab named Kenadia was sentenced to death for murder, and the guillotine was erected in the market square in Nouméa for his execution. The following account of what happened is taken from *The Illustrated Police News* of 27 January 1906:

The executioner had not before served in that capacity,

and was, so it was alleged, nervous about doing the duty which confronted him. The condemned man appeared bound, and his head was placed under the knife. It fell before time, however, with the result that only part of the man's skull was removed.

The spectacle was horrifying. The unfortunate Arab could be seen writhing in agony. Hurriedly the executioner hoisted the knife into position. For the second time it fell with a dull thud, removing another part of the man's head. The cord had broken, and the Arab had to endure frightful agony until it was mended, and the knife again placed in position. When it fell the third time the remainder of the man's head was cut off.

The execution was carried out before a large crowd of people, who became incensed at the bungling and made a rush at the executioner. Had there not been troops present to keep order, he would almost certainly have been lynched.

Stabbed to death
- and then guillotined

Besides the bunglings and mishaps, there were some ghastly incidents at the guillotine caused by resistance on the part of the condemned. One such case was that of Claude Montcharmont, a twenty-nine-year-old poacher convicted of murder at Chalon-sur-Saône, in central France, in the spring of 1851.

Montcharmont was a good-looking, powerfully-built man reduced to a state of abject terror by the fate which awaited him. During the forty days which he spent under sentence of death, he let out piteous cries for hours on end, begging for mercy or screaming for help whenever anyone came near him. But all of this was to no avail, and on the morning of 10 May he was told to prepare himself for death.

There were two executioners, one presumably an assistant to the other. When they came for him, they had difficulty opening the cell door, as he had managed to wedge it from the inside. Not only that, he had taken off all of his clothes and refused to put them back on. During the struggle which ensued, Montcharmont's screams could be heard outside the prison.

The executioners – one old, the other weak – eventually succeeded in dressing him. Having bound him hand and foot, they then carried him out to the waiting cart, and he was conveyed thus to the foot of the scaffold. But when his bonds were loosened so that he could climb the ladder, he pushed his legs between the rungs and gripped it in such a way that he could not be moved.

A desperate struggle followed. The condemned man, crying for help, clung to the ladder with a grim determination, while the executioners tried frantically to make him let go of it. Nobody came to his aid: the crowds merely watched in horror as the spectacle went on and on. But at last it became clear that the executioners were not going to get the better of him, and after thirty-five minutes the execution was abandoned. Montcharmont then let go of the ladder and was taken back to prison.

No commutation of sentence followed: Montcharmont had merely put off the fatal hour. And he had not put it off for long, for no sooner was he back in his cell than the authorities sent for the Dijon executioner, evidently to show the others how to do their work properly. He arrived in the town some hours later, and the condemned man was taken out to the scaffold for the second time.

Securely bound, he was this time carried up to the guillotine, unable to put up any resistance at all. With his neck in position under the blade, all he could do was call on God to pardon him. Then the blade was released and Montcharmont's ordeal ended.

But the shocking affair led to newspaper attacks on the Government, the most violent being one by Charles Hugo, the son of the famous novelist, in *L'Evénement*. This, in turn, led to the seizure of the paper and the prosecution of those primarily responsible.

Hugo was sent to prison for six months.

Eighteen years after Montcharmont's death, Jean-Baptiste Troppmann, a twenty-eight-year-old mass murderer, lay under sentence of death in Paris. One morning – it was 19 January 1870 – a small group of men entered his cell shortly before dawn. They found him awake and dressed, as if he had been waiting for them.

On being told that his hour had come, Troppmann remained calm. He declined to make a confession of his crimes, claiming that they were the work of accomplices whom he could not name. However, he accepted the service of the chaplain, whose daily visits he had evidently welcomed.

Soon it was time for the straps round his arms to be buckled and for the hair to be cut from the back of his neck, so that the execution could be carried out as swiftly as possible. It seems that he broke down during these final preparations, but soon regained his composure.

Outside the prison, in the Place de la Roquette, the guillotine awaited him. Noisy crowds stood in the cold, held back by troops and *gendarmes*, while well-to-do observers watched from windows overlooking the scene. Suddenly, the gates opened and the condemned man appeared, recoiling instinctively at the sight of the scaffold.

Encouraged by the priest, supported by the executioner's assistants, he walked the last few yards to the place where he was to die. At the foot of the steps he embraced the priest twice, but persisted in denying the crimes for which he had been condemned. The priest then retired and Troppmann ascended the steps, Heinderech, the executioner, pushing him from behind.

During the last few moments of his life, Troppmann's attitude of resignation suddenly vanished and terror took possession of him. Stretched out on the plank before the *lunette*, he twisted himself violently to the side, trying to avoid having his neck enclosed. Then, after being pushed back, he drew himself up in an astonishing display of strength and suppleness, and thrust himself so far forward that he got his shoulder into the semicircular aperture.

But with an assistant in front of him, clinging to his hair,

and the powerful executioner grasping his neck, Troppmann was quickly overpowered. In a final act of ferocity,
he sank his teeth into Heinderech's hand before his neck
was forced into position and the upper part of the *lunette*
lowered. Then the heavy blade fell and struck off his head.

It was still scarcely daybreak, and from where the
crowds stood little could be seen, as by now was always the
case. The execution was nonetheless followed by shouts of
approval, and two or three men who had slipped through
the cordon dipped handkerchiefs in the pools of blood
under the scaffold. They afterwards ran off, with a *gend-
arme* in pursuit.

Greece adopted the guillotine after becoming independent
of the Turks in 1829. But finding a suitable person to fill
the post of executioner was no easy matter, in view of
the disdain with which such functionaries were regarded
there. Eventually, though, the authorities succeeded in
finding somebody, and the carrying out of capital sentences began.

One such execution took place early in 1847, probably
in Nauplia. Two brothers, Demetrius and Theodosius
Tryphoupoulos, who had been condemned for brigandage,
were brought out to the place of execution to die together.
Both allowed themselves to be conducted to the foot of the
scaffold, but (as *The Times* reported)

> at the moment the executioner was about to tie Deme-
> trius to the fatal plank he, being a man of extraordinary
> strength, broke his bonds, and, throwing down the
> executioner and his assistants, attempted to escape.

They tried to secure him, but Demetrius fought desperately
and 'cruelly ill-treated them'. After a long and unavailing
struggle, the executioner drew a knife from his pocket and
plunged it into the condemned man's heart. Demetrius was

killed instantly and was then decapitated as though he were still alive.

Theodosius gave the executioners no such trouble. Trembling convulsively, he submitted himself to them in a spirit of resignation, and so was decapitated in the normal way.

Demetrius Tryphoupoulos's grim struggle was not the only spectacle of its type to occur in Greece about this time. According to Edmond About, a contemporary French author, there were many of them. 'The law ordains that he (the condemned) shall walk freely to punishment, and that his hands shall not be bound,' About tells us in *Greece and the Greeks* (English translation, 1855).

> Now the greater part of those that are sentenced, brigands by profession, are vigorous men, who never fail to struggle with the executioner. Every execution begins by a duel, in which justice always has the upper hand, for she is armed with a dagger.

He goes on to say that when the culprit has received 'eight or ten' wounds, and has lost all his strength with his blood, he goes freely to execution and his head falls. The witnesses afterwards ask themselves how they can best kill the executioner.

Louis Deibler beheaded a corpse inadvertently in France in 1898. An Italian mushroom grower named Carrara had been sentenced to death for killing a man his wife had lured into their house. But as he was thrown under the guillotine, he suddenly died of fright. One of the executioner's assistants noticed this and called to his chief to warn him. As he spoke, however, the blade fell.

Life after decapitation

On 25 June 1905, a doctor named Beaurieux attended an execution in Orleans for a very bizarre purpose. He had obtained permission to conduct an experiment with the victim's severed head, with a view to proving that life continues after decapitation. How he tried to do so was quite astonishing, and naturally resulted in a lot of publicity – none of which was to his own liking.

The execution was that of Henri Languille, a bandit who had terrorized parts of central France for some years before being brought to justice. It was carried out without difficulty, the condemned man remaining calm and resolute in the face of death, and when his head fell into a tray at the front of the guillotine, it landed in an upright position. This enabled the doctor to perform his experiment without actually touching it.

Beaurieux observed that for the first five or six seconds after the execution had taken place, Languille's eyelids and lips contracted spasmodically: a phenomenon with which he was already familiar. He waited until the face finally relaxed, with the eyes half-closed, then called out in a sharp voice, 'Languille!'

At this, the executed man's eyes opened slowly and fixed themselves on the doctor's, with the pupils focusing. They were, as Beaurieux declared in his own published account, 'undeniably living eyes' – and after staying open for several seconds they half-closed again of their own accord, the face taking on the same appearance as before.

Continuing his experiment, Beaurieux called out Languille's name for the second time, and elicited the same response. Languille's eyes opened and fixed themselves on his ('with perhaps even more penetration than the first time'), then half-closed again a few seconds later.

The doctor called out for the third time, but this time there was no movement at all. Languille's eyes took on the glazed look of the dead, and Beaurieux brought his experiment to an end.

It had lasted for twenty-five to thirty seconds, and the doctor was convinced that Languille's sight and hearing had both survived for most of that time. In writing his account for publication, he argued that the survival of conscious perception was a distinct possibility: a horrifying idea of which he was neither the first nor the last person to take seriously.

Three hundred years before Beaurieux's strange experiment, the severed head of a thief executed in Nuremberg behaved in an even more remarkable manner than Languille's. George Praun was beheaded with a sword by Franz Schmidt, the Nuremberg hangman, on 14 September 1602. According to Schmidt's diary, when his head was placed 'on the stone' (presumably the stone platform of the city gallows) it 'turned several times as if it wanted to look about it, moved its tongue and opened its mouth as if wanting to speak, for a good half quarter of an hour'.

Schmidt recorded only the briefest details of this amazing incident and made no attempt to explain it. He concluded by stating that he had never seen anything like it before.

The last public execution in France was that of Eugen
Weidmann, a coldblooded German killer guillotined
in front of the Palais de Justice in Versailles on
16 June 1939. The execution, which took place just
before five o'clock in the morning, was attended by
an unruly crowd, and women dipped their handkerchiefs in the dead man's blood before it was hosed
away. Newspaper photographs of the event, taken
from windows overlooking the scene, caused such an
outcry that public executions in that country were
brought to an abrupt end.

F. Tennyson Jesse, who was among the observers at
Weidmann's execution, tells us in *Comments on Cain*
(1948) that the crash of the blade was followed by
'the whistling that always sounds when a head is cut
off'. She adds: 'For the neck gives out a gasp as the
last breath of air leaves the lungs, though the head be
already in the basket. It is the man's windpipe and not
his tongue that protests.'

Deibler in print

Anatole Deibler, the French executioner, wrote the following *Account of an Execution* for Alfred Morain's book *The Underworld of Paris* in 1929. The guillotine used at this time was a model adopted in 1875.

As soon as the appeal for reprieve has been rejected, the Chancellerie sends a summons to the Executioner in Chief of Arrested Criminals, ordering him to present himself as soon as possible, that is to say, within a few hours. The day of execution is then fixed and the Executioner is given three orders. The first of these runs as follows: 'Monsieur Deibler, Executioner in Chief of Arrested Criminals, will proceed immediately to X— to receive the orders of the Attorney-General (or the Public Prosecutor) in regard to the execution of X— sentenced to death for murder, etc., by order of the Assize Court of X—, dated . . .

'He will be accompanied by three assistant executioners (or four if this is a double execution).

'He will show this document to the Attorney-General.

'Issued in Paris on . . .
'Le Directeur des Affaires criminelles et des Grâces.'

The second order requires the Railway Company of X— to give transportation in both directions, in a reserved compartment of the 2nd Class, to the Executioner in Chief of Arrested Criminals and his three (or four) assistant executioners.

The third order deals with the transportation to and fro of the scaffold.

As soon as he receives these orders, the Executioner goes to the railway station, obtains tickets for himself and his assistants, and then proceeds to the forwarding office to order the flat-bottomed waggon needed for the transportation of the guillotine. Afterwards he instructs his carmen to have the carriage containing the scaffold brought from the Santé prison to the station, where it is placed on the waggon and covered with a cloth. This operation is supervised by the Chief Executioner. The waggon is then placed on a siding to await the hour of departure. The Executioner and his assistants take a fast train in order to arrive on the day before the execution. On arrival, he orders a vehicle for the next day to transfer the carriage from the station to the place where the guillotine is to be erected. Then he goes to the Public Prosecutor's office, where he shows the first order and where he receives the necessary information concerning the place of the execution, the hour of the calling of the guard composed of garrison soldiers, police, gendarmerie, or local police, the hour of the awakening of the prisoner and the hour of execution. The Public Prosecutor must, in concert with the Executioner and according to Article 376 of the Penal Code, demand the assistance of armed forces to maintain order. He must requisition alike police and soldiery, as the assistance of the gendarmerie is in any case indispensable. The municipal authorities have to decide the actual spot where the execution will take place, but they must be in agreement with the Executioner and the Public Prosecutor.

On the demand of the Executioner, the place of execution has lately been near, or in front of, the gate of the prison. In the event of difficulties the Préfet de Police interposes. Without interfering with the arrangements of the Service d'Ordre, the Public Prosecutor requires the Service to abide by the following regulations:

The place chosen for the erection of the guillotine must be cleared of the public.

Access to this space is forbidden.

Only duly qualified persons, such as the Executioner and his assistants, magistrates, public functionaries, and journalists who can justify their presence, are admitted. For this purpose the Public Prosecutor provides admittance cards.

Three or four hours before the time fixed for the execution, the Executioner and his assistants go to the railway station in order to take delivery of the carriage containing the scaffold. He contrives to reach the place appointed for the execution a little while after the arrival of the Service d'Ordre.

The erection of the guillotine begins at once. About three-quarters of an hour must be reckoned for this purpose, according to the slope of the ground. The essential point is that it should be on a horizontal plane. For this purpose, wooden blocks of various sizes and levelling instruments are used.

When the guillotine is ready the Executioner and his assistants go into the prison to await the hour of the waking of the prisoner, at which they can attend if they choose. More often they wait in the clerk's office for the moment of the making of the last toilet. This consists in a simple cut into the collar of the shirt, the binding of the arms behind the back, and the fettering of the legs with a cord that permits of paces of about eight inches. This formality, made as a measure of security, takes three or four minutes.

The Executioner certifies the removal of the entry in the prison books and the condemned person is led to the scaffold. He arrives at the foot of the guillotine. He is placed in such a way that the abdomen rests against the vertical timber called the bascule. *The assistants, while supporting him, at the same time push his shoulders. The plank tips over, the prisoner loses his foothold and lies in a horizontal position. The plank supporting the body, moving on rollers, is pushed forward until the head of the condemned person passes beyond the main posts of the guillotine.*

At this decisive moment, the Executioner, standing to the left of the guillotine, must have his left hand on the spring of the lunette *(which encloses the head) and his right hand on the lever of the knife. He presses simultaneously with both hands.*

The lunette *falls and secures the head. The knife follows immediately afterwards and carries out the decapitation.*

A slight push on the body causes it to fall into the basket placed alongside the bascule.

The tin pail containing the head is emptied into the basket, which is covered and placed in the carriage. Then, accompanied by an escort of mounted gendarmes, *it is taken to a cemetery where, in the presence of the Executioner, it is put into a coffin and buried. Meanwhile the assistants take down the guillotine. On the return of their chief, the machine is reloaded on to the carriage, which then returns to the railway station.*

The return to Paris is made in the same manner as the outward journey.

Reprieved murderer
lived to be 101

Anton Nilsson, a revolutionary socialist, was the last man to be sentenced to death in Sweden. He lived to be 101 years old.

In 1908, at the age of twenty, Nilsson was convicted of causing an explosion aboard a ship in the port of Malmo, killing one person and injuring twenty-one others. The casualties were all English labourers who had been brought over to break a dock strike.

After he had been tried and condemned, a guillotine was imported from France for the purpose of carrying out his execution. But his sentence was commuted to life imprisonment, and in 1917 he was pardoned by King Gustaf V.

Nilsson then trained to be a pilot, but in 1918 went to the Soviet Union and joined the Red Army. He fought against the White Russians along the Finnish border.

After some years in the USSR, he returned to Sweden, and began lecturing and writing about his experiences. Despite serious doubts about Stalinism, he remained a revolutionary, and although he joined the Swedish Social Democratic Party, he was frequently in disagreement with the official line.

He died in August 1989, asking from his deathbed for revolutionary songs to be played at his funeral.

The English murderess Constance Kent was sentenced to

death in 1865, for a brutal murder committed five years earlier. She too lived to be a centenarian.

Constance was one of many children of a twice-married inspector of factories. On the morning of 30 June 1860, her half-brother Savill, aged three years and ten months, was found dead in a privy at the family's home in the village of Rode, in Somerset. His throat was cut and he had a stab wound in his chest, but he may actually have died of suffocation.

Suspicion fell upon Constance, who was then a sullen and troublesome girl of sixteen, but when she was charged with the crime the local magistrates released her for lack of evidence. A second suspect, a nursemaid in the household, was later arrested, but she was also discharged. Eventually, the case was abandoned, and remained unsolved for the next five years.

Constance, in the meantime, had undergone a religious conversion, and suddenly confessed to the crime; she said that it had been an act of revenge against her stepmother, whom she hated. On appearing for trial at the Wiltshire Assizes in Salisbury, on 21 July 1865, she pleaded guilty and was sentenced to death. Her sentence, however, was commuted to life imprisonment and she spent the next twenty years in jail.

Released in 1885, she travelled to Australia the following year under the name of Ruth Emilie Kaye, by which she was to be known for the rest of her life. She entered the nursing profession in 1890, and after completing a two-year training course in Melbourne, held a succession of posts in different towns. She spent the last twenty-two years of her working life running a nurses' home in Maitland, New South Wales, before retiring at the age of eighty-eight in 1932.

A respected member of the community, Constance later entered a rest home in nearby Strathfield, where she celebrated her 100th birthday on 6 February 1944. She died on 10 April the same year, almost seventy-nine years after the death sentence had been passed on her.

Her real identity was not discovered until long afterwards.

He survived the firing squad

Wenceslao Moguel, a Mexican student, was shot by a firing squad in 1915, in the aftermath of an unsuccessful attempt by rebel troops to seize control of the state of Yucatán. But eight bullet wounds failed to kill him and he survived even the *coup de grâce* given by the officer in charge. 'El Fusilado', as he was afterwards called, lived to become a well-known figure.

The affair began when the rebels attacked the Government Palace and other key targets in the city of Merida. The state at that time wanted independence, but the rebels were resisted by Government forces and within two days were forced to retreat. In doing so, they passed through the grounds of the university and took a large number of students captive. The students – Moguel among them – were divided into small groups and forced to fight alongside rebel soldiers.

'I was placed on board a train, with a gun and fifty bullets,' Moguel told an American journalist thirty years later. 'Soon we got off at a little village which had been deserted by the frightened inhabitants. The enemy attacked, and my friends fell dead. Then, after many hours of fighting, the Government forces took us prisoners and we were all sentenced to death summarily. We faced the firing squad two by two.

'When my turn came, I was trying to think of something

to give me courage but my throat was dry and I could neither breathe nor speak. I looked at the firing squad and it seemed to me as if they also looked at me. And then, in what was supposed to be my last moment on earth, I thought – I don't know why – of St James, and it dawned on me that a miracle might happen.

'I heard the shots and felt as if my body and my face had been hit by a hail of blows. I fell, and all around me there were the bodies of the dead soldiers and those of my university friends, and although I was half conscious, I could see the officer in charge advance, gun in hand, to fire the final shot into the heads of the dying.

'The officer came to me and put the gun to my face and pulled the trigger. Then all went blank. By all tokens, I should have been dead, but I wasn't.'

Instead of entering his head, that final bullet had shattered his jaw. But nobody noticed that he was alive, and Moguel was left lying among the bodies for some hours, until the soldiers left the village. Eventually, the villagers returned and some women came to the site to bury the dead. Finding Moguel still alive, they called a doctor in time to save him.

In 1945, when the journalist R.J. Urruela interviewed him for a New Orleans newspaper, 'El Fusilado' was, in Urruela's own words, one of two 'human attractions' in Merida – the other being a man who knew *Don Quixote* off by heart. He had written a booklet describing his adventures and had once made a trip to New York in order to be presented to a national radio audience.

But, despite his fame, Wenceslao Moguel was a poor man. He lived in an adobe on the outskirts of Merida, with his wife and several children. For the support of his large family, he relied on assistance from the Governor of Yucatán.

When two senior police officers were sentenced to death

for bribe-taking in Liberia in 1982, the country's military ruler, Samuel Doe, ordered that the firing squad which executed them should be composed of policemen who could swear that they themselves had never been guilty of any corrupt practice.

This proved an impossible requirement to meet, for Liberian police had long seen bribe-taking as a natural way of supplementing their salaries. Before long, the search for honest policemen was abandoned and the two condemned, Deputy Director Sam Massaquoi and Lieutenant Colonel Sam Kamara, were released from prison and reinstated in their posts.

The Director of Police and the Minister of Justice were both dismissed for damaging the credibility of the force.

Buried alive at sea

In the penal colony of French Guiana, where the guillotine was used, there were generally two executioners. One served the mainland settlements, the other the three little islands off the coast: Royale, St Joseph and Devil's Island. Both were invariably convicts, hated by their fellow prisoners, and isolated for their own safety. Despite this precaution, they lived in constant fear of being murdered.

But the posts were not difficult to fill, as their occupants enjoyed certain privileges which were denied to the rest of the convict population. So when one of them became vacant early in 1940, it was not seen as surprising that a killer named Serge Corbière should get himself appointed to it. Corbière, however, had no wish to remain an executioner for the rest of his life – and was not destined to, either.

Since his arrival in the colony in 1933, Corbière had been interested in one thing above all else: how to escape. He had already made several unsuccessful attempts, the last of which had ended with his recapture just a few weeks earlier. At that time he had been quite deranged and was suspected of cannibalism, but he had since regained his sanity as a result of hospital treatment at St Laurent, on the mainland.

During the time that Corbière was in hospital, George Bonfils, the island executioner, tried to escape from the Isle

Royale, where he was stationed. He had evidently been planning the attempt for some time, but was surprised by a guard while digging up a canoe which he had hidden. In his determination to get away, Bonfils killed the guard, but was then captured while trying to launch the boat.

A new executioner was therefore needed, not just to replace Bonfils but to execute him, and when Corbière agreed to accept the post he was obviously aware that this would be his first task. The execution was duly carried out on 10 February 1940, and Corbière was afterwards left to prepare the dead man's body for burial at sea. But instead of doing so, he hid the body and wrapped himself in the shroud, so when the guards returned they unwittingly took him out to sea and threw him overboard.

This, of course, was what Corbière had intended, and on finding himself in the sea, he swam back unobserved to a part of the island where Bonfils had hidden a second canoe – as the old executioner had confided to him while under sentence of death. Corbière used this to make his own escape, and, heading south-east, was eventually picked up by a coastguard cutter of the Brazilian Navy. He was given asylum in Brazil, but later made his way to France, where he arrived in March 1941.

Corbière spent the rest of the Second World War fighting in the French Resistance, and in 1945 surrendered to the authorities, hoping for a pardon. But instead he was committed to prison, and remained there until a group of friends broke into the jail and rescued him. A fugitive again, he left the country in haste and settled in Mexico, in the old French colony of San Raphael. He is known to have been still living there in 1968.

Another former executioner of French Guiana was stabbed to death in Paris in 1938, a year after being repatriated. Léon La Durrell had been the mainland executioner for fifteen years, his predecessor, like Corbière's, having been executed for murder. La Durrell's own murder was never solved.

Three wartime executions

On the morning of 31 January 1945, Private Eddie D. Slovik, of the Twenty-Eighth Division of the US Army, was shot by a firing squad for desertion in the small town of Ste Marie aux Mines, in eastern France. The execution was carried out in the walled garden of a closely-guarded house, before a large group of the condemned man's fellow soldiers. The firing squad was made up of twelve riflemen, one of whom had a blank cartridge in his gun.

Slovik, who had a record of petty crime in civilian life, had disappeared from his company while it was engaged in heavy fighting in Elboeuf on 8 October the previous year. On returning the following day, he confessed that he had been frightened, and said he would desert again rather than go into combat. He was sentenced to death by a court-martial.

After the sentence had been carried out, Slovik's body was buried in the Oise-Aisne American Cemetery near Château-Thierry, where for the next forty-two years he shared a plot with ninety-five other Americans who had been hanged for raping or murdering civilians. In 1987, his remains were taken back to America and reburied in his home town of Detroit.

Private Slovik was just one of forty thousand American servicemen who deserted during the Second World War, but the only one to be executed for that offence. No other

Americans have been put to death for desertion since the Civil War.

Britain's last execution by shooting took place in August 1941, when Josef Jakobs, a German officer, faced a firing squad at the Tower of London. His crime was spying.

Seven months earlier, Jakobs had landed in England by parachute, equipped with a short-wave radio transmitter, a loaded pistol and £500 in cash. His mission was to obtain information about weather conditions, for use in planning bombing raids. But, unfortunately for him, he broke his ankle and was quickly captured.

As a serving soldier, he was tried by court-martial and, on conviction, sentenced to be shot rather than hanged. His execution took place on a small rifle range, with the condemned man strapped to a chair. He died instantly.

Belgium's only execution for a non-military offence since 1863 was that of Camille Verfeuille, a soldier guillotined in Furnes in March 1918 for the murder of a servant girl. The execution was to have taken place in public, in the marketplace, but as the town was under enemy bombardment at the time it was decided that it should be carried out within the walls of the prison instead. The French executioner, Anatole Deibler, had travelled to Belgium with his assistants – and his guillotine – especially for the occasion. They left in haste after finishing their work.

Thirty-two years on Death Row

Sadamichi Hirasawa, a prominent Japanese tempera painter, was sentenced to death in 1950, following his conviction for a bizarre mass poisoning. Though never commuted, the sentence was never carried out, and Hirasawa lived to become the oldest and longest-serving Death Row prisoner in the world. He protested his innocence to the end, and was widely believed to have been convicted on the basis of fabricated evidence and a false confession. For many years, a determined group of supporters campaigned tirelessly for his release.

The crime for which he was condemned had taken place on 26 January 1948, when a man arrived at the Shiina-machi branch of the Teikoku (Imperial) Bank in Tokyo at closing time. Posing as a health official, he told the staff that there had been an outbreak of dysentery in the area and that he had come to administer an anti-dysentery medicine to each of them. He thus induced everyone on the premises to drink a solution of potassium cyanide, as a result of which twelve people died. The man escaped with about 180,000 yen in cash and cheques.

Hirasawa, aged fifty-six, was arrested seven months later, and was unable to explain a large sum of money found in his possession. Of the four bank employees who had survived the poisoning, three said only that he bore a

passing resemblance to the bogus health official, while the
fourth said that there was no likeness at all. Hirasawa was
nonetheless convicted, and his death sentence was confirmed by Japan's Supreme Court in 1955, after a review
of the case. The condemned man was then moved to Death
Row, to await execution.

But for some undisclosed reason, successive Justice
Ministers – some two dozen of them – refused to sign the
necessary order. So Hirasawa just went on waiting there,
year after year, with no way of knowing when or even
whether the execution would be carried out. He was still
under sentence of death when he died of natural causes at
the age of ninety-five.

The Save Hirasawa Committee, formed in 1962,
claimed that the condemned man had been framed by the
Japanese police, who knew the identity of the real killer but
were prevented from bringing him to justice by a sinister
cover-up ordered by General MacArthur's post-war Occupation Forces. They said that the Teikoku Bank robber had
had a knowledge of poisons, and a skill in handling them,
which Hirasawa did not have, and named a former member
of a secret chemical warfare unit of the Japanese Army as
the real culprit.

Lieutenant Colonel Saburo Suwa, who was drowned in
1949, had emerged as the prime suspect during the police
investigation. But instead of arresting him, the police,
according to Hirasawa's supporters, had succumbed to
pressure from MacArthur's General Headquarters to sup-
press the link between the army unit and the mass
poisoning. At the same time, Japanese newspapers which
tried to investigate the connection were censored on the
grounds of military security.

The allegation was based initially on disclosures made
in 1963 by the man who had headed the detective team
investigating the crime, but was reinforced just two or

three years before Hirasawa's death when the American author William Triplett unearthed a batch of the Occupation Authorities' own records in the National Archives in Washington.

Besides confirming that police inquiries *had* been concentrated on former personnel of the secret army unit, these revealed that at the time of the investigation MacArthur's GHQ had been protecting the unit's key members from prosecution as war criminals – for carrying out experiments on prisoners during the Second World War – in return for information of military value. This was obviously a deal which was in danger of being exposed if the original suspect were arrested, and so provided a motive for GHQ staff to protect him as well – as they apparently did.

In view of the controversy surrounding the case, there were times when campaigners seemed to have a good chance of securing the condemned man's release. But during his thirty-two years on Death Row, seventeen appeals for a retrial and five appeals for an amnesty were all turned down. Even an attempt, in 1985, to get him released under Japan's Statute of Limitations failed, the Tokyo District Court accepting the Justice Ministry's interpretation that the thirty-year limit on carrying out the death penalty applied only to accused persons who had not been captured and prisoners who had escaped.

In his old age, Hirasawa legally adopted Takehiko Morikawa, the son of the novelist Tetsuro Morikawa who had led the Save Hirasawa Committee for many years. His own children (he had five of them) had all disowned him after his conviction, when their mother obtained a divorce, but Takehiko was as staunch a supporter of Hirasawa's cause as his father had been. He became Hirasawa's adopted son for legal reasons, so that he could continue the struggle to clear his name in the courts after the painter's death.

Sadamichi Hirasawa spent his last two years, frail and often bedridden, at the Hachioji Medical Detention House outside Tokyo, having been transferred there from Sendai Prison in northern Japan. He died of pneumonia, thirty-seven years after his conviction, on 10 May 1987.

Between July 1983 and July 1984, three other prisoners who had spent many years under sentence of death in Japan were declared innocent and set free after long legal battles. In all three cases, the original verdict hinged on a confession which the accused said was false.

Sakae Menda, aged fifty-seven, was acquitted after a retrial in Yatsushiro, in south-western Japan, thirty-two years after being sentenced for two murders. It was the first such reversal in the country's history.

Shigeyoshi Taniguchi, aged fifty-three, was similarly acquitted in Takamatsu, also in south-western Japan, in March 1984. He had been under sentence of death since his conviction for the murder of a black-market rice dealer thirty-three years earlier. His appeal for a retrial was granted in 1976.

Yukio Saito, aged fifty-three, had served twenty-seven years after being condemned for the murder of four people in Matsuyama, near Sendai. He had confessed to the murders after being arrested in connection with a different offence.

There was a fourth such case a few years later, this time in Tokyo. Masao Akabori, aged fifty-nine, had been sentenced in 1958, for the murder of a six-year-old girl in 1954. He spent twenty-six years on Death Row before the Tokyo High Court ordered a retrial and suspended his sentence.

On 12 March 1984, Shigeyoshi Taniguchi left the District Court in Takamatsu, on the island of Shikoku, after being cleared of the murder for which he had once been sentenced to death. It was the end of an ordeal which had lasted thirty-four years.

Outside the courthouse, a crowd of supporters greeted him excitedly, and the former Death Row inmate, clearly relieved by the court's decision, threw up his arms and joined in their cries of jubilation.

'Everything I see is glittering,' he told reporters. 'All I want now is to go back to my village and till the land.'

It was his first day of freedom since March 1950, when, as a youth of nineteen, he was accused of killing and robbing a sixty-three-year-old black-marketeer a month earlier.

At his trial, which was held the following year, Taniguchi said that the police had used force to make him confess to the crime, and he challenged evidence that blood found on his trousers matched that of the victim. He was, however, found guilty, and his death sentence was upheld by the Supreme Court in 1957.

Nineteen years later, after repeated appeals, the Supreme Court finally granted his request for a retrial, sending the case back to the District Court. But it was not until another eight years had elapsed that Taniguchi heard Chief Judge Kiyoshi Furichi rule that the evidence against him was not sufficient for a conviction.

Among the crowd which gathered outside the Takamatsu courthouse to hear the result of the retrial was Sakae Menda, another former Death Row prisoner.

Menda had himself been acquitted after a retrial just a few months earlier. His ordeal had also lasted thirty-four years.

In January 1989, the retrial ended with his acquittal, and it was reported that Akabori would receive a record 120 million yen (£500,000) from the state in compensation.

The most celebrated prisoner currently on Japan's Death Row is Norio Nagayama, a serial killer and prize-winning novelist whose case was at the centre of a campaign to abolish capital punishment during the mid-1970s. As a nineteen-year-old coffee-shop waiter during October and November 1968, Nagayama killed four people on separate occasions, using a stolen handgun. He was arrested the following year, and has been in prison ever since.

In 1981, after he had been on Death Row for some years, the Tokyo High Court reduced his sentence to life imprisonment. But his prosecutors then appealed to the Supreme Court, and the lower court was directed to reinstate the death penalty. The 1981 decision was accordingly reversed in 1987, and in 1990 the Supreme Court was reported to have rejected Nagayama's final appeal. So he may yet be hanged after all this time.

Nagayama's autobiographical novel, *Wooden Bridge*, won the New Japan Literary Prize in 1983 and became an instant bestseller. A second novel, *Tears of Ignorance*, followed, and this also sold many copies. Besides his fiction, Nagayama has written a book about Marxism and translated the works of a leading Dutch criminologist into Japanese. He has used some of the proceeds of his writings to compensate the relatives of his victims.

Chinese executions convenient for transplant surgery

In recent years, China has regularly used organs from the bodies of executed criminals for transplant surgery, without the consent of either the prisoners or their relatives. Many of the organs are sold to rich overseas buyers: a practice which has led to criticism that they are being used as a source of hard currency.

What usually happens is that a buyer registers with a hospital for the operation he needs – generally a kidney transplant – and waits for the required organ to become available. The police then notify the hospital when an execution is to take place, so that arrangements for the operation can be made beforehand.

Executions are by shooting, and many are carried out in public. Usually the prisoner is shot in the back of the head, but if his eyes are needed he is shot in the heart instead. Immediately the execution has taken place, the prisoner's body is conveyed to a nearby ambulance, so that his organs can be removed and rushed to the hospital.

China has many crimes which are punishable by death, including murder, rape, robbery, drug-trafficking and political offences, and hundreds of people are executed there every year. The practice of using such offenders as organ donors was carried on in secret for some years, until exposed in 1990. By that time it was already well established.

Besides supplying its own hospitals, China sells kidneys to surgeons in Hong Kong. Some patients – even ones from abroad – prefer to have transplants in the colony rather than in China itself. In such cases, the condemned may be moved from one part of China to another, in order to be nearer to Hong Kong when he is shot. This is because the transplant has to be carried out within twelve hours of death.

The practice of using organs from executed prisoners without their permission was defended in 1990 by Dr Man Kam Chan, a prominent Hong Kong kidney specialist, who said that it was important to put it in perspective and not judge it by Western standards. 'These are criminals,' he said. 'What do you want to ask their consent for when you are going to execute them?'

This view, however, was not endorsed by Hong Kong's medical association, which was quick to declare itself *against* the trade in organs, and to express concern about the number of sick foreigners which it was attracting to the colony.

Death for adultery - and an executioner with twenty-four wives

In November 1977, a Saudi Arabian princess was publicly executed for committing adultery. Princess Misha, the twenty-three-year-old granddaughter of Prince Mohammed Ibn Abdulaziz, King Khalid's elder brother, was shot in the head before a large crowd of people in a Jeddah square. Her lover was beheaded with a sword immediately afterwards, the executioner, according to one report, severing his head only at the sixth attempt. The onlookers nonetheless cheered loudly as he finished his grim task.

The beheading was secretly photographed by an Englishman using a camera concealed in a cigarette packet. 'Only the viewfinder and the lens were showing, because if anyone sees you with a camera there it is usually confiscated,' Barry Milner told the *Daily Express* when he returned to Britain the following January. His story made sensational news – to the annoyance, no doubt, of the Saudi Royal Family.

Two years later, the case was in the news again, this time following a controversial television documentary, *Death of a Princess*, screened in Britain on 9 April 1980. This contained a reconstruction of the executions and claimed that other members of the same family, both male and female, committed adultery regularly. According to the programme, they only objected to it if it caused a scandal.

King Khalid was furious. Having personally ordered in 1977 that Islamic law be strictly observed throughout Saudi Arabia, he saw *Death of a Princess* as an attack on both his regime and his religion. Britain was promptly threatened with the breaking-off of Anglo-Saudi relations and the suspension of oil exports and business contracts worth hundreds of millions of pounds.

The threat caused alarm in London, and elicited from Britain's Foreign Secretary, Lord Carrington, a personal message to the Saudi Government, expressing his 'profound regret' for the offence which had been caused. But the threat of retaliation was not lifted until several weeks later, after further moves on the part of Britain to placate the Saudis. By that time, plans to show the programme in a number of other democratic countries had been abandoned.

The usual punishment for adultery in Saudi Arabia is not shooting or beheading but death by stoning. Such executions are not reported in the newspapers there, but the manner in which they are carried out is familiar to the country's Western residents.

The offender is buried up to the waist in the ground and pelted with stones of increasing size. If he or she manages to wriggle out of the earth, the execution is discontinued, as it is then regarded as the will of Allah that the offender should go free. But such escapes are rare; normally, the condemned suffers a painful and protracted death.

It was reported from Amman after Princess Misha's execution that some members of the Royal Family had wanted both her and her lover to be put to death in this terrible way. They had, however, allowed less harsh penalties to be inflicted, at the request of the Princess's grandfather.

Death by beheading – or shooting, in the case of women – is the penalty for a number of other capital offences, including murder, drug-trafficking and apostasy; rapists are also executed by this method in some cases, though in others they are stoned. In 1980, sixty-three Shi'ite Muslims were beheaded in one day, for taking part in an armed occupation of the Grand Mosque at Mecca. Generally, though, there are an estimated twenty-five beheadings a year.

During a newspaper interview in 1989, Saudi Arabia's chief executioner, Saeed Al Sayaf, revealed that in the course of a career lasting almost four decades, he had personally executed 600 criminals and cut off the hands of sixty others. He said that he carried out beheadings with a special sword, following the writings of the Prophet Mohammed, and used sharp knives to amputate the hands of thieves. The reason that he had to execute women by shooting was 'to avoid removing any part of the cover on the upper part of the woman's body', he explained.

Al Sayaf was aged about sixty, a man with twenty-four wives and twenty-five children. He told his interviewer that he had sometimes lain awake all night before an execution, worrying that he might fail to carry it out satisfactorily. He did not say whether he was the executioner of Princess Misha and her lover, but claimed that he normally succeeded in cutting off a man's head at the first attempt.

Despite fears of failure, Al Sayaf was enthusiastic about his work. He did not mind his friends and relatives joking about it, and had begun training one of his sons for the calling. He said that after an execution he experienced delight and satisfaction, and gave thanks for the power which he believed God to have given him.

Asked whether he had faced any unusual scenes during the course of his grim career, Al Sayaf recalled a bizarre case in which two men were to be beheaded for killing a colleague. Neither of their faces were covered, as there was no rule about the covering of faces at that time.

'Following the announcement, I chopped off the head of one of them and it fell directly in front of the other criminal,' said the executioner. 'When I went towards the other to finish the job, he stared at me very strangely.

'I had no sympathy at that moment and was about to lift my sword when suddenly the man collapsed and fell to the ground. A doctor examined him and said that he had had a heart attack.

'While he was being carried to the cemetery to be buried, his voice was heard asking for water.

'I was called immediately, and when I looked at him he uttered a few words: "Won't you spare me?"'

Instead of going on with his story, Al Sayaf suddenly brought it to an end, saying, 'This was a very strange scene and I remember it vividly.'

Readers of the *Arab Times*, for which newspaper the interview was conducted, were left to imagine the rest.

Not all convicted murderers are executed in Saudi Arabia: some are spared in compliance with the wishes of the victim's relatives. This happened in the case of a British maintenance engineer and his Irish wife in 1989, when they were found guilty of a brutal murder committed in the mountain town of Taif, in the Hejaz, three years earlier.

Peter Hall, aged forty-one, and Monica Hall, thirty-eight, were convicted of battering to death Helen Feeney, the Irish matron of a maternity hospital, in April 1986. Helen Feeney, who was forty-eight, had been beaten to death with a blunt instrument, and a large sum of money – about £9000 – was afterwards found to be missing from her flat.

When the couple were arrested three months later, they both confessed to the crime; it therefore seemed almost certain that in due course they would be executed. But before they were put on trial, the dead woman's sister, Mrs Teresa Tonry, of Boyle, County Roscommon, appealed to the Saudi authorities for mercy to be shown in the event of their conviction. Because of this, Peter and Monica Hall were given prison terms of ten and eight years respectively, instead of being sentenced to death.

In such cases, Islamic law requires the murderer or murderers to pay a large sum of money to the bereaved, to compensate them for their loss; in Saudi Arabia, at this time, the sum was 120,000 riyals (about £20,000). The Halls had no way of raising this sort of sum, but it was speculated that the British and Irish governments might pay it for them. However, it was never paid, probably because Helen's relatives had made it known that they did not wish to benefit from her death.

Despite the callous nature of their crime, Peter and Monica Hall did not stay in prison for long. In May 1989, just three months after their conviction, they were un-expectedly granted clemency by King Fahd (the successor to Khalid, his half-brother, who died in 1982). Their release was seen as a friendly gesture towards Britain, at a time when Anglo-Saudi relations were at their most cordial for years.

4

Some American Cases

Franz Schmidt, hangman of Nuremberg, carrying out an execution by beheading in 1591.
(From a contemporary pen-and-ink sketch.)

The Hangman's Bridge in Nuremberg, about the beginning of the seventeenth century,
from a contemporary engraving. The hangman lived in the small tower and the part of the
bridge to the left of it.

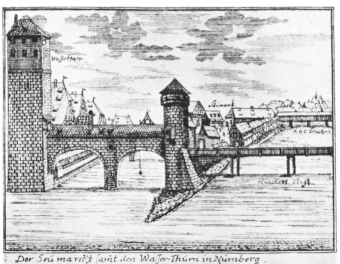

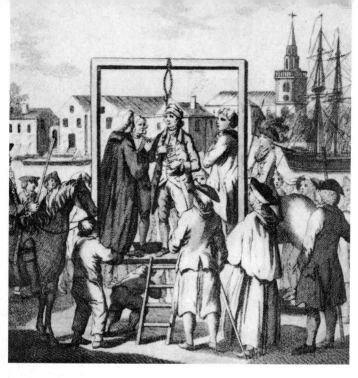

A pirate hanged at Execution Dock. (From an old print.)

The Halifax Gibbet, a forerunner of the guillotine. (From an old print.)

Earl Ferrers hanged at Tyburn in 1760, for the murder of his steward.

After being dissected, his body was put on public display.

The execution of the Cato Street conspirators, who were hanged and beheaded in 1820.
(From an old print.)

An unsuccessful attempt to rescue Robert Johnston from the gallows in Edinburgh in 1818, after his execution was bungled. (From *The Life and Recollections of William Calcraft*, 1870.)

The hanging of thirty-eight Indians at Mankato, Minnesota, in December 1862. (From *Frank Leslie's Illustrated Weekly*.)

The execution of a sow, from *L'Homme et la Bête* by Arthur Mangin (Paris, 1872).

Hangman John Ellis, who later killed himself in a fit of madness.

James Berry, who tried unsuccessfully to hang John Lee of Babbacombe.

Tokichi Ishii, the Japanese murderer who protested at his own acquittal.

Louis Deibler, the French executioner, and his wife.

Theodore Durrant, San Francisco's 'Demon in the Belfry' killer, hanged in 1898.

The gallows at San Quentin Prison.

Jimmy Thompson, tattooed executioner of Mississippi, with America's first portable electric chair. (From *Life* magazine.)

Celebrities of Death Row

America's Death Row has had many celebrated inmates. Their cases excited intense public interest at home and made headline news around the world. Some were famous because they were convicted of sensational crimes; others because their cases were, for one reason or another, controversial. The following are probably the best-known of them all:

- Nicola Sacco and Bartolomeo Vanzetti, two Italian immigrants who had been active in the anarchist movement, were convicted in 1921 of a double murder committed during the course of a payroll robbery in South Braintree, Massachusetts, in April the previous year. The evidence against them was not conclusive and many believe that they were convicted because of their unorthodox political views. But after six years under sentence of death, during which time a number of appeals were made on their behalf, they were electrocuted at Charlestown Prison on 23 August 1927. Fifty years later, a proclamation issued by Governor Michael S. Dukakis denounced the prejudice which had prevailed during their trial but stopped short of declaring the two men innocent.

- Ruth Snyder, a Queens, New York, housewife, persuaded her lover, Henry Judd Gray, to help her kill her husband Albert, by whose death she stood to gain $96,000 from a life insurance policy. When they stood trial together, she accused Gray of the crime, and he admitted taking part in it, but said he had done so under her domination. The details of their affair caused much excitement, and while on Death Row, Ruth received many proposals of marriage. But on 12 January 1928, she and Judd Gray were both electrocuted at Sing Sing Prison, a press photographer taking a secret photograph of Ruth at the moment of death. The photograph took up the entire front page of the following day's New York *Daily News*.

• Bruno Richard Hauptmann, an illegal German immigrant, was convicted of the murder of Charles Lindbergh Jr, the nineteen-month-old son of the famous aviator, of Hopewell, New Jersey. The child had been kidnapped on 1 March 1932, and was later found dead after a large ransom had been paid for his return. Hauptmann, an unemployed carpenter, was arrested in September 1934, and part of the ransom money was found in his garage. At his trial, the case for the prosecution seemed overwhelming, but records unearthed in recent years show that much of the evidence produced against him was false. Denying the offence to the end, Hauptmann was electrocuted at Trenton State Prison on 3 April 1936.

• Julius and Ethel Rosenberg, a married couple with two children, were sentenced to death in March 1951 for transmitting top-secret information about the atom bomb to the Russians. The case aroused much controversy, because no other Americans had ever been executed for spying in peacetime, and many people believed that the punishment was too severe. The Rosenbergs were actually promised a reprieve in return for a full confession, but both maintained that they were innocent of the crime. They were electrocuted at Sing Sing on 19 June 1953.

- Barbara Graham, an occasional prostitute with a criminal record, was sentenced to death with two men in 1953 for the murder of Mrs Mabel Monahan, a sixty-two-year-old widow of Burbank, California. Though a prosecution witness accused her of personally battering the victim with a pistol, many people believed that she was innocent and a campaign was started to save her from the gas chamber. But this was unsuccessful, and on 3 June 1955, Barbara and the two men convicted with her were executed at San Quentin Prison. Three years later, a film about the case, *I Want to Live!*, starring Susan Hayward, asserted that she *was* innocent, and accused the police of using underhand methods to ensure her conviction.

- Caryl Chessman, a habitual criminal, was sentenced to death in 1948 on two counts of kidnapping, under California's 'Little Lindbergh Act'. Arriving on San Quentin's Death Row, he began a marathon struggle to get his convictions reversed, making one appeal after another. His own account of his case, published in 1954, became a bestseller, and this and subsequent books provided him with funds to hire a team of lawyers. But he eventually went to the gas chamber on 2 May 1960, denying to the end the crimes for which he had been condemned. His execution, after twelve years under sentence of death, caused widespread horror and dismay.

- Gary Gilmore, a violent criminal and double murderer, became famous for just the opposite reason to Chessman. On being sentenced to death in the State of Utah, he fought off repeated attempts by others to save his life and insisted on having the sentence carried out. He was shot by a firing squad at Utah State Prison, near Salt Lake City, on 17 January 1977, the execution taking place in a disused cannery in the prison grounds. Prior to 1983, the condemned in Utah were given the choice of being hanged or shot, and most of them, like Gilmore, chose the latter. The hanging option was then abandoned in favour of execution by lethal injection.

Hangings no bar
to the Presidency

On two occasions in the early 1870s, hangings were carried
out at the city jail in Buffalo, New York, by a man who was
destined to become President of the United States. Grover
Cleveland, a lawyer by profession, was then Sheriff of Erie
County, to which post he had been elected after completing
a term as Assistant District Attorney. The two executions
were apparently the only ones to take place in that county
during Cleveland's tenure of office.

The first was that of Patrick Morrissey, a twenty-eight-
year-old Irishman who had killed his mother with a carving
knife. The crime, which was unpremeditated, had been
committed during the course of a violent quarrel while the
culprit was under the influence of drink. Because of this,
Morrissey maintained to the end that his punishment was
unreasonably harsh.

Shortly after midday on 6 September 1872, the day of
his execution, he was brought out into the jail yard,
wearing a black robe and with the noose round his neck.
Escorted by the Sheriff, his deputies and three priests, he
walked to the scaffold with a firm step and took his place
on the trap. The part of the yard where the scaffold stood
had been covered with a canvas awning to protect the scene
from the public gaze.

Morrissey, who was resigned to his fate, accepted the
services of the priests, repeated a prayer and said he was

ready to die. The Sheriff stood at the foot of the gallows, waiting to release the trap by pressing a spring lever. The condemned man's arms and ankles were bound, and he said goodbye to all who were present. Then the black cap was drawn over his eyes.

At fourteen minutes past twelve, Cleveland received the signal that he was waiting for and opened the trap. Morrissey fell through and, in an instant, hung lifeless and rigid. His body was left hanging for twenty-five minutes before being lowered and placed in a coffin.

Though Cleveland had been responsible for the conduct of the execution, there had actually been no need for him to carry it out personally. His predecessors had been in the practice of paying a subordinate to spring the trap for them, and he could easily have done so as well. However, he chose instead to perform the degrading task himself, and apparently had no regrets about it afterwards. He did the same thing a few months later, when his other victim, Jack Gaffney, was hanged at the same jail.

Gaffney had killed a man named Patrick Fabey in May 1872 – another crime committed under the influence of drink – and feigned insanity in the hope of saving his own life. On the day of his execution, 14 February 1873, there was snow and ice on the ground, and officials had to sprinkle salt and sand in the yard, to make sure that nobody slipped on the way to the gallows.

Standing on the trap, Gaffney made a short speech in which he begged the forgiveness of those he had wronged. Like Morrissey, he was hanged without incident, his death, according to the *New York Times* taking place almost instantaneously. His body was afterwards taken back to his home, with a crowd from outside the jail following it.

Though there was nothing remarkable about either of these executions, the fact that Grover Cleveland later became President gives them a special interest. His political opponents tried to use them to get him disqualified from holding office, but did not succeed. Elected in 1884, he was duly inaugurated as America's first Democratic President for twenty-eight years.

To this day, he remains the only US President known to have personally carried out an execution of any sort.

Panic in the
execution chamber

The electric chair was used for the first time on 6 August 1890, when William Kemmler, a convicted murderer, was executed at Auburn State Prison, New York. The execution was carried out in an atmosphere of great tension before twenty-five witnesses, several of whom were distinguished doctors. The condemned man, however, was unperturbed, and went to his death calmly.

The execution at first appeared to have been performed satisfactorily, though some who were present found the proceedings disturbing. But after the initial current had been switched off in the belief that he was dead, Kemmler was found to be still alive. The officials involved then began to panic, and a second charge, administered for longer than necessary, caused burns to the prisoner's body.

Despite the outcry which followed, New York persisted with its new method of execution, and before long other states began to follow its lead: Ohio in 1896, Massachusetts in 1898 and New Jersey in 1906. Edwin F. Davis, the prison electrician who had supervised the construction of the chair used at Auburn, became the official executioner of New York, and later of New Jersey and Massachusetts as well. He carried out over 240 executions before retiring in 1914.

The change to electricity was made in the belief that it was more humane than hanging, and from the outset attempts were constantly being made to improve both apparatus and procedure. But mishaps and mechanical failures still occurred from time to time, and have continued to do so to the present day.

On 27 July 1893, again at Auburn, William G. Taylor was executed for the murder of a fellow convict. At the first surge of electricity, his legs stiffened, breaking off the part of the chair to which his ankles were strapped. So the current had to be switched off, and it was not until one of the guards brought a box to place underneath the chair that the execution could be resumed.

When it was finally thought to have been completed, the condemned man, like Kemmler, was found to be still breathing. The executioner was therefore ordered to throw the switch again, but when he did so nothing happened. The machinery had apparently broken down because the prison generator was taxed beyond capacity.

So Taylor was taken from the chair and placed on a bed which had been brought into the execution chamber. Drugs were administered to him, to prevent pain in the unlikely event of his regaining consciousness, and electricians began to pass wires over the walls of the prison from the city's power plant. But an hour elapsed before they were ready to go on with the execution – and by that time Taylor was dead.

However, his body was strapped into the chair again, and a current was passed through it for half a minute. Only then were the prison authorities satisfied that he had been properly executed, as the law prescribed.

Ten years later, on 1 October 1903, three brothers named Van Wormer were electrocuted at Dannemora Prison for the murder of their uncle. Afterwards, in the room adjoining the execution chamber, Fred Van Wormer, the youngest of the three, was seen to move and his heart was found to be still beating. So he, too, had to be carried back to the chair and given a further charge.

A distressing incident of a different sort occurred at Sing Sing Prison shortly after Dr Amos O. Squire became Acting Chief Physician there in 1900. Antonio Ferrarea, whom Squire describes in his memoirs as 'a rough, animal type, who spoke only broken English and persistently refused to wear anything in his cell except his under-clothing', could not be pronounced dead until after he had been given seven charges. The experience, says Squire, was horrible in every way.

But even this is not the worst such case on record, for at the execution of James Wells, a black murderer, in Little Rock, Arkansas, in 1922, *twelve* charges were needed. According to the *New York Times* of 11 March that year, Wells sang in the chair until the first jolt silenced him. The need for so many subsequent charges is attributed to inexperience on the part of the executioner.

And on 3 May 1946, in St Martinville, Louisiana, an attempt was made to execute a black youth of seventeen which resulted in complete failure. Willie Francis, who had murdered a local drugstore owner eighteen months earlier, was saved from the fatal current by a loose or burnt-out wire. The State, however, insisted that this did not entitle him to a commutation of sentence, and after a twelve-month legal battle, Willie Francis was successfully executed on 9 May 1947.

One of the worst cases of recent years was that of John Louis Evans, a thirty-three-year-old man put to death in Atmore, Alabama, on 22 April 1983. Evans, who had been convicted of the murder of a pawnbroker, was subjected to three charges over a ten-minute period. During the first, the

July 10 came. Not that I believed I was going to the hot seat. Like I have said, I never once believed that. Yet we were young, we didn't know the law, my folks could have been wrong, anything bad could happen.

If I live to be a hundred I will never forget that day because the juice was turned on in the death chamber. The state of Alabama burned Will Stokes, an axe killer, a few minutes after midnight. He was the first to get the chair since we were in the death row. Him going and us staying made us feel how life can hang by a hair. You can't forget when a man tells you what night you're going to die.

When they turned on the juice for Stokes we could hear the z-z-z-z-z-z of the electric current outside in the death row. The buzz went several times. After the juice was squeezed into him a guard came out and gave us a report. 'Stokes died hard. They stuck a needle through his head to make sure.' I sweated my clothes wet.

For a day or so I couldn't look into the Bible. But I held it so in my hands till from sweat the pages hung together.

Haywood Patterson, *Scottsboro Boy*, 1950

electrode attached to his left leg burnt through and fell off, after which prison doctors said he was still alive.

When the switch was thrown for the second time, smoke and flame erupted from his left temple and his leg. The doctors then put stethoscopes to the condemned man's chest, but said they were still not certain that he was dead. At this point, with some of the official witnesses showing signs of distress, an appeal for clemency was made to Governor George Wallace, but this was rejected.

The third jolt was then administered, and four minutes later, the prisoner was officially pronounced dead. His attorney, Mr Russell Canan, afterwards declared that John Evans had been 'burnt alive' and 'tortured ... in the name of vengeance and in the disguise of justice'.

Other recent cases include the botched execution of Jesse Tafero, in Starke, Florida, on 4 May 1990. Tafero, who had been sentenced for murdering two police officers in February 1976, was given three jolts of electricity. Each time the switch was thrown, flame shot out of the headpiece and a cloud of smoke rose to the ceiling. Ashes fell on to the prisoner's shirt as he was pronounced dead, six minutes after the first charge.

Four executed without knowing why

On 12 August 1912, at Sing Sing Prison, four Italian immigrants were executed for a crime at which they had not been present, and which had been committed without their knowledge. One after another, they went to their deaths, quite unable to understand why they had ever been convicted. Yet no miscarriage of justice was taking place – not, at any rate, within the accepted meaning of the term – for as the law stood, all were guilty of a capital offence.

Nine months earlier, five men had forced their way into a farmhouse in Westchester County, New York, and robbed the occupants, while a sixth kept watch nearby. There were three women and two children in the house at the time, and during the course of the robbery one of the women was brutally murdered in an upstairs bedroom. Only two of the intruders had taken part in the murder, and the rest left the premises unaware that it had occured. But all six men were legally guilty of it, as it had stemmed from a felony in which they were all involved.

Five of the men, Santa Zanza, Angelo Guista, Vincenzo Cornu, Felipe Demarco and Lorenzo Cali, all from Brooklyn, were arrested, tried and sentenced to death within the space of a month. The sixth man, Salvatore Demarco, was apprehended a few weeks later, and in due course joined his companions in the condemned cells. From statements made by the six men, it was clear that Zanza and Guista were the ones who actually committed the crime, and Zanza, who was executed a month before the others, admitted his part in it shortly before his death.

Guista was executed the same day as the other four, as were two other murderers unconnected with the case. So there were seven electrocuted altogether that day: the largest number in any one day in Sing Sing's history. And to make the occasion even more ghastly, the four who considered themselves innocent howled and screamed in the cells as they waited their turn to die.

'All of us in the execution chamber – witnesses and officials – could hear them, as could those of the seven who went first,' the prison physician Amos O. Squire later recalled. 'The shrieking and wailing I heard that day is indescribable. The whole thing was like a nightmare, unreal and yet horrible. I'm sure that all of the witnesses in the room were indeed sorry they were there.'

When the executions were over, and the autopsies required by law had been carried out, the bodies of all five Italians were taken back to Brooklyn by friends and relatives. There they were put on display, spectators paying small sums to be allowed to view them. Before long, however, health officers intervened, and at their insistence the corpses were buried.

The Scottsboro Boys

In the notorious case of the Scottsboro Boys, which began on 25 March 1931, nine black youths aged between twelve and twenty were accused of raping two young white women aboard a freight train on which they had travelled illegally from Chattanooga, Tennessee to Paint Rock, Alabama. Doctors who examined the two women could find no evidence of rape, but the youths were put on trial in Scottsboro, Alabama, within a fortnight of the alleged crimes, and an all-white jury found all of them guilty. All except the youngest one were sentenced to death.

The affair sparked off many protests at home and abroad, and the socialist International Labour Defence (ILD) came to the youths' aid by providing lawyers to represent them. In March 1932, the Alabama Supreme Court reversed the conviction of the second youngest (who was still only fourteen) but upheld those of the other condemned. In November, however, the US Supreme Court ruled that the original court had failed to provide adequate counsel for the prisoners' defence and ordered that they should be retried.

One of the youths, Haywood Patterson, was put on trial again on his own towards the end of March the following year. This time only one of the women gave evidence for the prosecution: the other appeared as a defence witness, telling the court that she and her companion had made up the story about being raped, in order to avoid being charged with vagrancy. In spite of this dramatic development, Patterson was again found guilty – and again sentenced to death.

Two months later, Judge James E. Horton, before whom the trial had been held, granted a defence motion to set aside the conviction, on the grounds that it was not justified by the evidence. Patterson was thus put on trial for the third time, before a different judge, on 20 November 1933 – and on 1 December he was convicted and sentenced to death for the third time. Immediately afterwards, Clarence Norris, another of the Scottsboro Boys, was put on trial for the second time. A week later, he, too, was convicted and sentenced to death.

With defence lawyers continuing their struggle to save the two youths from the electric chair, the Alabama Supreme Court upheld the sentences in both cases in June 1934. But the following April the US Supreme Court reversed both convictions on the grounds that black people had been barred from serving on the juries which indicted and tried the defendants, in violation of the Constitution. This important decision ended Alabama's practice of automatically excluding blacks from jury service.

But the prosecution refused to accept defeat, and in November 1935, the grand jury in Scottsboro, whose eighteen members now included one black, returned fresh indictments for rape against all of the youths, including the youngest two, whose cases had been transferred by Judge Horton to the Juvenile Court. A two-thirds majority was all that was needed to return an indictment.

The following month, the youths' defence was taken over by the newly-formed Scottsboro Defence Committee. This was composed of representatives of the ILD and several other organizations – including the National Association for the Advancement of Coloured People and the

American Civil Liberties Union – all of which had already actively supported them.

In January 1936, Haywood Patterson was put on trial for the fourth time; this time blacks were called as potential jurors, but none actually served. Patterson was convicted and sentenced to seventy-five years' imprisonment. A number of appeals followed, but all were turned down.

In July 1937, Clarence Norris was convicted and sentenced to death for the third time – a sentence afterwards commuted to life imprisonment. Two of the other youths, Andrew Wright and Charles Weems, were retried, convicted and given prison sentences of ninety-nine and seventy-five years respectively. A third, Ozie Powell, was given a twenty-year sentence for slashing a deputy sheriff with a sharp instrument – a crime committed on the day after Patterson's fourth trial ended – but in his case the rape charge was dropped.

Following Powell's conviction, the Alabama Attorney General's Office announced that the rape charges against the other four youths, Willie Roberson, Olen Montgomery, Roy Wright and Eugene Williams, were also being dropped.

The prosecution now accepted that neither Roberson nor Montgomery had been in the car in which the alleged rape had taken place, and that neither of them would have been capable of committing such a crime: Roberson because he was suffering from a severe form of venereal disease which would have made the act too painful, and Montgomery because he was practically blind.

The prosecution also accepted that Wright and Williams were innocent, though both had been travelling in the car in which the crime had allegedly been committed. Wright was twelve years old at the time; Williams was thirteen. The State apparently took the view that they could not have been involved in the crime because they were too young.

But in declaring four of the Scottsboro Boys innocent, the State placed itself in an untenable position, for the evidence against those four was the same as that used against four of the others who were still in jail. So if they were innocent, the others must have been innocent as well.

Governor Bibb Graves recognised that this was so, and in negotiations with the Scottsboro Defence Committee said that he intended to release the rest of the group on parole as soon as their cases were 'out of the hands of the judiciary'. At one point, he set 24 October 1938 as the date for their release, but as that date drew near he postponed it to 31 October – and then put it off indefinitely. It was apparently political considerations which caused him to change his mind.

Just before Christmas, Dr Allan Knight Chalmers, Chairman of the Defence Committee, published an open letter to Graves in which he gave details of their negotiations and accused the Governor of reneging on a gentleman's agreement. But the following year, due to growing international tension and the outbreak of the Second World War, public interest in the case subsided. By 1942, the Defence Committee had become inactive and the ILD could do little more than send regular sums of money to the five Scottsboro Boys who were still in prison.

Clarence Norris and Andrew Wright were eventually released on parole on 8 January 1944, Charles Weems shortly afterwards and Ozie Powell two years later. But within a year of their release, Norris and Wright were back in jail for parole violation, Wright being returned for the second time on the same charge in 1946. Norris also broke parole after his second release, but was not apprehended. He went to New York, where he led a fugitive existence, working as a warehouseman.

Haywood Patterson remained in prison until 1948, when he escaped and made his way north. His autobiography,

Scottsboro Boy, was published in England in 1950, but he died of cancer two years later. At the time of his death, he was in jail for killing a man in a bar-room brawl.

Clarence Norris never gave up hope of clearing his name, and after a long campaign backed by the NAACP, finally succeeded in 1976. By this time, he was sixty-four years old and believed to be the only one of the Scottsboro Boys still alive. His pardon was signed by Governor George Wallace, after the Alabama Pardon and Parole Board declared him innocent of the crimes of which he had first been accused forty-five years earlier. He died in 1989, leaving a wife and two daughters.

No one to take his picture

On the night of 15 February 1933, Giuseppe Zangara, a thirty-two-year-old Italian immigrant, tried unsuccessfully to shoot the President-Elect, Franklin D. Roosevelt, at a public meeting held under the floodlit palms of Bayfront Park, Miami. Though Roosevelt escaped injury, five other people were hit in the attempt, including Mayor Anton J. Cermak of Chicago, who died from his wound nineteen days later. The culprit was disarmed and arrested at the scene of the crime.

Zangara was an unemployed bricklayer, just five feet tall, who lived on dwindling savings in a Miami boarding-house. He had a hatred of capitalist society, which he blamed for the chronic stomach-ache which had afflicted him for most of his life, and had at first planned to take his revenge on it by assassinating the outgoing President, Herbert Hoover. He only decided to kill Roosevelt instead as a matter of convenience, when he heard that the President-Elect was about to visit Miami.

On being questioned after his arrest, Zangara freely admitted that he was the man who had fired the shots. Voluble and defiant, he said repeatedly that he was sorry he had not succeeded in killing Roosevelt and that all he now hoped for was another chance. He left investigators in no doubt that his own life was of little importance to him.

When he appeared for trial five days later, Zangara

pleaded guilty to four counts of assault on others in an attempt to assassinate the President-Elect, and for these crimes he was sentenced to eighty years in jail. But on 9 March he was put on trial for murder, Cermak having died three days before; and this time, having again pleaded guilty, he was sentenced to death.

Disdainful of the whole judicial system, he made no appeal, and so was executed at Raiford State Prison on 20 March, just thirty-three days after the shooting had taken place. He remained unrepentant to the end, having somehow convinced himself that his crime would benefit the world's poor.

On the morning of his death, he entered the execution chamber haughtily, boasting that he was not afraid, and smiled as he sat in the electric chair. 'See, I no scared of electric chair!' he said proudly.

He was surprised to find that there was nobody with a camera present, for having been the subject of much publicity since his arrest, he had assumed that there would be press photographers at his execution – and perhaps newsreel cameramen as well. The realization that there were none came as a disappointment to him.

'Lousy capitalists!' he grumbled. 'No picture! Capitalists! No one here to take my picture! All capitalists lousy bunch of crooks!'

Following this memorable statement, a black cowl was placed over his head, but he went on speaking through it, keeping up his show of indifference until the switch was thrown.

Zangara left an autobiography, written in three notebooks, which gave an idealized account of his case. 'I go contented because I go for my idea,' he had said in conclusion. 'I salute all the poor of the world.'

The question of his sanity was given little consideration at the time, as no plea of *in*sanity was ever made on his behalf. But twenty years later, in an interview with Robert J. Donovan, author of *The Assassins* (1956), a Miami psychiatrist who had examined Zangara before he was put on trial remarked: 'I am sure that if he were alive today and we had the modern facilities for examining him psychiatrically, he would have been adjudicated as a very insane person – and probably hopelessly insane.'

In a letter to Donovan on the same subject, Dr T. Earl Moore later expressed the view that had he not been executed, Zangara might have settled down within five years to 'little more than a vegetative existence'.

Leo Jankowski, who was executed at Sing Sing in 1920, kissed the electric chair before sitting in it and, with tears running down his face, said that he was 'never so happy to see anything'. A tuberculosis sufferer, he had been eagerly awaiting death as a relief from the pain of his illness.

Last public hangings

The last person to be hanged in public in the United States was Roscoe 'Red' Jackson, who was executed in Galena, Missouri, on 21 May 1937, for a murder committed three years earlier. Jackson, aged thirty, was executed inside a stockade on Galena's public square at six o'clock in the morning. There was a crowd of about 2,000 people present, including women and children.

'This is the end of me,' the condemned man said in a farewell speech from the scaffold. 'I'm the cause of all this public confusion. I guess it's asking too much for everyone concerned to forgive me, but I want all to know that I meet death with a heart free of all hatred. I blame no one for this but myself, and the law is merely doing its duty.' A Catholic priest prayed with Jackson before the trap was sprung, the condemned man repeating calmly, 'Jesus Christ, have mercy.' After the noose was adjusted around his neck, he called to the spectators, 'Be good, folks!' Then the trap opened and he fell to his death.

Jackson had been condemned for the murder of Pearl Bozarth, a travelling salesman of Evansville, Indiana, in August 1934. Bozarth had stopped to give him a lift in his car while he was hitchhiking and had bought him a meal in Brandson, Missouri. Jackson afterwards killed him.

Not long after Jackson was hanged, Missouri changed its mode of execution to lethal gas. The change was prompted by the behaviour of spectators on a number of occasions during the previous year.

'Within the past year there have been several public hangings by county officers which have shocked and embarrassed Missourians who believe that an execution is no occasion for a Roman holiday,' the *New York Times* of 30 May reported. 'In at least three instances small communities have become carnival spots for the day as hundreds of persons for miles around came to town to see the spectacle.'

Neighbouring Kentucky's last public hanging took place on 14 August 1936, when Rainey Bethea, a twenty-two-year-old black man, was put to death in Owensboro for the assault-murder of a seventy-year-old white woman.

The event attracted a crowd of 10,000 white people, some of whom jeered the condemned. After the trap had been sprung, sixteen and a half minutes elapsed before Bethea was pronounced dead; then, despite a cordon of guards, some of the spectators managed to tear off pieces of the black hood to keep as souvenirs.

Kentucky had actually changed its method of execution to the electric chair many years earlier, but the State Legislature had retained hanging as the punishment for criminal assault, leaving county officials to decide whether the execution should take place in public or in private. In this case, they decided that it should take place in public, without disclosing their reasons for doing so.

Kentucky finally abolished public hanging in 1938.

Executed for 'messin' around'

Roosevelt Collins, a twenty-two-year-old black man, was executed in the electric chair in Montgomery, Alabama, in 1937, following his conviction for raping a white woman. The offence had allegedly taken place on a Webster County farm, where the woman in question – the farmer's wife – had been digging potatoes when Collins appeared on the scene. She afterwards claimed that he had raped her at gunpoint, threatening to kill her if she put up any resistance.

Collins denied the allegation, saying that he had had intercourse with his accuser with her consent. There was little real evidence to the contrary other than the testimony of the woman herself, but when he appeared for trial at the County Court, a hostile crowd gathered outside and the attorneys appointed to defend him made no serious attempt to secure his acquittal. The prisoner's own evidence caused outrage among the spectators, and the woman's husband tried to shoot him in the courtroom.

In spite of all this, Collins stuck to his story and remained unshaken throughout his cross-examination. But the result of the trial was a foregone conclusion, and the all-white jury took just four minutes to return the verdict which sent him to his death. Several of the jurors told a journalist afterwards that they believed the prisoner to have been speaking the truth, but thought he deserved to die anyway, for 'messin'

around' with a white woman. The judge also said unofficially that he believed Collins to be innocent.

It appears from an account of the case written by
William Bradford Huie (the journalist who recorded these
statements) that the farmer's wife had actually been caught
committing adultery with Collins by two other women, and
that she accused him of rape in order to save her reputation.
Huie further suggests that the gun fired at Collins while he
was giving evidence may have been smuggled into the
courthouse by the woman herself, as her husband was
thoroughly searched for weapons before being admitted.

Other black men who have been executed for raping, or
allegedly raping, white women include William Henry
Anderson and Willie McGee, both of whom have, like
Collins, been cited as victims of judicial murder.

Anderson, who was executed in Florida in 1945, had
been convicted in a case in which the woman had made no
attempt to resist his advances or to call for help. Evidence
was produced on his behalf to show that he and his 'victim'
had been having an affair for some months prior to the
incident which led to his prosecution, but the State
Governor rejected his plea for clemency. The Governor is
known to have received a letter from the Sheriff of
Broward County, asking for 'special attention in this case
before some sympathizing organization gets hold of it'.

McGee was executed in Laurel, Mississippi, in 1951,
having been convicted of raping a young housewife five
and a half years earlier. The crime was alleged to have
taken place at the woman's home, while her husband and
two children slept in the next room, but the defence
contended that McGee had been having an affair with her
for several years and that she had falsely accused him of
rape after her husband found out about it. A confession had
been extracted from McGee after he had spent thirty-two
days in custody.

The case attracted worldwide attention. McGee was actually tried, convicted and sentenced three times, his first two convictions being quashed, on technical grounds, on appeal. His execution was carried out in the state's portable electric chair, in the courtroom in which the final trial had taken place (as was the custom in Mississippi).

Hanging on his mind

A year or so before the State of California adopted the gas chamber as its official mode of execution, a young man named William G. Smith arrived at San Quentin Prison to serve a term for burglary. Smith, a native of Los Angeles, had set out to be an actor, but turned to crime when success eluded him. He soon began to show an unusual preoccupation with the method of execution then in force.

Hanging around the furniture factory in which the gallows room was housed, he asked many questions about execution procedures. Such details as the way in which ropes were stretched and hardened before use, or the condemned measured and weighed for the drop, were of great interest to him. He also liked to talk about San Quentin's most famous murderers, and how they had behaved in the face of death.

Before long, he began to hint that he, too, was a killer of some note; that he would have been hanged himself had the police been smarter – and that he knew exactly what he would say if ever he *were* hanged. Eventually, he told a cellmate that he had shot a man in Sacramento, a boast which the cellmate reported to one of the guards without delay. It proved to be true.

Following inquiries, Smith was indicted and put on trial for the murder of Elmer Cox, a Sacramento Post Office employee, during an attempt to rob the home of one of Cox's neighbours in January 1936. He was convicted, sentenced to death and hanged at San Quentin on 8 September 1939, maintaining a stunned silence during his last moments of life. He was twenty-four years old.

Recalling the case in 1950, Clinton Duffy, then Warden of San Quentin, commented: 'The psychiatrists might say Smith was merely a man acting under a compulsion to seek punishment for his crime, thus accounting for his abnormal interest in the noose. That may be true and scientifically sound, but around San Quentin we still think of Smith as the man who literally talked himself to death.'

William Smith was actually hanged *after* California changed its method of execution to lethal gas. The change had taken effect on 27 August 1937, and San Quentin's gas chamber was used for its first executions on 2 December 1938. But the gallows had to be kept in working order for Smith and one other man – Robert 'Rattlesnake' James – who had both been sentenced to die by hanging.

'Rattlesnake James', a barber who had murdered his wife in order to benefit from her life insurance policies, was hanged in 1942.

Music in the Death House

Prior to his execution on 28 January 1944, Farrington Graham Hill spent several months on San Quentin's Death Row. A thirty-one-year-old double murderer with a long criminal record, he kept himself to himself, ignoring his fellow inmates and speaking to guards as little as possible. He showed no remorse for his crimes and refused to see any minister of religion.

On the evening before he was to die, he asked for no special meal; no books or newspapers. He did not write any letters or inquire about the possibility of a last-minute reprieve. He merely stood in his holding cell, a few yards from the gas chamber, smoking one cigarette after another as he waited for his last night on earth to pass.

After he had been there for four and a half hours, Warden Duffy came to see him and asked whether there was anything he could do for him. Despite his coldness, Duffy felt sorry for him and hoped that there was some way in which he could help to make his last hours easier.

At first it seemed that there was nothing he wanted, and when Duffy suggested that he should let the Death Watch officers play a record for him on their phonograph, the condemned man said that they did not have what he liked. The Warden asked *what* he liked, saying that he might be able to get it for him, and after some hesitation, Hill suddenly asked whether they had 'something about Vienna'.

'*Tales from the Vienna Woods*?' asked Duffy.

'Yeah,' said Hill. 'Yeah, that's it. *Tales from the Vienna Woods*.'

Duffy did not know if the prison had a copy, but said he would try to find one for him. There was no copy among the stack of records kept in the corridor outside the cells, so he went to look in the prison library. But there was no copy there, either.

By this time, it was past eleven o'clock at night, but with the execution scheduled to take place at ten o'clock in the morning, Duffy was determined to get hold of the record the prisoner wanted. It was the only thing that Hill had asked him for in all the time that he had been under sentence of death. Duffy therefore went to his office and began telephoning record shops, in the hope of finding one open, but failed to do so.

He then arranged for his wife to make inquiries among her friends, to find out whether any of them had a copy, while he asked guards and prison officials who he knew had phonographs at home. By half-past twelve, however, he had exhausted every possible means of finding a copy at that time of night and had to accept that he would not be able to find one anywhere in time for the condemned man to hear it.

But instead of giving up, the Warden went to see 'Major' John Hendricks, the organizer and conductor of the prison orchestra, to ask for his help. The orchestra had its own radio show, *San Quentin on the Air* (theme song: 'Time on my Hands'), which was broadcast nationwide. It had its own recording machine, which was used in connection with the broadcasts, and Duffy hoped to arrange for it to record the piece Hill wanted to hear at short notice.

Hendricks, who was serving a life sentence for murder, agreed to try, and the Warden had the other members of the orchestra woken up and brought to the small mess–hall where they held their practices. When they had all arrived, Hendricks told them why they were there.

'Listen, gang,' he said. 'There's a guy checking out in the morning and we're going to play *Tales from the Vienna Woods* for him.'

'Without a score?' one of them asked.

'We don't need a score,' said Hendricks. 'I'm going to give it to you myself.'

He whistled the tune for the pianist, then went through the parts played by each of the other instruments in turn. When they were all familiar with it, they rehearsed the piece as a whole until Hendricks decided that they could play it well enough to cut the record.

Some time after two o'clock, Duffy entered the Death House and looked into Hill's cell. Hill was lying on his back, smoking and staring at the ceiling.

'I've got your song, son,' said Duffy.

Hill got to his feet. He was pleased: so pleased, in fact that for once he was smiling. He and Duffy listened to the record together, and by the time it came to an end they both had tears in their eyes. At the condemned man's request, it was played over and over again for the rest of the night.

In the morning, with the record still playing, Hill accepted the services of the chaplain and prayed with him in his cell. When the Warden arrived to supervise his execution – a task which Duffy, as an opponent of capital punishment, hated – he greeted him cheerfully. The two men talked to each other for a few minutes, and during the course of their conversation, the prisoner said, 'I suppose you'd kind of like to know why I wanted that number so badly, Warden?'

'Tell me if you'd like to,' replied Duffy.

'Well,' said Hill, 'I was running away from the cops after a hold-up over in the Sunset district one night, and I hid in the bushes near the bandstand at Golden Gate Park.

I heard them announce something about Vienna, and then they started playing the song. I sort of liked it and wished I could stay, but the cops were after me, so I had to get out of there.'

He dragged on his cigarette for a moment, then added: 'I never did hear the ending of it, Warden – not until now. And, you know, it's just as pretty as the beginning.'

Shortly afterwards, while the final preparations were being made for his execution, Hill asked if the guards could go on playing the record for him while he was inside the gas chamber. 'Maybe I won't be able to hear it after you close the door, but I'll feel better if I know it's still on,' he said.

Duffy assured him that it would still be on.

With his wrists strapped together and a stethoscope attached to his chest, Hill then asked Duffy to thank the orchestra for him. 'Tell them – tell them they helped me find something I never had before,' he said. 'And tell them the last thing I did was say a prayer for them. I never talked to God before – never.'

It was now time for the execution to be carried out. The condemned man had one last request: he asked the Warden to send a Bible to his brother, who was then serving a term of imprisonment. 'I think he can use it,' he said. 'Tell him it came from me.'

Hill showed no fear as he was escorted to the octagonal chamber of death. He paused at the open door and listened to the music for a moment, smiling. Then he stepped inside. 'So long, Warden!' he said.

'So long,' said Duffy.

With the official witnesses watching through the windows, guards unstrapped Hill's wrists, strapped him into one of the two metal chairs and fastened a long tube to the stethoscope. They then left the airtight steel room and closed the door.

With the Warden standing beside him, the executioner pulled a lever controlling a suction fan, to draw some of the air out of the chamber. He then gave a signal to an assistant waiting in the mixing room, which adjoined the gas chamber, and sulphuric acid was released into the wells under the two chairs. At a nod from the Warden, the executioner then pulled a second lever, lowering cyanide pellets into the two wells of acid, and the deadly gas fumes started to rise.

Hill had entered the gas chamber at 10.02 a.m. It was not long before he lost consciousness, but his head lolled back and forth for some time afterwards. At 10.13 the doctor listening through the stethoscope nodded to the Warden to indicate that the condemned man was dead.

The music which had been played throughout the execution was then switched off.

A boy of fourteen

On 16 June 1944, George Stinney Jr, a fourteen-year-old black boy, died in the electric chair in Columbia, South Carolina. He had been sentenced by an all-white jury, after ten minutes' deliberation, for the murder of two white girls, one aged eleven and the other eight. The girls had been beaten to death following an unsuccessful attempt to rape one of them, while they were out picking wild flowers together.

George Stinney, who confessed to the crime, was represented by a court-appointed attorney, who made no attempt to save him once the sentence had been passed. During the days leading up to his execution, the State Governor, Olin D. Johnston, received many letters and telegrams pleading with him to spare the young killer's life. But Johnston, who had a primary election to face in July that year, refused to exercise clemency on his behalf.

Stinney was five feet one inch tall and weighed less than seven stone. Newspapers reporting his execution stated that the guards 'had difficulty strapping the boy's slight form into the wooden chair built for adults' and that the condemned 'was such a small boy that it was difficult to attach the electrode to his right leg'. But the execution was carried out, and Stinney became – as he has remained ever since – the youngest person to be executed in the United States this century.

'We ought to remember George Stinney, because if this country ever goes back to executing children, it will happen much as it did in his case,' wrote David Bruck, a criminal defence lawyer, in a *New York Times* article forty years later.

Those who assume that the courts and public opinion will prevent such executions from taking place today will be proved right – most of the time. Few juveniles will ever be sentenced to death, and most of those who are will eventually be spared by successful appeals. In the end, only a handful will be left to die, and because many of their crimes will have been truly appalling – as was George Stinney's – they will have few defenders.

At the time Bruck was writing, there were at least thirty prisoners on Death Row nationwide who had been seventeen or younger at the time their crimes were committed. Ten of these inmates – one a girl – had been sixteen; one had been only fifteen.

Seven years later, in October 1991, an Amnesty International report criticized the United States for sentencing more juvenile offenders to death than any other country except Iraq and Iran. By this time, ninety young people had been condemned there since the 1970s for crimes committed between the ages of fifteen and seventeen, and four had been executed since 1985, the report stated.

Most of the prisoners in question were from deprived backgrounds, and some had histories of mental illness which had not been presented at their trials. In several cases, defence lawyers had been unable to obtain independent psychiatric evaluations of their clients, due to lack of funds.

The man who blamed God

On the morning of 6 April 1956, a convicted murderer was carried, struggling and shouting, into San Quentin's gas chamber after an unsuccessful attempt to take his own life. With blood flowing from a gash in his throat, Robert O. Pierce, aged twenty-seven, fought ferociously to avoid being strapped into the chair in which he was to die. As he did so, he protested his innocence, calling out to God to help him:

'I'm innocent, God! ... I tell you I'm innocent! ... God, you know I'm innocent! ... God, don't let me go like this!'

A strong man with massive shoulders, he went on struggling desperately for several minutes until the five guards managed to strap his wrists down. The shocked witnesses knew nothing of Pierce's suicide attempt, but could hardly have failed to notice that his shirt was becoming soaked with blood. A jacket draped over his back soon had blood seeping through it as well.

'Oh, Lord Jesus, let me die – but not like this!' cried Pierce.

With his wrists secured, the guards – who now had blood on their own clothes – quickly strapped his ankles. A second condemned man, Smith E. Jordan, aged twenty-eight, was then brought into the execution chamber. Jordan was Pierce's partner in crime: they were both to die for the murder of a cab driver in Oakland three years earlier.

But Jordan did not struggle, and did not even seem perturbed by the sight of Pierce's wound. Indeed, he grinned, winked at the witnesses and gave a V-for-Victory sign. As soon as he had been strapped into the second chair, the guards left the chamber, slamming the steel door after them.

'All right, Lord, if this is the way you want it!' shouted Pierce. He then turned on the witnesses: 'You sent me here! ... I did wrong, but I never killed nobody!' Suddenly, he made a supreme effort to burst his bonds, and for some seconds it seemed that he might succeed. When he did not, he blamed God for his plight: 'God, you're a dirty son of a bitch, because I'm innocent!' he raved.

When the cyanide pellets were released into the acid, he at first watched the rising fumes with some curiosity. But then he went back to shouting at God – and continued doing so until he succumbed to the gas. Jordan, however, waited with his eyes closed and his head held high, determined to die in a dignified manner. Ignoring the cries of his accomplice, he remained calm to the end.

In February 1924, two prison guards in Carson City, Nevada, strapped a condemned man into a chair in the death chamber for America's first execution by lethal gas. One of them was so nervous that, having completed his own part of the task, he inadvertently shut his companion in with the prisoner. The second guard, unable to open the door himself, banged on it until it was opened from the outside.

Nine minutes after the pellets had fallen, both men were dead. The witnesses went on sitting in silence, until a prison lieutenant addressed them, saying, 'That's all, gentlemen!' They then got up to leave.

Pierce's suicide attempt had been made in his holding cell less than one minute before he was due to enter the gas chamber. He had earlier said that he would die 'fighting, kicking and screaming', and prison officials had expected that that was what would happen. For this reason, extra security measures were taken.

Yet somehow he was able to keep a piece of broken mirror concealed about him when he was moved from Death Row, for there were no mirrors in the holding cells. And as the prison's Roman Catholic chaplain gave him the last rites, he suddenly slashed his own throat. He came close to killing himself outright before he was forcibly restrained.

Another condemned prisoner who went to his death fighting was Leandress Riley, a thirty-two-year-old killer from Sacramento, who was executed at the same prison on 20 February 1953.

A small, wiry man, Riley writhed and kicked as he was taken from his holding cell, shrieking and moaning alternately. The guards carried him into the gas chamber, strapped him down, then came out and closed the door. But because of his size, Riley was able to slip his arms free of the straps and release himself from the chair before the signal for his execution was given.

The guards re-entered the chamber and strapped him down again, but he again got free and had to be strapped down for a third time. Even then, as the signal was given for the pellets to be dropped, Riley freed one of his hands – and used it to release the other.

Still shrieking and moaning, he undid the chest strap and was trying to undo the waist strap when the rising gas stopped him. He died with his eyes open, holding both hands over his face in a vain attempt to avoid inhaling the fumes.

At an execution in Raleigh, North Carolina, in November 1943, the mechanism for releasing the cyanide pellets failed and the executioner had to go into the gas chamber and release them by hand. The Warden, Ralph McLean, held the door open for him, so that he would not be impeded in his dash for safety.

Caryl Chessman's final ordeal

Caryl Chessman spent twelve years on San Quentin's Death Row, fighting to avoid the gas chamber. It was a remarkable struggle which made him a media star and bestselling author, and gained him the support of distinguished people at home and abroad. He claimed to the end that he was innocent of the crimes for which he had been condemned – and many believed that he was telling the truth.

The case began in January 1948, when police in Los Angeles received reports of a number of 'lovers' lane' hold-ups committed by a gunman driving a car with a red spotlight. This 'Red Light Bandit', as the press called him, would rob couples in parked cars, sometimes abducting and sexually abusing the woman. Generally, he approached his victims posing as a police officer.

Chessman, a violent twenty-six-year-old robber, burglar and car thief, had already served several prison terms, and had been released on parole only a few weeks earlier. On 23 January, he and another ex-convict were arrested after a car chase, and Chessman was accused of being the Red Light Bandit.

He confessed to the crimes, but later claimed that he had only done so because he had been brutally beaten, denied sleep and subjected to various threats by the Hollywood district police.

Identified by some of the Red Light Bandit's victims, Chessman was charged with violating California's 'Little Lindbergh Act' of 1933. This allowed the death penalty to be imposed for kidnapping, regardless of whether any ransom had been demanded. And it was so loosely worded that it even applied to some cases of armed robbery.

At his trial, which lasted from 29 April to 21 May, Chessman conducted his own defence, but was convicted on seventeen counts of felony. He was sentenced to death on two of these and given prison sentences for each of the others.

Undismayed by the outcome of the trial, he began studying law, to try to get his convictions quashed. During the next few years he won much admiration as a knowledgeable and meticulous jailhouse lawyer; and from 1954 onwards, thanks to the sales of his books, he was able to hire attorneys whose services he could not otherwise have afforded.

He appealed, in all, sixteen times to the United States Supreme Court, nine times to the California Supreme Court, five times to the US Court of Appeals, six times to the US district courts, once to the California District Court of Appeals and twice to the Marin County Superior Court. He also obtained six hearings in the Los Angeles county courts.

With all this activity, Chessman succeeded in staving off his execution several times, but he was never granted a retrial or a commutation. The 'Little Lindbergh Act' was actually revised a few years after his trial, to ensure that it applied only to cases of kidnapping in the usual sense of the word. But this was not accepted as an invalidation of his sentence; nor was it seen as providing grounds for clemency. So it did not help him at all.

After seven reprieves, his execution was fixed for 19 February 1960. By this time, Chessman appeared to have exhausted all legal means of challenging his conviction, but ten hours before he was due to die a further stay was granted at the request of the US State Department. The reason for this was that President Eisenhower was about to make a scheduled visit to South America – where the condemned man had many active supporters – and it was feared that he would be greeted with hostile demonstrations if the execution was carried out.

Seventy-three days later, however, on the morning of 2 May, Chessman finally went to the gas chamber. His attorneys went from court to court in a desperate attempt to get him a last-minute reprieve, but a few minutes before the end he was told that no reprieve had come through. He accepted the news calmly.

'Well, I guess this is it,' he said. 'I'm ready to go.'

With fifty-nine witnesses looking on, and hundreds of protesters holding a vigil outside the prison, he entered the glass-panelled chamber at two minutes past ten. He put up no resistance as four guards strapped him to one of the metal chairs, and showed no fear when they left the chamber, sealing the door after them. Turning to one of the witnesses, he began to move his lips, conveying a message to her:

'Take it easy. It's all right. Tell Rosalie goodbye.'

The message was addressed to a woman reporter who had supported him in his struggle for survival. The person referred to was Rosalie Asher, one of the attorneys still acting on his behalf.

At three minutes past ten, the cyanide pellets were released, and the gas began to rise. At that very moment, or just a few seconds later, news of a ninth reprieve reached the prison. A federal judge in San Francisco had agreed to order a brief stay of execution – thirty minutes to one hour – so that he could hear arguments on a new petition. But his secretary misdialled the San Quentin telephone number and so failed to put him through to the prison in time to halt the proceedings.

Even so, Chessman was still alive and clearly conscious when the call came through, and could have been rescued from the gas chamber had the appropriate instructions been given. But the Warden, Frederick R. Dickson, failed to give these instructions – an omission which led one of Chessman's supporters to describe the execution as 'illegally and immorally hasty'.

Six minutes after the pellets had dropped, the condemned man, still conscious, turned to another reporter, Will Stevens of the *San Francisco Examiner*. He had agreed to give Stevens a signal by moving his head up and down if, as some suspected, this form of death was agonizing. He gave the signal – and then lost consciousness. Three minutes later, he was pronounced dead.

Death Row writings

Chessman's first book, Cell 2455, Death Row, *was auto-biographical. Published in 1954, it became a bestseller and was translated into fourteen other languages. But its success embarrassed California's prison authorities and led to an announcement that Death Row inmates would no longer be allowed to write for publication. Writings removed from Chessman's cell at this time included a novel, a novelette, some short stories and three articles about the causes of crime.*

A second autobiographical book, Trial by Ordeal, *was smuggled out of the prison for publication not long after the ban was announced. After that, Chessman's cell was subjected to daily and sometimes twice-daily searches, but he still managed to write a third such book, typing it on to carbon paper in order to prevent its discovery. The publication of* The Face of Justice *was followed by an unsuccessful attempt to prosecute his literary agent, publisher and lawyers for helping him to smuggle it out.*

These three books are estimated to have brought their author in a total of $50,000 in royalties – all of which was spent on fighting his case. His confiscated novel, The Kid Was a Killer, *was eventually released by court order, but not published until after his death.*

Chessman's published writings together form only a part of his Death Row output. He also wrote many appeal briefs (some of them book-length), a 200-page text on habeas corpus *and a 400-page text on federal practice and procedure as it related to state court convictions.*

Probably, he was San Quentin's most industrious prisoner, as well as its most famous.

Too much haste
at Huntsville

On the night of 4 October 1983, James D. Autry, a convicted murderer, lay strapped to a hospital trolley in the execution room at Huntsville State Prison, Texas. With intravenous tubes in both forearms, and a saline solution flowing through his veins, he was waiting to die by lethal injection. But he had been prepared with undue haste, and thirty-one minutes before the execution was due to be carried out, the unexpected happened. The condemned man was reprieved.

The reprieve was granted by a US Supreme Court Justice, following a last-minute plea from an American Civil Liberties Union lawyer. The ACLU had pursued appeals in several different courts that day on Autry's behalf – after the Supreme Court had dismissed an earlier one the day before – but all had been rejected. The new petition, however, raised a constitutional issue which could not be ignored. The judge had therefore to stay the execution.

The news caused dismay among prison officials in Huntsville and the condemned man was left strapped to the trolley for another half an hour, in case the stay was reversed. Autry himself had been resigned to his fate, but made no comment and displayed no emotion when told that he had been reprieved. Apart from giving a nod to show that he understood what had been said to him, he did not react in any way.

Autry, a twenty-nine-year-old oilfield worker with a long criminal record, had been sentenced to death for the murder of a night sales clerk at a food store in Port Arthur on 20 April 1980. According to evidence given at his trial, he had shot the clerk between the eyes rather than pay her $2.70 for six cans of beer which he had picked up. He had then shot two witnesses, killing one and disabling the other, before leaving the scene of the crime.

With his execution scheduled to take place at one minute past midnight, Autry was conducted into the death chamber shortly before 11 p.m. He put up no resistance, and was quickly strapped to the trolley. The Warden, Jack Pursley, received word of the reprieve at 11.37, and informed Autry of it two minutes later. By that time, the witnesses were ready to enter the execution room and a crowd outside the prison was chanting, 'Kill him! Kill him!'

At eight minutes past midnight, after the news had been officially confirmed, Autry was unstrapped and returned to his holding cell. Later that morning, he was taken back to Death Row, to await the outcome of his appeal.

But the appeal was turned down and, four months after his ordeal in the death chamber, a new date was set for the condemned man's execution. His attorneys went on trying to get his sentence overturned, but without success, and on the morning of 13 March 1984 he was again driven from Death Row to the building which housed the execution room, fifteen miles away. There he was informed that a final appeal to the Supreme Court – this one on the grounds that he had been subjected to cruel and unusual punishment – had been rejected.

He was not surprised. He had had little hope of obtaining either a commutation or a fresh reprieve, and was again resigned to his fate. He had, in fact, requested that his execution be televised, as a warning to others. But the Texas Board of Corrections had refused to allow this, for fear of placing the death penalty itself under threat.

Shortly after midnight, Autry again lay strapped to the trolley, this time in the presence of the witnesses. There was no last-minute intervention, and the lethal drugs were released into the saline solution at 12.26 a.m. But Autry complained of a pain in his arm and did not die for ten minutes. For much of that time he remained conscious.

It is unclear why the execution took so long. Medical experts suggested that the drugs may have been diluted or the tube clogged, but inexpert use of the needle was another possible cause. Had the drugs been injected into muscle tissue instead of a vein, they would have been absorbed more slowly and so had a delayed effect.

Whatever the reason for it, Autry's slow and painful death showed that this new method of execution, which had only ever been used once before in America, was not necessarily as humane as its advocates had expected it to be. And the following year, in the same prison, an even worse case occurred.

Stephen Peter Morin, aged thirty-seven, had been convicted of the murder of three women and accused of two other murders. He had once been one of the FBI's ten most wanted criminals.

His execution, on the morning of 13 March 1985, was carried out with great difficulty, as years of drug-taking had caused extensive damage to the condemned man's veins. It was only after repeated attempts, lasting over forty minutes, that medical technicians were able to find one suitable for the injection.

Morin, a drifter from Rhode Island, had told his lawyers not to try to get him reprieved. Despite his long ordeal, he died calmly, but it was not until eleven minutes after the needle had been inserted that he was pronounced dead. It was Huntsville's sixth execution by this method since the resumption of capital punishment in Texas in 1982.

A prison spokesman said afterwards that the difficulty which had been experienced would probably lead to a review of procedures for administering the drugs in such cases. But nothing apparently came of this idea, for two years later, again at Huntsville, another man's final ordeal was similarly protracted.

Elliot Rod Johnson, a Port Arthur handyman aged twenty-eight, had been convicted of murdering a Beaumont jeweller during a robbery in 1982. His execution, on 24 June 1987, followed three reprieves and the rejection of a number of appeals for a fourth. He claimed to have had no part in the crime for which he was sentenced.

Like Morin, Johnson had a history of drug-taking. In his case, the search for a suitable vein took thirty-five minutes and the execution was not completed until almost an hour had elapsed.*

Yet another distressing scene occurred on 13 December 1988, when Raymond Landry, who had been convicted of murdering a Greek restaurant owner, became the twenty-ninth person to die by lethal injection at Huntsville.

Two minutes after the execution began, the tube attached to the prisoner's right arm sprang a leak, spraying the solution in the direction of the witnesses and halting the proceedings. It was not until another twenty-two minutes had elapsed that Landry was finally pronounced dead. In the meantime, he was heard murmuring and groaning.

'It was a mechanical and physical problem,' a spokesman for the Texas Attorney General's Office said later. 'Landry was very muscular and had Popeye-type arms.

---

* A further case in which this difficulty was encountered was that of Billy White in 1992 (see p. 246).

When the stuff was flowing, it wouldn't go into the veins and there was more pressure in the hose than his veins could absorb.'

The spokesman, Ron Dusek, went on to describe the prolonged execution as an accident. 'There's not much you can say about it,' he continued. 'This has been done twenty-nine times now without any major screw-up or problem. It couldn't be helped.'

Just how bad a mishap would have to be for the Attorney General's Office to regard it as a 'major screw-up or problem' was not explained. Presumably it would have to be more serious than *any* of the incidents which had already occurred.

Death Row's
biggest breakout

On 31 May 1984, six convicted murderers at Mecklenburg Correctional Centre, in Boydton, Virginia, staged the biggest Death Row breakout in American history. Armed with makeshift knives, they overpowered a number of guards, changed into their uniforms and drove out through the gates in an official van, pretending that they were removing a bomb that had been found in the cellblock. They were well away from the prison by the time the alarm was raised.

The leaders of the breakout were Linwood Briley, a thirty-year-old man awaiting execution for the murder of a disc jockey, and his brother James, aged twenty-seven, who had been sentenced for murdering a pregnant woman and her young son. Both were notorious killers who had taken part in a murder spree in the Richmond area in which eleven people had been killed, and the news that they and four other desperate men had escaped caused much concern.

A large-scale search began, and a number of private telephone lines were placed under electronic surveillance. Within twenty-four hours, two of the escapees were recaptured in Warrenton, North Carolina, where the prison van had been found abandoned. Earl Clanton and Derick Peterson were apprehended in a coin laundry and convenience store, to which calls they had made had been traced.

They were seized by police officers as they sat in the shop, eating and drinking.

For the next few days the manhunt was concentrated in the Warrenton area, with searchers conducting door-to-door interviews. Teams of bloodhounds were used, and a trail was picked up which led back to the Virginia state boundary, but no further arrests resulted. On 8 June, however, two more of the fugitives, Willie Jones and Lem Tuggle, were captured in Vermont. They had been making their way to Canada.

Linwood and James Briley remained at liberty until 19 June, when they were arrested by FBI agents outside a car repair shop in Philadelphia. The FBI knew that the two men had relatives in the area and, as well as the repair shop, had had a house there staked out for some days before they appeared. The two brothers were taken by surprise when they arrived at the shop in connection with one of the cars there, and were apprehended without incident. Over twenty heavily armed agents were involved in their capture.

The escape was naturally the subject of an official investigation, during the course of which it became clear that there had been a general breakdown in security at the prison. When the findings of the investigators were reported, five guards were dismissed for violation of prison procedures, and the Warden and Deputy Warden were suspended for ten days without pay. There was no evidence that any of the guards were guilty of criminal acts in connection with the breakout.

Four months after his recapture, Linwood Briley was put to death in Virginia's electric chair. His execution took place at the State Penitentiary in Richmond on the night of 12 October 1984, the condemned man declining to have a clergyman accompany him as he left his cell to walk his last thirty paces. His ten-year-old son, whose name was not revealed, was among those who saw him during his final hours.

James Briley died in the same chair on 18 April the following year, after two last-minute appeals had failed to save him. Earlier that day, his fellow inmates had sought to disrupt the execution by rioting, and nine guards and one prisoner had been injured. At least four of the guards had to undergo surgery for stab wounds to the abdomen.

Linwood and James were not the only members of the Briley family involved in the crimes which led to their condemnation. A third brother, Anthony, had also taken part, and he, too, had been convicted of murder. He, however, had escaped the death penalty and was serving a sentence of life imprisonment.

Derick Peterson, who had been sentenced for the murder of a grocer in 1982, was executed at the Greensville Correctional Centre in August 1991. He was given a charge of 1725 volts for ten seconds, followed by 240 volts for ninety seconds, but had then to be given a further jolt when his heart was found to be still beating. The chaplain who had attended him afterwards complained that their last moments together in private had been interrupted by prison guards.

Murder on Death Row

On 6 September 1991, Donald Henry Gaskins, a fifty-eight-year-old serial killer, was executed in Columbia, South Carolina, for the murder of a fellow prisoner nine years earlier. Rudolph Tyner, a black man aged twenty-four, was himself under sentence of death when he was killed by a home-made bomb at the Central Correctional Institution on 12 September 1982. He was Gaskins's fourteenth victim.

Tyner, a native of New York, had been sentenced for killing a middle-aged couple, William and Myrtie Moon, during a robbery at their convenience store in 1978. It was thought at first that he had blown himself up by accident while making the bomb as part of an escape plan. But an investigation revealed that he was the victim of a contract killing instigated by Myrtie Moon's son, Richard Tony Cimo.

Cimo, a bricklayer, was a married man with two children. He was very bitter about the murder of his mother and stepfather, and resented the use of legal technicalities to save their killer from the electric chair. At some stage, he decided to take the law into his own hands and began trying to find another inmate of the prison whom he could hire to kill Tyner for him. Eventually, he was introduced to Gaskins.

Gaskins, nicknamed 'Pee Wee' because he was only five

feet six inches tall, was at that time serving ten life sentences. He had confessed to stabbing, shooting or drowning thirteen people, including eight whose bodies had been found in shallow graves near the rural community of Prospect, in South Carolina's tobacco belt. For one of those crimes, he had initially been sentenced to death, but the sentence had since been commuted.

Gaskins had a hatred of black people which was so intense that he had once drowned a white woman because she was pregnant with a black man's child. He readily agreed to help Cimo, and apparently made several unsuccessful attempts to poison Tyner before resorting to the use of explosives. The bomb with which he finally accomplished his design was disguised as a radio.

Convicted of first-degree murder, Donald Gaskins was sentenced to death for the second time. Tony Cimo was convicted of conspiracy to murder and given an eight-year prison sentence. In June 1983, Cimo, then aged thirty-six, gave an interview to the *Chicago Tribune* in which he said that even if he had known he would be caught and sent to prison, he would still have done the same thing. He served only six months before being released on parole, and was later portrayed in a CBS television film, *Vengeance: The Tony Cimo Story*.

Gaskins put up a long fight to avoid execution, using – like Tyner – whatever legal means were available to him. A few hours before he was escorted to the electric chair, he slashed his wrists with a razor blade which he had swallowed and then coughed up the week before. He had to be given twenty stitches.

His execution was unusual in that it was the first time that a white man had been put to death in America for killing a black person since 1944. As such, it served to underscore the extent to which the death penalty is discriminatorily applied there, with one lawyer remarking that Gaskins's ten life sentences for previous murders were 'the sort of criminal record a white man needs to be executed for the murder of a black'. Forty-two of the other 152 people who had been executed since 1976 were all blacks who had killed whites.

The release of Tony Cimo, after he had served only six months of his sentence, was also highlighted as an example of racial discrimination. Describing the killing of Tyner as 'a high-tech lynching', David Bruck, chief lawyer of the South Carolina Office of Appellate Defense, added: 'About all you can say about South Carolina's efforts to correct racial disparities in this case is that Tony Cimo served six more months than he would have half a century ago.'

Cimo had no criminal record prior to this offence. He suffered a severe head injury in a boating accident in 1977, and was only able to return to work a short time before his mother and stepfather were murdered. Following his conviction, his neighbours held a barbecue and lottery to raise money to help his family. Many of them said they supported Cimo's action in arranging for Tyner to be killed.

Execution videotaped
by judicial order

On the morning of 21 April 1992, Robert Alton Harris, a thirty-nine-year-old double murderer, was executed at San Quentin Prison after spending thirteen years under sentence of death. The execution followed a last-minute legal wrangle, in which one reprieve after another was granted and overturned. When the condemned man finally entered the gas chamber for the second time that day, it took him fourteen minutes to die. His death throes were recorded on videotape, by order of a federal judge.

It was California's first execution for twenty-five years, and the excitement it caused was reminiscent of the hangings once carried out in public. Intense media interest brought hundreds of satellite lorries to the vicinity; television producers paid local people thousands of dollars for the right to use their bungalows as 'death watch' headquarters. As in other well-publicized cases, opponents of capital punishment held a vigil outside the prison, while supporters called for the law to take its course.

Harris had been sentenced to death in 1979, for the brutal murder of two teenagers in San Diego the previous year. Accompanied by his younger brother Daniel (who later testified against him), he had kidnapped the youths from a fast-food restaurant, forced them to drive to a secluded spot, and there shot both of them dead. His sole reason for doing so was that he and his brother wanted their car to use for a bank robbery. After the murders, according to his own account, he sat down and ate the hamburgers that his victims had left unfinished.

'It seemed fun at the time,' he told a police psychiatrist.

Harris, who suffered from foetal alcohol syndrome – brain damage caused by his mother's alcoholism – had a history of crime. Beaten, abused and neglected as a child, he had taken to glue-sniffing at an early age, and while in his teens was twice convicted of stealing cars.

One night in 1975, after drinking heavily, he picked a fight with one of his neighbours and beat him to death. Pleading guilty to a charge of manslaughter, he spent the next two and a half years in jail, but was then released on parole – despite warnings from the Imperial County Sheriff's Department that he was 'in need of psychiatric attention' – just six months before the shooting of the two youths.

During his long years on Death Row, Harris's lawyers filed many appeals on his behalf; his case was also taken up by the American Civil Liberties Union. Four times his execution date was fixed and then cancelled: on one occasion, in April 1990, he came within hours of death before being reprieved. Two years later, as his fifth and final date drew near, the fight to save him continued.

Three days before he was due to die, District Judge Marilyn Hall Patel granted Harris a ten-day stay of execution, so that she would have time to hear a lawsuit filed by the ACLU – on behalf of all of the inmates of California's Death Row – claiming that the use of cyanide gas amounted to cruel and unusual punishment. This was overturned by a federal appeals panel, following an appeal by lawyers acting for the state.

On the evening of 20 April 1992, with Harris's execution scheduled to take place at one minute past midnight, a judge of the Ninth US Circuit Court of Appeals in San

Francisco ordered a seven-day reprieve, to allow the court
to vote on new evidence that the condemned man's brother
may have killed one of the two youths himself. But the
state appealed to the US Supreme Court in Washington and
got the ruling reversed.

A second stay was then imposed by the same federal
appeal court on the basis of the ACLU claim of 'cruel and
unusual punishment'. When this was overturned, a third
was ordered on the same grounds. But this, too, was
quashed by the Supreme Court and the execution was then
rescheduled for 4.01 a.m.

At 3.49 a.m., Harris was strapped to a chair in the gas
chamber and the witnesses assembled. There were forty-
nine official witnesses altogether, including twelve 'repu-
table citizens' selected by the Warden. Harris was wearing
a blue work-shirt and a pair of jeans. Seemingly relaxed, he
looked at the witnesses, nodding and winking at people he
knew.

But as he sat waiting, a nearby telephone rang and it was
learnt that the federal court had granted yet another stay of
execution, the judge referring the 'cruel and unusual
punishment' question to California's State Supreme Court.
Harris had therefore to be unstrapped and taken back to his
cell a few yards from the execution chamber.

Again the state appealed to the US Supreme Court – and
again the ruling was reversed. This time the Supreme Court
voted seven to two to bar the lower federal courts from
issuing any further reprieve without its approval, saying
that there was 'no good reason for this abusive delay'. The
two dissenting judges described the use of lethal gas as
'barbaric'.

Shortly before 6 a.m., Harris was led into the gas
chamber again. After the strain of his prolonged ordeal, he
was now subdued and gloomy. The gas was released about
seven minutes past six and the condemned man pro-

nounced dead fourteen minutes later. The eighteen journalists present differed in their impressions of how long he took to lose consciousness: some said it was one and a half minutes, others that it was as long as seven minutes.

'This was torture,' said Kevin Leary of the *San Francisco Chronicle*. 'I'm not sure of my stand on the death penalty any more.'

Steve Baker, the father of one of the victims, watched the proceedings silently, from a distance of six feet. He said afterwards that Harris had mouthed the words 'I'm sorry' as he began to inhale the deadly fumes.

Harris was the 169th person put to death in America since 1976. Details of his last meal – a giant tub of Kentucky fried chicken, two pizzas and a bag of jelly beans – were released by prison authorities in a media briefing. His last formal statement was a quotation from the film *Bill and Ted's Bogus Journey*: 'You can be a king or a street sweeper, but everybody dances with the grim reaper.'

The execution was videotaped by order of Judge Patel, who said the film could prove to be crucial evidence in the lawsuit brought by the ACLU, as state lawyers had challenged the reliability of reports on the suffering caused by lethal gas. She specified that the tape should be deposited under seal with the court and that no copies should be made of it unless ordered by a judge. It was the first such recording ever made of an American execution.

The previous year, a San Francisco television station had sued the Warden of San Quentin and the state prison authorities after being denied permission to film the event for broadcasting. KQED, a non-profit making educational station, had claimed that the public had a right to witness the execution and that an important constitutional issue – freedom of the press – was at stake. The Warden, Daniel Vasquez, however, argued that a camera in the gas chamber would turn the proceedings into an undignified spectacle and disrupt his attempts to make the occasion as solemn and respectful as possible.

The federal judge who heard the case in June 1991 ruled against allowing the execution to be televised.

Harris was not America's longest-serving Death Row inmate. At the time of his execution there were eight capital offenders nationwide who had been under sentence of death since 1974. One of them, William Andrews, has since been executed: he was put to death by lethal injection in Salt Lake City, Utah, in July 1992. Andrews, aged thirty-seven, died for his part in a robbery in which three people were killed.

In June 1991, Jerry Joe Bird, aged fifty-four, was executed by the same method in Huntsville, Texas, eight days after suffering a stroke. He had been sentenced seventeen years earlier for the murder of an antique-gun collector during the course of a burglary.

In September 1991, in the same prison, James 'Sugarman' Russell was executed for kidnapping and murdering a shop manager, also in 1974.

Yet another of Huntsville's long-term Death Row inmates was put to death on 23 April 1992, just two days after Harris. Billy White, a thirty-four-year-old rubbish-van driver, had been sentenced fourteen years earlier. It took him nine minutes to die, after technicians had spent forty minutes finding a suitable vein.

None of these executions caused anything like the furore unleashed by Chessman's case in 1960, though all of the prisoners concerned spent longer – some of them a good deal longer – on Death Row before their sentences were carried out. Apart from Harris, none of them was even very well known.

The fact that a human being can be subjected to such a terrible ordeal in the name of justice does not seem to matter as much nowadays as it did a generation ago.

When Jimmy Lee Gray was executed in Mississippi's gas chamber in September 1983, he had convulsions for eight minutes, gasped eleven times and struck his head repeatedly against a pole behind the chair to which he was strapped. When the witnesses were asked to leave, it appeared to some of them that he was still not dead.

5

Some
Executioners

How the hangman
got his name

English hangmen of the eighteenth and nineteenth centuries were commonly called Jack Ketch (or Catch), after the executioner of the Duke of Monmouth. It has been claimed by some authors that the name is a corruption of Jacquet, but this is quite untrue. The real name of Monmouth's executioner was John Ketch, as the hangman's own burial record makes clear. He was an infamous figure, with a reputation for savagery and incompetence.

It is not known when his career as a hangman began. The last known holder of the London post before him – Edward Dunn, the executioner of the Regicides – died in office in 1663, but the earliest references to Ketch are to be found in tracts published in 1678. By then, however, his name was already a familiar one, so obviously his appointment had taken place somewhat earlier.

He remained the hangman for London and Middlesex for the next eight years, and during that time officiated at a great many executions. Most of the prisoners concerned were hanged in the normal way, but those who died for political or religious crimes were hanged, drawn and quartered – or, in the case of noblemen, beheaded. The victims of the 'Popish Plot' conspiracy of 1678, convicted on the basis of perjured evidence, were among those who suffered at his hands.

Besides executing capital offenders, Ketch was often

called upon to punish lesser criminals, generally by whipping them through the streets. In 1685, he whipped Titus Oates, the inventor of the 'Popish Plot', from Aldgate to Newgate on 20 May and from Newgate to Tyburn two days later: a punishment inflicted with such severity that those who witnessed it were amazed at the victim's survival. He also had to brand offenders who managed to escape the gallows by claiming benefit of clergy.

Of the two executions which he is known to have bungled, the first – that of Lord William Russell in 1683 – may not have been quite so shocking as was generally believed. One eyewitness account informs us: 'The hangman gave him 3 blows, besides sawing wth ye ax, before he cut his head of.' But another merely states that the prisoner's head was 'cut off at two strokes'.

Monmouth's execution, two years later, was a far worse case. On that occasion, the hangman was visibly agitated and had to make five attempts before he succeeded in finishing his work. He had to be guarded afterwards for his own safety.

Ketch was not a man noted for decorum. It was customary for noblemen facing the axe to give him a few guineas as a gratuity: that was one of the perquisites of his office. And when the amount which he received fell short of his expectations, as happened at the execution of Algernon Sidney, a few months after Russell's, he was not above spurning or grumbling about it. Quite possibly, as one contemporary pamphlet suggests, he was given to heavy drinking, and had to fortify himself with spirits for important occasions.

At the beginning of 1686, he was removed from office and committed to Bridewell (the house of correction) for allegedly affronting the Sheriffs of London. But at the end of May he was reinstated in order to hang his successor, a fellow named Pascha Rose. He then continued as hangman until his own death towards the end of November the same year.

Little more is known about him. It may be true, as one tract states, that he was briefly imprisoned for debt in 1679. But another claim, that he successfully struck for higher wages in 1682, seems to be based on very slender evidence.

It is, however, interesting to observe that a tract entitled *A Pleasant Discourse by way of Dialogue, between the Old and New Jack Catch* was published early in 1686. That was almost certainly the first time that the hangman's name, or its accepted variation, was applied to another member of the profession, and it occurred shortly after his place had been taken by Pascha Rose. Perhaps it was the only time it was so used during his own lifetime.

A German hangman's
chronicle of blood

Franz Schmidt was the hangman of Nuremberg from 1578 to 1617. During those thirty-nine years he carried out over three hundred executions, details of which he recorded in his private diary. Though generally shunned – as were all executioners of his time – he was an honest and conscientious man who gave his employers no cause for complaint. He believed in the efficacy of his work, and saw himself as a benefactor of society.

There were three main types of execution which Schmidt performed: hanging, beheading (with a sword) and breaking on the wheel. Hanging, which was considered a particularly shameful form of punishment, was usually reserved for thieves and criminals of low birth: some offenders who might have been subjected to it were beheaded instead, as a favour to them or their families. Beheadings, however, were carried out with the culprit unbound and without the use of a block. It was easy to bungle such an execution if the prisoner was distraught or refused to co-operate, and Schmidt did so on several occasions.

Breaking on the wheel was a more protracted form of execution, commonly used in France as well as Germany at this time, but never introduced into England. The offender, usually a murderer of the most brutal sort, was bound to a large wheel resting on a tripod and his bones were systematically broken with a sharp-edged bar. Sometimes in such cases – and, indeed, in some cases in which women were beheaded – the culprit was nipped with red-hot tongs before being put to death. This was obviously a spectacle no less hideous than the execution itself.

Besides these and other types of execution which he occasionally had to carry out – strangling, burning or drowning – Schmidt had many whippings to inflict, usually for petty theft, bigamy or (apparently) moral laxity. He was also called upon regularly to torture suspects who refused to confess to the crimes alleged against them. Of this part of his work, however, he made no record, probably because he felt bound by the secrecy in which the examinations took place.

In return for his services, he was paid a fixed salary, together with fees in respect of each duty performed. He was given free lodgings on Hangman's Bridge (a small tower and part of the bridge itself), bonuses at certain times of the year and compensation each time a prisoner was reprieved at the last minute. He was also provided with an assistant, whose own salary and fees were paid by the City Council.

Schmidt was the son of the hangman of Bamberg, in northern Bavaria. He had entered the profession as his father's assistant in 1573, and continued to serve in that capacity until his appointment to the Nuremberg post five years later. Though a man of little education, he not only kept a diary throughout his working life, he also had scientific interests which led him to dissect bodies from time to time, with the Council's permission. Sometimes he was even consulted on surgical questions.

In 1580, with the help of two priests, Schmidt managed to persuade his employers to substitute beheading for drowning in the case of three women convicted of child-murder. After that, there were no more cases of drowning for this type of offence in Nuremberg, though there was an instance of it eight years later, for a different sort of crime. Schmidt's influence in this matter is proof of his good standing with the Council.

In 1585, it befell his lot to execute his own brother-in-law on the wheel. We know from other sources that he carried out this grim task with his usual sense of duty, but we do not know whether he recorded it in his diary. If he did so, it was in a disguised form, as execution No. 88 (for all the entries are numbered, at least in the published version). This reads as follows:

> 88. February 11th. Frederick Werner of Nuremberg, *alias* Heffner Friedla, a murderer and a robber who committed three murders and twelve robberies. The first time he shot dead his own companion at Büch, the second time he killed and robbed a man in the Erlanger Wood, the third time he killed a journeyman, whom he attacked alone in the Fischbach Wood and knocked on the head with a stone, so that he died here in hospital. He likewise helped to rob his wife in the Schwabach Wood with the help of Herdtelt (already executed) and left her for dead. Drawn to execution in a tumbril, twice nipped with red-hot tongs, and afterwards broken on the wheel.

If this was indeed his brother-in-law's execution, it seems to have been the only occasion on which Schmidt felt any need to hide the sufferer's true identity. Normally, he was anxious to record the details of those who passed through his hands as accurately as possible.

The gallows on which most of Nuremberg's executions were carried out in Schmidt's time stood several hundred yards outside the city wall. The gibbet, composed of four wooden uprights fitted with crossbeams, stood on a massive stone platform, and those hanged were generally left hanging until their bodies rotted or were eaten by birds. Sometimes, though, they were mutilated, as in this instance which Schmidt recorded in 1588:

118. September 3rd. George Solen of Nuremberg, a blanket-weaver, *alias* Leck-Küchner, brought up in the Foundling Hospital, a thief who broke into houses and gardens many times and stole from them: was whipped out of the town three months ago. Hanged here and left on the gallows only eight days, for someone cut down half his body with the breeches and left the rest hanging. The body was finally thrown into the gallows pit next day, as it looked too horrible.

Jews sentenced for theft were hanged apart from other thieves, one of the crossbeams of the gibbet having been cut longer than the others for this purpose. In earlier times, they had also been forced to wear caps lined with hot pitch on the gallows, and to have dogs hanged alongside them.

In 1590, Schmidt recorded the execution of Frederick Stigler, who had been an assistant executioner, though whether he had been employed in this way in Nuremberg or in Bamberg is unclear. Stigler, at any rate, was one of the many offenders beheaded 'as a favour' at this time:

131. July 28th. Frederick Stigler of Nuremberg, a smith and executioner's assistant, for having brought accusations against some burghers' wives, for that, he said, they were witches and he knew it by certain signs – however, he wittingly did them wrong – also that they dealt in witchcraft and spells; likewise for having threatened his brother Peter, on account of which threat he had appeared before the court at Bamberg, but was

begged off; lastly, for having taken a second wife during the life of his first wife, and a third wife during the life of the second, after the death of the first – was beheaded with the sword here as a favour instead of being hanged.

It is believed that Schmidt helped not only to end the drowning of women for child-murder, but also to prevent the persecution of witches, then prevalent in other parts of Germany, from taking root in Nuremberg. But he can hardly be considered a humane person, for he had little sympathy for lawbreakers in general and few misgivings about the terrible punishments he was called upon to inflict. In 1594, for example, he was able to record a case of burning entirely without comment:

158. August 13th, Christopher Mayer, a weaver of fustian, and Hans Weber, a fruiterer, both citizens of this town, who for three years had practised sodomy together and were informed against by a hookmaker's apprentice, who caught them in the act behind a hedge. The fruiterer had practised this for twenty years, that is with the cook Endressen, with Alexander, and others. The weaver was first beheaded, then his body was burnt with the fruiterer, who was burnt alive.

In 1603, a close friend of Schmidt's was sentenced to be whipped out of the town. On this occasion, Schmidt avoided carrying out the sentence himself, and the *löwe* (assistant executioner) officiated in his place. Schmidt nonetheless recorded the event in his usual matter-of-fact way – and no doubt held himself in readiness for his next task.

Though always eager to serve the ends of justice – and elicit the approval of his employers in the process –

Schmidt was by no means indifferent to the social ostracism which was inevitably the hangman's lot. On his retirement in 1617, after so many years of revolting work, he noted in his diary that he was now, once again, a 'respectable' person. And Nuremberg society, having shunned him for so long, soon began to accept him as such.

At his death, in 1634, he was given an honourable burial.

A family of executioners

During the eighteenth and early nineteenth centuries the most famous executioners of France were all members of the Sanson family. This remarkable line lasted six generations, and provided *bourreaux* (as these officials were commonly called) not only for Paris but also for many provincial towns. Between them they carried out countless executions, numbering many notable figures among their victims.

The founder of the family was Charles Sanson, known as Longval, a former soldier born in Abbeville in 1635. Charles entered the profession as an assistant to Pierre Jouënne, the executioner of Dieppe, Rouen and Caudebec-en-Caux, in 1663, through his marriage to Jouënne's daughter Marguerite. A quarter of a century later, on 23 September 1688, he was appointed executioner of Paris by royal commission.

He was not a wholehearted member of the profession, for he disliked the grim tasks that executioners of his time were expected to perform, and hankered after respectability. Following Marguerite's death in 1681 – she died after giving birth to their one child, a son also named Charles – he may even have tried to find himself a different occupation. But the disesteem in which executioners were held made such a course immensely difficult, if not impossible.

So for another eleven years he administered the various punishments then in force, including torture, mutilation and whipping, in addition to several different methods of execution. But, as if to make amends for these revolting duties, he then practised medicine and surgery as a sideline, evidently with some success. He thus developed a dual role which his descendants were to continue.

In 1699, at the age of sixty-four, Charles Sanson married again, his bride on this occasion being the daughter of a master carpenter. About this time, his son took over his duties as executioner, but the elder Sanson remained the official holder of the post until his death in 1707. He therefore had to be present at executions in order to legalize them.

An Executioner Aged Seven

Eventually, Charles Sanson the younger became executioner in his own right. By this time, he was twenty-six years old and newly married to his stepmother's sister. He accepted the appointment willingly, without suffering any pangs of conscience. Of all the Sansons, he was the only one who was not ashamed of his work.

Charles had three children, the eldest a girl and the other two boys, but they died in 1726, before any of them reached adulthood. In his will, he left his post to his elder son, Charles-Jean-Baptiste, as it seems he was entitled to do, and after his death the son in question, though only seven years old, was named as the new executioner of Paris.

Charles-Jean-Baptiste would not have been allowed to carry out his duties himself at that age, even if he had been physically capable of doing so. But as the official executioner, he still had to be present when they were carried out on his behalf – generally by a man named François Prud'homme – in order to give them legality. It was not until he was eighteen that he carried out an execution himself.

Charles Sanson's widow later married into a family of executioners from Metz; his daughter married the executioner of Soissons; his second son became executioner of Rheims. Charles-Jean-Baptiste, who married twice, had ten children in all; his seven sons are all believed to have found employment as executioners, executioners' assistants or torturers, while at least two of his three daughters are known to have married executioners. For the women as well as the men, the family profession was virtually inescapable.

In 1754, at the age of thirty-five, Charles-Jean-Baptiste retired, after suffering a stroke, and his eldest son, Charles-Henri, was appointed his successor. Charles-Henri could not be formally invested with the office because his father was still alive, but was allowed to officiate at executions, in spite of being only fifteen years old: he did so for the first time in January 1755, when a man named Ruxton was broken on the wheel. Until he was eighteen, however, the main part of the work was done by his assistants.

Charles-Jean-Baptiste, whose stroke had left his right side paralyzed, managed to recover the use of his limbs. But he made no attempt to resume his duties as executioner of Paris, and in 1778, when he was near to death, he obtained the King's permission to resign his office, so that his son could accede to it. Charles-Henri thus received his commission, after holding the post unofficially for twenty-four years.

Executions From Dawn to Midnight

A handsome, rather ostentatious man, with a wife and two sons, Charles-Henri was destined to be the keystone of the Revolution, the executioner of the King and one of the busiest members of his profession in history. But at the time of his appointment he was doing much the same work as his great-grandfather had done, and could hardly have foreseen the momentous changes that were about to occur.

Charles-Henri lived an outwardly respectable life, resenting the view that executioners were men of low station. He dressed stylishly, hunted, played the violin and cello and twice a year gave dinner parties at his home for the entire Sanson family. It is believed that he was called by his quasi-official title of Monsieur de Paris at these gatherings, and that the other executioners present were similarly addressed, according to the towns in which they practised.

During the years of unrest which preceded the fall of the Bastille, Charles-Henri was seen as a symbol of tyranny and injustice, and on one occasion, in August 1788, the populace actually prevented him from carrying out an execution.

The condemned man, a young revolutionary named Louschart, had been sentenced to be broken on the wheel for killing his father (evidently by accident), but the crowds were on his side. In an explosion of public feeling, the scaffold was destroyed, the prisoner carried off and the executioner attacked. Louschart was afterwards pardoned and the wheel abolished.

When the Revolution finally began, there was widespread opposition to the continued use of the death penalty in any form, and Charles-Henri became worried that his livelihood might soon disappear. But the Constituent Assembly was not in favour of abolition, and instead decided that a single method of execution was needed: one which was both quick and painless. The machine named after the proposer of this reform, Joseph Ignace Guillotin, thus came into use, replacing all other methods, in 1792.

After the storming of the Tuileries Palace, on 10 August of that year, Charles-Henri and two of his brothers, both of whom had been working as his assistants, were arrested on suspicion of harbouring royalist sympathies. For a while they were in danger of being guillotined themselves, but were soon released to execute others. Only a week or so later, Charles-Henri officiated at the most tragic execution of his career.

Three men, the Abbé Sauvade and two others, had been condemned for forging *assignats*, a paper currency issued by the Revolutionary Government. When their executions had been carried out, Charles-Henri's younger son Gabriel, acting as his father's assistant, went to pick up one of the severed heads, to show it to the crowd. But in doing so he fell from the scaffold and fractured his skull: an injury from which he immediately died.

His parents were so shocked and grief-stricken by his death that neither of them ever fully recovered.

Thereafter, Charles-Henri went about his work with a growing distaste. Just a few months later, on 21 January the following year, he had what was to him a particularly shocking duty to perform: the execution of Louis XVI. And it seems that on this occasion he was obliged to operate the guillotine himself, though he normally left this part of the execution to one of his assistants.

Even so, the event proved to be even more distressing than he might have expected, for the King's neck was too thick to fit properly into the *lunette*, and the descending blade failed to cut right through it. It was only when Charles-Henri's assistants threw their weight on to it that it completed its work.

That evening, and every other evening for the rest of his

life, the remorseful executioner prayed for the dead King's soul. But the Revolution continued apace, and during the 502 days from 11 March 1793 to 27 July 1794, an estimated 2,632 people were executed under his direction, including Marie Antoinette and several of the Revolution's leading figures. During the Reign of Terror, which began in October 1793, executions were carried out from dawn to midnight, with Charles-Henri having to employ seven assistants instead of his usual four.

After the death of Robespierre, who was himself executed on 28 July 1794, the Terror came to an end. The populace demanded the punishment of Robespierre's supporters, and some of them were, in fact, executed in the months that followed. These included Antoine Fouquier-Tinville, the former Public Prosecutor, who was led to the scaffold amid scenes of jubilation.

Strangely, there were no demands for Charles-Henri to be punished, and he continued as executioner until 30 August 1795. He then retired after forty-one years' service, to be succeeded by his one surviving son, Henri. He died eleven years later, at the age of sixty-seven.

The Guillotine in Pawn

Henri Sanson, born in 1767, had begun helping his father at executions when he was eleven years old. He left the profession during the late autumn of 1793 to join the National Guard, but returned to it at the time of his father's retirement. He was formally commissioned after Charles-Henri's death in 1806, and remained in the post until his own death in 1840.

A well-educated man with a wife and four children, Henri lived a quiet, orderly life. He spoke English fluently, played the piano and had other interests which included opera and the theatre. He also distributed bread to the poor of his neighbourhood every Saturday and gave medical treatment free of charge to those who could not afford to pay for it.

Though the use of the death penalty diminished during the course of his career, Henri officiated or assisted at over 360 executions. Henri-Clément, the elder of his two sons, began to assist him at the age of sixteen, and later, when Henri succumbed to an attack of pleurisy, took his place as executioner. The last of the Sanson line, Henri-Clément took over the post officially at his father's death, but held it for only seven years before losing it in very unusual circumstances.

While Henri disliked his work intensely, Henri-Clément found it almost unbearable. On his first appearance as executioner in his father's place, he was so sickened by the task to be performed that he had to get one of his assistants to assume command. Even then, standing at the foot of the scaffold steps, he was seen to flinch as the blade fell.

During the third decade of the nineteenth century, Henri-Clément often had to officiate on account of his father's ill health. He never ceased to be disgusted by the work he had to do, and when an execution was imminent his face would become blotchy and he would be overcome by fits of trembling. He longed to find some other way of earning his living, but knew that he would never be able to. When the time came for him to be appointed executioner, he accepted the post in a spirit of resignation.

Henri-Clément was a married man with two daughters; his only son had been killed in a carriage accident in infancy. He had a large household, including impoverished relatives (as well as servants and assistants), to maintain, but, unlike his forbears, made little attempt to appear respectable. Between executions, he closed his mind to the horrors of his work by drinking, gambling and frequenting brothels; and while squandering money at an alarming rate, he gave up the practice of medicine which his family had traditionally used as a second source of income.

Getting into financial difficulties, he began selling his possessions – the guillotine blade with which Louis XVI had been beheaded among them. But even then his excesses continued, and in 1846 he was arrested for debt and imprisoned. It was only by pawning the guillotine that he managed to secure his freedom – and then he was unable to raise enough money to get the machine back.

Eventually, the inevitable happened: the guillotine was needed for an execution. Henri-Clément pleaded for its return, but without success; he therefore had to ask the Ministry of Justice for 3800 francs, to enable him to redeem it. In the circumstances, the Minister had no choice but to authorize the payment, and on 18 June 1847, the execution (the 111th of Henri-Clément's career) was duly carried out. The forty-eight-year-old executioner was afterwards dismissed from office.

There were, by this time, few such posts in France, as the number of executions continued to decline. So there was no shortage of applicants to fill the vacancy which his dismissal had created, and little or no chance of Henri-Clément finding a similar position elsewhere. With the work which he hated no longer available to him, his outlook was indeed bleak.

Henri-Clément's daughters were now both married, and his wife had left him after years of friction. Not long after his dismissal, his house in Paris was sold by his creditors, and he and his mother retired to a small village in the country. There, living under an assumed name, Henri-Clément was constantly in fear of being recognized as the former executioner. But his terrible secret was never discovered, and after his mother's death in 1850, he remained in the village for another seven years.

He returned to Paris in 1857, and in the early 1860s was paid 30,000 francs for the six-volume *Memoirs of the Sansons*, a highly unreliable work published under his name in 1862. In his old age, he lived in Versailles with his widowed elder daughter, Marie-Emilie, whose neighbours called him 'Monsieur Henri'. He died, in his ninetieth year, on 25 January 1889.

Mutton Curry - the sheep thief who became a hangman

William Curry, alias William Wilkinson, a labourer from Thirsk, in the North Riding of Yorkshire, was sentenced to death at the York Assizes in March 1793 for stealing three sheep. The sentence was later commuted to seven years' transportation, and this he served aboard the prison hulks in Woolwich. He was released in March 1800.

A year later, he appeared for trial on a similar charge – the theft of five sheep – and, on admitting the offence, was again sentenced to death. This time the sentence was commuted to fourteen years' transportation, which was then changed to fourteen years' imprisonment. He served this second term in York Castle.

In 1802, Curry was offered the post of hangman of York, which was traditionally filled by a pardoned felon. He accepted it, and carried out a triple execution (one of the offenders was a fellow sheep thief) shortly afterwards. He remained in the Castle, however, until 1814 or 1815, being brought out only when his services were required.

In all, 'Mutton' Curry, as he was then called, held the office of hangman for thirty-three years, carrying out several dozen executions in York and others in different parts of the north of England. Most of these executions seem to have been carried out as efficiently as one could expect in those days, but on occasions the hangman's performance was marred by drink.

Probably the worst of these incidents was one which took place on 14 April 1821, when a robber named William Brown was hanged at York's City Jail. Curry was so drunk on that occasion that he made an exhibition of himself on the scaffold and proved quite incapable of performing his duty.

First he had difficulty pulling the cap over the condemned man's face; then, finding the rope too short, he had to hold up the proceedings while he lengthened it. After that, he tried unsuccessfully to put the noose round the prisoner's neck, removing the cap at each attempt. Eventually, the Jailer and one of the Sheriff's Officers went to his assistance, and it was only with their help that the execution was accomplished.

Although it was raining, there was an unusually large number of spectators present, and the hangman's conduct shocked and infuriated them. Afterwards, as he made his way home, Curry was attacked and knocked down repeatedly.

At a multiple execution carried out at York Castle (the county jail) in September the same year, Curry had an unpleasant experience of a different sort which may also have been caused by his excessive drinking. With the five condemned waiting for the platform to fall, he inadvertently placed one foot on it himself before drawing the bolt which released it. Consequently, he fell to the ground, to the delight of the spectators, and suffered severe bruises.

Following this second incident, Curry remained hangman for another fourteen years, during which his conduct seems to have given no further cause for serious concern. Upon retiring from the post, in or about November 1835, he entered the parish workhouse in Thirsk, where he spent the last six years of his life. His burial entry, dated 10 March 1841, gives his age as seventy-six, but other evidence suggests that he may only have been about seventy-one.

Curry was the last capital offender to be appointed hangman of York, though not the last criminal. The last criminal was his successor, James Coates, who, at the Summer Assizes in 1835, had been sentenced to seven years' transportation for larceny. Coates held the post until 1840, when he escaped from prison and was replaced by a coal porter named Nathaniel Howard.

Though Howard had no convictions, it is known that he carried out his first execution dressed as a prisoner. Perhaps his employers insisted upon this as a compromise with tradition.

Alexander Green - the monster of New South Wales

At the General Quarter Sessions in Shrewsbury, in January 1824, a twenty-two-year-old circus tumbler named Alexander Green was sentenced to transportation for life for stealing a piece of material from a mercer's shop. He arrived in Sydney six months later, and received a conditional pardon the following year.

Though this did not alter his sentence, it gave him considerable freedom of movement within the colony, so long as he reported his whereabouts to the constables and kept out of trouble. It also enabled him to seek work as he wished, rather than have it found for him.

In 1827, while working as an official flogger – one of many employed in the colony at that time – he became an assistant to Henry Stain, the public executioner. And when Stain died in January 1828, Green was appointed his successor.

He made his first appearance as executioner at a triple hanging in Sydney two months later. Two of the condemned died instantly, but the third man's rope broke and he had to be hanged again. Because of this, the new hangman was booed by the spectators and criticized in the newspapers, but he was apparently not discouraged by the experience. He went on to hold the post for twenty-seven years.

A powerfully-built but frightfully ugly man, Green

drank heavily and was inclined to violence. He soon became an object of hatred throughout the colony, and as such was sometimes subjected to violence himself. On one occasion, quite early in his career, he was assaulted during an execution in a quite extraordinary manner.

The incident occurred on the scaffold at Windsor on 23 August 1830, while Green was waiting to hang a young bushranger named Thomas Tiernan. The condemned youth had the rope round his neck and was speaking to the priest attending him, when suddenly he threw himself at the hangman and knocked him off the scaffold, strangling himself at the same time. He died hanging over the front of the gallows.

Green had fallen fifteen feet to the ground and broken his arm, but was prevailed upon to finish carrying out his duty just the same. Climbing back on to the scaffold, he dragged the youth's body back to the platform and released the trap in the normal way. The body was then left hanging for fifteen minutes, as the law required.

In December the same year, after carrying out a double execution in Port Macquarie, Green was returning to Sydney by schooner in company with fifteen absconders who had given themselves up. Realizing who he was, one of the prisoners seized an axe and struck him with it, inflicting a deep wound down one side of his face. When the wound healed, Green was left with a long scar which made him look more ghastly than ever.

In January 1831, his sentence was reduced to transportation for seven years. Green was therefore a free man, and could return to England if he so wished. But he chose not to do so, in spite of the dangers which he faced in Australia. Presumably, his post was more important to him than his safety.

Yet he seems not to have made any attempt to give a good impression of himself, for his appearance and conduct were often criticized in the newspapers of the day. Besides being ugly, he was often drunk, dirty and improperly dressed for the duties he had to perform. Moreover, he was abusive and needlessly rough in his treatment of the condemned.

Green's notoriety, in fact, was such that when he made an unsuccessful suicide attempt in October 1832, after being rebuffed by a member of the opposite sex, the *Sydney Herald* concluded its report of the affair by stating that with the help of half a pint from a nearby tavern, 'the monster, we are sorry to say, recovered'.

But the strangest feature of Green's case is the number of times he escaped punishment after being accused of criminal offences. In April 1827, he had been appointed an honorary constable in Port Stephens, only to be dismissed two months later, for aiding a fellow constable in an assault. Luckily for him, the matter was taken no further, and he was appointed official flogger at the George Street Barracks shortly afterwards.

In September the same year, he and another man were arrested after being found in possession of some stolen goods. When they appeared in court, they claimed that they had found the goods on a vacant allotment and were taking them to the constables when a constable arrived on the scene. The court gave the prisoners the benefit of the doubt, and Green was able to continue his ignominious occupation. This time he managed to stay out of trouble for nine years.

Then, in 1836, he was arrested after an incident at the lodgings of Ester Howell, a widow whom he found attractive but who did not find him so. Green had tried to win Mrs Howell over with presents, but when she refused to have anything to do with him, he flew into a rage and apparently threatened to kill her. After being charged however, he was released on bail – upon which, he returned to the widow's home and caused a second disturbance.

Mrs Howell fled in terror. The hangman was again arrested and this time charged with aggravated assault. But he did not appear for trial and, in his absence, was merely bound over to keep the peace and stay away from Mrs Howell. This he seems to have done.

In January 1840, in company with two women (he and one of them were both lodgers at the home of the other) he was charged with stealing a quantity of groceries. The charge was eventually dropped, but only after he had spent two months in custody. Six months after that, he was given a short prison sentence for assaulting a woman described as his wife.

In July 1841, Green moved into a whitewashed cottage in Green Park, adjoining the new Darlinghurst Jail. But he was regularly baited by hooligans, and on the night of 1 March the following year was forced to defend himself with a constable's staff against a mob of twenty or thirty of them. During the affray, the cottage was set on fire and the hangman almost burnt to death. After that, he took up residence in the jail for his own protection.

On 24 December 1843, he returned to the cottage in a state of insobriety and found a man sleeping there. Throwing the man out, he left him lying on the ground, then came back with a large sandstone block and broke his leg with it. In the morning, he was arrested and charged with attempted murder, but the case was not officially filed against him. So, amazingly, he was again not brought to trial.

Upon his release, Green was suspended from duty. But finding somebody suitable to replace him was no easy matter, and his suspension was soon lifted. He then went back to live in the cottage, and remained there for several years, baited by hooligans as regularly as before.

During those years, he was twice dismissed from his

post, but reinstated each time. The first time was in January 1847, when the reason given for his dismissal was gross insolence; the second was in May 1853, when it was for misconduct at a double hanging in Bathurst. At the time of this second incident, Green was showing signs of madness, but still no suitable person could be found to take his place. Green thus continued as hangman for another two years.

But on 28 February 1855, at Darlinghurst Jail, he finally carried out his last execution. The condemned man, the 490th offender to be hanged by Green, was a murderer named William Ryan, who had killed his wife in a revolting manner while under the influence of drink. He was the first person to be hanged inside the walls of the prison.

The hangman, according to Sheriff John O'Neill Brenan, was by now quite insane, and it was only with great difficulty that he had been 'got to conduct himself with common decency' at Ryan's execution. On 4 May that year, at Brenan's request, he was committed to the Tarban Creek Lunatic Asylum, where he probably spent the rest of his life. Nothing more was ever heard of him.

This time a new hangman *had* to be found, and after a delay of five months a frail old man named Robert Elliott was appointed. Elliott, a prisoner nearing the end of his sentence in Darlinghurst, had agreed to accept the post in return for his freedom. His release was thus procured, and his appointment took place on 2 October. But within a year he was arrested for stealing and sent back to prison.

A solitary fellow named Bull was then appointed, and with him the authorities were more fortunate. He gave them no trouble, as far as we know, and served as hangman until his retirement in 1872. He spent his last years in the Liverpool Asylum.

Bull's successor, Robert Howard, was as grotesque in appearance as Alexander Green. A former cabman, he had been kicked in the face by a horse, as a result of which he had no nose. This made it difficult for him to go on earning his living as a cabman, as so many people found it unpleasant to look at him. But it did not affect the number of offenders he was called upon to hang.

Despite his dreadful calling and his physical peculiarity, Howard was a good-natured man, who helped discharged prisoners and prisoners' families who were in distress.

He hanged, in all, between sixty and seventy people before retiring on a pension some years prior to his death.

The hangman who could not kill chickens

John Ellis, the well-known English hangman, was a native of Rochdale in Lancashire. Born in 1874, the son of a hairdresser, he went to work in a spinning mill after leaving school, and later earned his living at a large textile-machine maker's in the nearby village of Castleton. But he eventually became unfit for heavy labour, owing to an accident at the mill from which he had never fully recovered. He thus became a hairdresser himself, setting up his own business in Oldham Road, Rochdale.

In 1901, he embarked on his career as an executioner, which was to last for twenty-three years. It began with a one-week training course at Newgate Prison, at the end of which he had to take an efficiency test, to show that he had mastered the technique of hanging. With this passed satisfactorily, his name was added to the official list of executioners approved by the Home Office (for hangmen were no longer the full-time employees they had been in earlier times) and he was then allowed to assist at executions wherever his services were required.

Ellis served as an assistant executioner for seven years, and then as chief executioner for sixteen years, carrying out executions all over the country. He hanged, among others, Dr Crippen in 1910; Frederick Henry Seddon (another notorious poisoner) in 1912; George Joseph Smith, the 'Brides in the Bath' murderer, in 1915; Sir

Roger Casement, the Irish nationalist convicted of treason, in 1916, and Edith Thompson, one of the so-called 'Ilford Murderers', in 1923. He also travelled to Ireland on a number of occasions, to hang members of Sinn Fein.

In all, he officiated or assisted at the execution of 203 people, receiving fees and expenses in respect of each of them. As assistant, his fee was £2 2s for each person hanged; as chief executioner, it was £10 10s (or £15 if the execution was in Scotland). Between executions, he went on working as a hairdresser, his shop becoming more and more of an attraction to sightseers as his fame increased.

A slightly-built man with a bushy moustache, Ellis was married with four children. He loved dogs, bred poultry and took a keen interest in boxing and football. In the evenings, he liked to go to a public house and play cards or dominoes with friends. He was kindly by nature and often gave generously to charities and good causes.

Ellis's resignation from the Home Office list in March 1924 gave rise to rumours that he was 'haunted' by the hanging of Edith Thompson fourteen months earlier. Mrs Thompson had been hanged while practically insensible after collapsing in Holloway's condemned cell, and Ellis himself admitted that the execution had been his most upsetting experience. But he denied that he had given up being a hangman because of it, and this was almost certainly the truth.

For Ellis had a more prosaic reason for resigning: that was his desire to sell his memoirs to a newspaper. As a serving hangman, he was forbidden to publish information about his official duties, but there was nothing to prevent his doing so after he retired. His life story, commissioned by *Thomson's Weekly News*, began to appear just a week after his career came to an end, and Ellis was undoubtedly well paid for it. But five months later, he tried to kill himself.

The attempt was made at his home in Kitchen Lane,

Balderstone Fold, Rochdale, during the early hours of Monday, 25 August 1924. Ellis, who had been drinking, shot himself with an automatic pistol, fracturing his jaw. Mrs Ellis, who was in the house at the time, called a policeman, to whom the ex-hangman admitted that he had inflicted the wound himself. Ellis was taken to hospital.

Two days later, with his face bandaged, Ellis appeared before Rochdale magistrates, charged with attempted suicide. The case attracted a lot of public interest, and hundreds of people had to be turned away, as there was not enough room for them in the courtroom. Ellis admitted the offence, but declined an opportunity to explain it. He did, however, give an undertaking that he would make no further attempt to take his own life. This satisfied the Bench and the Chairman addressed him as follows:

'I am sorry to see you here, Ellis. I have known you for a long time. If your aim had been as true as the drops you have given, it would have been a bad job for you. Your life has been given back to you, and I hope you will make good use of it, and lead a good life in atonement.'

The prisoner again promised not to repeat the offence, and also agreed to give up drinking. The court bound him over to keep the peace for twelve months, and he was released. But he was not destined to keep either of his promises indefinitely.

The unexplained suicide attempt was naturally taken in some quarters as confirmation that he was indeed haunted by the hanging of Edith Thompson. But three years later, in December 1927, an unremorseful Ellis began appearing in a play, *The Life and Adventures of Charles Peace*, at the Grand Theatre in Gravesend. The play was a melodrama with a gallows scene, and Ellis played the hangman.

'I am feeling more nervous now than at any real execution,' he told a reporter in his dressing room shortly before making his début. 'I hope it all goes all right.' He

added (referring to the actor who played the condemned):
'If Mr Morris complains afterwards he will be the first one
that I have handled who has ever done so.'

The play caused great excitement, but there were many
protests and the matter was raised in the House of
Commons. After a very short run, it was taken off. Ellis,
who apparently had some of his own money invested in the
venture, sold all the props except the model scaffold and
returned to Rochdale. He stored the scaffold in a garage
near his home and went back to working as a hairdresser.

Early in 1932, he began a lecture tour of fairgrounds up
and down the country, taking the scaffold with him, to use
for demonstrations. His shows were popular, and he did
well out of them. At the end of the tour, about June or July,
he put the scaffold back into storage and again resumed his
regular occupation.

But his health was deteriorating. He had suffered from
neuritis and insomnia for some years – this was probably the
real reason for his suicide attempt in 1924 – and now had
heart trouble and 'nerves' as well. His drink problem was as
acute as ever; he was subject to fits of violent temper, and
more than once he threatened to commit suicide.

Finally, on the evening of 20 September 1932, Ellis
arrived home from work earlier than usual. He had been
drinking, but was not drunk. He sat down in a chair in the
front room and slept for two hours, then had some tea in the
kitchen. After that, he went back into the front room to
have a smoke.

Mrs Ellis remained in the kitchen, sewing, in the
presence of her daughter Amy. Suddenly, her husband
came into the room again, took off his collar and tie and
took his razor from a shelf. Rushing at his wife with it, he
shouted, 'I'll cut your head off!'

Mrs Ellis ran from the house in terror, but Amy stayed
and asked her father what was the matter. Instead of

answering, he turned on her. 'I can't cut your mother's head off,' he said. 'I'll cut *yours* off!'

Amy pushed him away and screamed. Ellis suddenly stopped threatening her and went back into the front room. Amy stayed in the kitchen on her own.

Before long, Mrs Ellis returned, accompanied by her son Austin, who had been at his brother's house in the same neighbourhood. The old hangman stood waiting at the front door as they approached, his throat bleeding and the razor still in his hand. Before they reached him, he turned and walked back into the front room, where he cut his throat for the second time, his son entering a moment too late to stop him.

He died lying face downwards in a pool of blood after Austin had rushed out to summon a doctor.

At the inquest the following afternoon, Mrs Ellis said that her husband, who was fifty-seven years old, had been worried about the state of his health, but had, as far as she knew, no other worries. She told the court of his suicide threats and agreed that he had tried to kill himself some years earlier. But when asked whether she had ever before seen him in the condition that he was in when he rushed at her, she replied, 'No, it struck me he had suddenly gone mad.'

'I am quite of the opinion that he did this rash act in a sudden frenzy of madness,' said Mr J.H. Chadwick, the Deputy County Coroner. He recorded a verdict that the deceased had committed suicide while of unsound mind.

That Ellis had killed himself 'in a sudden frenzy of madness' was undoubtedly true. He was not a brutal man by nature – in fact, he could not even bring himself to kill his own chickens – and although he *had* tried to kill himself before, he had not on that occasion tried to harm anybody else.

That he should suddenly threaten his wife and daughter

with a razor, without the slightest provocation, was a clear
sign that he had become mentally ill, after years of physical
illness, worry and heavy drinking. His suicide was thus
almost certainly prompted by the realization that he was
now a danger to those around him.

It nonetheless served to reinforce the rumour that he was
haunted by the hanging of Edith Thompson, even though his
own statements on the subject suggest otherwise.

It would be useless for me to attempt to ascribe any
particular reason as actuating me in my desire to
adopt such an unusual profession as that of hangman.
I simply wanted to be one – and that was all!

It wasn't any love for the gruesome, for I was not
attracted by things of that nature. Perhaps it may be
difficult to believe, but it is nevertheless true that
never in my life have I been able to steel myself to
drown a kitten or kill a fowl.

Only once did I try to drown a kitten, and I was
upset for the rest of the day. After that, whenever
things like that had to be done in our house, either
Mrs Ellis or somebody else, had to do them. Yet I
have never had the slightest uneasiness over executing the sentence of the law upon a murderer.

Still, despite my helplessness when faced with the
drowning of a kitten, I stuck to my secret project of becoming a hangman, and at last made a definite move in
the matter. Before doing so I threw out a sort of "feeler"
on the subject to my wife, but she objected so strongly
that I dropped the subject – or rather, pretended to – for
I was determined to take up the work.

John Ellis, *Thomson's Weekly News*, 22 March 1924

Executioner against
the death penalty

Robert Greene Elliott, a fifty-one-year-old electrical contractor, was appointed executioner to the State of New York in January 1926, following the unexpected resignation of his predecessor, John Hulbert. A former chief electrician of Clinton Prison, he had once served for two years as an executioner's assistant, and during that time had been trained to carry out executions by electricity himself. He thus knew what the work entailed and was able to start as soon as his services were needed.

He did not have long to wait, for New York had many executions in the 1920s, all of them carried out at Sing Sing Prison. An honest, law-abiding man and a regular churchgoer, Elliott went about his work conscientiously, receiving a fee of $150 for each person he put to death. By the end of the year, he had become the official executioner to Massachusetts, New Jersey and Pennsylvania, as well as New York – and later in his career he added two other states, Vermont and Connecticut, to the number he served.

In thirteen years he executed, in all, 387 people, including some of America's best-known Death Row inmates of all time: Sacco and Vanzetti in 1927, Ruth Snyder and Henry Judd Gray in 1928 and Bruno Richard Hauptmann in 1936 (see the chapter *Celebrities of Death Row*). Because of the part he played in such cases, Elliott became a well-known figure himself and received many death threats.

On one occasion, on the night of 18 May 1928, there was an explosion at his house in Richmond Hill, New York. The front of the two-storey building was wrecked; a section of the roof was hurled thirty feet, landing on the garage, and all of the windows were blown out. Luckily, nobody was hurt, but a man loading a milk truck nearly a block away was knocked down by the impact. The police were unable to discover who was responsible for the explosion.

Elliott was personally opposed to the death penalty, believing that it was merely a form of revenge and therefore served no useful purpose. He also accepted that the judgment of juries was not infallible, and dreaded executing somebody who was innocent. But he did not feel guilty about his career as an executioner, and in his autobiography, written shortly before his death in 1939, he summed up his attitude towards his work as follows:

The decision that a man must pay with his life for the crime he committed has been made long before his appointed hour with death. It has been made by the commonwealth which has chosen me to carry out the sentence of the court. My job is to see that this is done as humanely as possible. Outside of that, my responsibility for this individual's untimely death is no greater than that of any other member of a society which endorses or condones capital punishment.

Elliott claimed that death by electricity was painless and certain – 'as humane as ordered death can possibly be'.

The first terrific shock of 2000 volts shatters the person's nervous system instantly and beyond recall, and paralyzes the brain before the nerves can register any pain. Medical experts declare that unconsciousness is produced in less than one two-hundred and fortieth of a second.

He said he felt sure that nearly every condemned person, if allowed, would choose to die in the electric chair rather than by any other method of execution then in use.

Elliott, who was born in January 1874, was a native of rural New York, and spent his early years on a large fruit farm in Monroe County. After studying electricity at school, he went to work at the electric light factory in Brockport, and later entered the prison service as an electrician.

In 1903, he was appointed assistant to Edwin F. Davis, the then New York executioner, witnessing his first execution in November of that year and throwing the switch himself for the first time, under Davis's direction, in June 1904. However, he gave up assisting Davis in February 1905, and was not directly involved in any more executions for another twenty-one years. During those years he changed jobs several times, leaving the prison service altogether towards the end of the First World War.

Davis retired in 1914, and was succeeded as executioner by Hulbert, who had assisted him since 1905. When Hulbert suddenly resigned in 1926, Elliott was among the hundreds of people who applied to fill the post which he had left vacant. And being by now the only person in New York, other than Hulbert himself, with experience of this sort of work, he was the obvious choice.

A married man with three children, Elliott had been running an electrical contracting business in partnership with his son Robert since 1920. He was to continue in this line for the rest of his life, taking time off whenever he was needed to perform an execution.

Elliott was not the only executioner, or former executioner, to declare himself against the death penalty. His own autobiography reveals that Davis was another:

> One of my predecessors, Edwin F. Davis, also saw no good reason why any person need die for the safety of the rest of us. On the day in 1903 when he electrocuted the three Van Wormer brothers, Davis told a newspaperman: 'I believe and hope that this execution will sound the beginning of the death knell of capital punishment in New York.' I know he was sincere, for I often heard him express himself in a similar manner.

A third was James Berry, the English hangman who tried unsuccessfully to execute John Lee of Babbacombe, 'the man they could not hang', in 1885. Following his resignation in 1892, Berry spoke in opposition to the death penalty in a series of lectures to theatre audiences, some of them accompanied by lantern slides. Later he became a lay preacher, and denounced it vehemently at revivalist meetings all over the country.

The best-known case of all, however, was that of Albert Pierrepoint, the retired hangman who died in 1992, at the age of eighty-seven. Pierrepoint, like Elliott, wrote an autobiography in which he announced that he was now opposed to capital punishment. Like Elliott, he did not accept that it was a deterrent, and expressed the view that executions achieved nothing but revenge.

Pierrepoint was the third member of his family to serve as an executioner. In his twenty-five-year career (1931–56), he hanged over 400 people, including fifteen spies during the Second World War and many war criminals afterwards. Ruth Ellis, the last woman to be hanged in Britain, was also one of his victims.

Throwing the switch
for the first time

In June 1904, under the direction of Edwin F. Davis, Robert
Greene Elliott threw the switch for the first time, putting a
murderer named Albert Koepping to death. This is how he
later recalled the event.

*After the witnesses were seated, Davis tested the chair with
a board of lights. I stood immediately to the right of the
death seat, the head electrode in my hand. I was trembling.
Davis noticed this, and said, 'Steady, Bob, steady.'*

*Koepping was brought in, and walked firmly to the
chair. As he sat down, he reiterated his earlier statement
that he was expiating the crime of another. I placed the
electrode on his head. I could feel him shudder as several
drops of water ran down the back of his neck. Next I went
over to the switch ten feet away. Davis was there, and he
put his hand on my shoulder reassuringly. I reached out for
the switch, and my right hand closed around it.*

*While I waited for the signal, I heard the nervous cough
of one of the witnesses. There was the shifting of feet, and
a terse, quiet word spoken by an official. My temples
throbbed.*

*The prison physician then gave the signal by a wave of
his hand. I glanced at the chair to be sure that nobody was
standing too near it. 'Now,' whispered Davis. I threw the*

switch, and the condemned man stiffened under the straps. In a few seconds, Davis said, 'Cut it down.' I reduced the amount of current, and the body slumped. Finally, after the necessary number of shocks, it was decided that justice had been done. I went over and unfastened the head electrode. What had once been a living man was removed from the chair, and wheeled into the autopsy room. I had killed him.

Jimmy Thompson
- executioner and hypnotist

Jimmy Thompson was executioner of Mississippi in the early 1940s, after the state gave up hanging in favour of electrocution. A former showman with a criminal record, he operated the country's first portable electric chair, receiving a fee of $100 for each execution he carried out. He was proud of his job and, unlike Elliott, enjoyed being the centre of attention.

A native of D'Lo, in Simpson County, Thompson was born in 1896. He attended the Agricultural High School in nearby Mendenhall and served in the US Army in the First World War. After trying his hand at various other occupations, he eventually set himself up as a stage hypnotist.

Calling himself Dr Alzedi Yogi – or Dr Stingaree or Dr Zogg – Thompson gave one-man shows around the country. He wore a turban for these performances, and exposed the upper part of his body, which was covered with tattoos. He was evidently a very good hypnotist, but his shows came to an end when he was convicted of highway robbery and given a prison sentence.

Pardoned in 1939, he was appointed executioner the following year by Paul B. Johnson Sr, the new State Governor. Johnson was a close friend and birdshooting companion of Thompson's, and chose him from a list of six applicants.

The State Legislature had that year voted to change

Mississippi's method of execution. There had been demands for a change for several years, following a bungled hanging in the early 1930s, but the residents of Sunflower County, where the state penitentiary was situated, objected to the idea of having *all* of the state's executions carried out there. They feared that Sunflower would become known as the 'death county'.

The Legislature therefore called for the construction of a movable electric chair, so that executions could still be performed in county prisons. The chair was duly ordered from a firm in Memphis, and was completed in September 1940, costing the state $4000. But the authorities were so pleased with it that they had it placed on public display outside the State Capitol in Jackson, where it attracted a lot of attention.

'Crowds saw a big silver truck, a portable generator and a sturdy chair complete with helmet, straps and electrodes,' *Life* magazine of 7 October reported.

> Beside it stood Mississippi's new executioner, Jimmy Thompson, ex-sailor, marine, carnival man and high tension expert. No less proud of his chair than of the black cat, snakes and strawberries tattooed on his velvety skin, he explained that he and his volts would travel from county to county as business required.

There was, however, a lot of adverse publicity as well, with some newspapers denouncing the display as barbarous. 'Everything was exhibited but a victim,' the Memphis *Commercial Appeal* complained.

Those prisoners who were under sentence of death at the time the law was changed were given the choice of being hanged or electrocuted. Five of Thompson's first nine victims were persons who had been given this choice, and the new executioner was glad of the work he obtained as a result of their decisions.

'Brother, I sure appreciate your trade,' he told each of them (or so he claimed in an *American Mercury* interview). 'I'm going to show my appreciation by giving you a nice clean job. I'm going to give you the prettiest death a guy can have.'

Jimmy Thompson performed his first execution of all in Lucedale on 11 October 1940, the victim being a wife-killer named Willie Mae Bragg. The other eight of those first nine victims – three of whom were black men condemned for rape – were all put to death during the next year or so. The three rapists were all executed before large crowds of black people, all of whom were present against their own will.

Thompson was convinced that the condemned were always grateful for his assurance of 'a nice clean job'. 'I guess I just have a talent for this sort of thing,' he told the *American Mercury*. 'Condemned men seem to trust me, and I never let them down.' He also boasted that his 'fry parties', as he called them, were never marred by sparks or scorched flesh.

In other respects, his conduct was equally bizarre. It is known, for example, that after his first two or three executions, he began sleeping with his windows open at night, whatever the weather, to 'let the ghosts go in and out' without rattling them. However, a claim by one of his friends that Thompson was the sort who would get up at any time of the night to 'shoot a guy's guts out' was almost certainly untrue.

There had been one occasion, in the 1920s, when he had shot a neighbour for 'talking nasty' to his mother. He had been saved from prosecution then by an unwritten Southern law which gave a man the right to shoot another for the sake of his womenfolk. But that was the only incident of its type in which he is known to have been involved, so his friend's remark was clearly an exaggeration.

In spite of his dreadful calling and his boastful nature, Thompson was a colourful character with a lot of friends. Many people enjoyed birdshooting in his company and he often entertained them with pranks involving the use of hypnosis. One imagines that he was especially popular among white supremacists.

But how long he continued as executioner is not known for certain, for official records appear not to contain such information and the press seems not to have reported his leaving office. Probably somebody else was appointed in his place by Thomas L. Bailey, who became Governor of Mississippi in January 1944.

He was, at any rate, the 'former state executioner' by December 1946, when the *Jackson Daily News* reported that he had been 'painfully but not seriously' wounded in a shooting accident. This had occurred near his home while he was out hunting with his stepson, Frankie Kalberg. He was treated at the Veterans' Administration Hospital in Jackson.

At some stage after losing or relinquishing his post, Jimmy Thompson settled down to a life of farming, which he had presumably been intended for at the outset. But on 12 October 1952, he was involved in an accident of a different sort, and this time his injuries were fatal.

The accident occurred between Johns and Star in Rankin County when a pick-up truck in which Thompson was travelling as a passenger left a gravel road and one of its doors flew open. Thompson's head struck a tree and he was killed instantly; his head and his arm were both crushed. He was fifty-six years of age.

A report of the accident informs us that the old executioner left a sister and five brothers. But it is hard to believe that any of them were anywhere near as outlandish as him.

Some other executioners

Britain's longest-serving executioner was William Calcraft (1800–79), who was sworn in as hangman of London on 4 April 1829 and retired shortly after carrying out his last execution on 25 May 1874. During his long career, besides hanging a great many offenders at Newgate Prison, he frequently travelled to provincial towns where his services were required. In between carrying out executions he worked as a boot- and shoemaker.

Johann Michel Widmann was hangman of Nuremberg for an amazing seventy-one years, from 1665 to 1736, retaining his skill with the sword into old age. It is, however, recorded that on one occasion in 1717, in cutting off the head of a condemned man, Widman almost severed the hands of his assistant, who was holding the prisoner in position.

A Salzburg hangman of the eighteenth century, Franz Joseph Wohlmuth, entered the profession at nineteen and carried out his last execution – the beheading of a matricide – sixty years later. Like Franz Schmidt, he kept a record of all his executions, but this has not been published.

A French executioner named Desmorets, employed in the department of the Aisne, held his post for a similar length of time. In 1797, after he had been in office for almost sixty years, an official wrote to him to inquire whether it was true that he intended to resign. Desmorets, an octogenarian, replied, 'It is not true that I have ever spoken of relinquishing my office. I was born in it and hope to die in it.' He did so, and was succeeded by his nephew from Cambrai.

Britain's oldest known hangman was John Murdoch (1767–1856), a peripatetic functionary who carried on working to the age of eighty-four, officiating at almost all of Scotland's provincial executions from 1837 to 1851. His last execution was that of Archibald Hare, who suffered in Glasgow on 24 October 1851, for a murder committed in Blantyre. Murdoch, according to an obituary, was then lame with rheumatism, but nonetheless went about his work 'with nerves of steel'.

The youngest known executioner in England or Scotland was George Ormiston (1672–1702), who apparently succeeded his father John (an impoverished gentleman) as hangman of Edinburgh at the age of sixteen. George was removed from office in August 1700, for failing to carry out a public whipping satisfactorily, but was reinstated the following year, when the post became vacant. He died shortly before 1 July 1702, when a man named John Robertson was appointed hangman in his place.

A female executioner known as Lady Betty is said to have lived in Ireland during the early decades of the nineteenth century. According to an article in the January 1850 number of *The Dublin University Magazine*, she officiated at executions in the town of Roscommon and elsewhere in the province of Connaught, having previously been under sentence of death herself. She is described as a stout, middle-aged woman, of swarthy complexion, but by no means forbidding in appearance. Her real name is not given.*

Female executioners were not unknown in France. In 1785, in Sarralbe, in Lorraine, a man named Grosseholtz and his wife were both authorized to perform the functions of the executioner in that town, so presumably Mme Grosseholtz served as her husband's assistant or deputy. In 1615, according to Alister Kershaw's *History of the Guillotine* (1958), a *'bourelle'* (unnamed) carried out the execution of a young girl when the official executioner's nerve failed him. And in another case, Marie Ganier, née Ferey, the widow of an executioner, took over the post which her husband's death had left vacant – evidently without giving any cause for complaint.

In Freistroff, in Lorraine, in 1767, a child named Pierre Hoffre was appointed to succeed his father as executioner, on condition that his mother, Anne Dillembourger, ensured that his duties were carried out during his minority.

Of the many great families of executioners in France, the Desfourneaux were the oldest. Their connection with the profession extended back to the fourteenth century, some three hundred years before the first Sanson was appointed. Henri Desfourneaux, the family's last executioner, died in 1951, having held his post for twelve years.

The longest-serving family of executioners in Britain, as far as we know, was the Otway family of Taunton. Joshua Otway, who was hangman of that town in 1804, was the

---

* Inquiries made by this author have failed to produce proof that Lady Betty really existed.

great-grandson of the man who had held the same post at the time of the Bloody Assize. The office was believed to be hereditary.

Karl Huss was the son of the hangman of Most, in northern Bohemia. Born in 1761, he began assisting his father at the age of fifteen, and later succeeded his uncle as hangman of Eger, in Hungary. With the abolition of the death penalty there in 1787, he left the profession and took up anatomy and bonesetting, becoming one of the few ex-hangmen to overcome the prejudice of his contemporaries. He was a keen collector of coins and natural curiosities, and a friend of Goethe for many years.

Gregory Brandon, who was hangman of London in the early part of the seventeenth century, was granted a coat of arms in 1617, as a result of a trick played on a member of the College of Heralds. When the affair came to light, Garter King of Arms and York Herald were both imprisoned.

Gregory Brandon's son Richard, who succeeded his father as hangman about 1639, is generally thought to have been the executioner of Charles I. Richard Brandon had at first said that he would not execute the King, but allegedly did so after being subjected to bribes and threats. He died five months later, on 20 June 1649.

York's tradition of appointing a pardoned criminal as hangman led to some offenders being pardoned on condition of accepting the post. One such offender was Matthew Blackbourn, whose appointment was recorded in the *Gentleman's Magazine* of 1731. Perhaps it was he who, eight years later, hanged Dick Turpin.

John McClelland, a capital offender, was appointed hangman of Glasgow in 1605. He had earlier been banished from the town for theft, but had returned to commit further crimes. The Glasgow magistrates set aside the charges against him when he agreed to accept the vacant office.

In 1737, a burglar under sentence of death in Philadelphia was offered a pardon on condition that he hanged two other offenders, one of whom was a woman. Isaac Bradford agreed to do so, and hanged Catherine Conner and Henry Wildeman together on 2 July of that year. These two prisoners had also been convicted of burglary, Catherine Conner not for the first time. She had been sentenced to death the previous year, but had then been pardoned because she was pregnant.

In Aix-en-Provence, in south-east France, on 14 April 1714, a Madame Scrignan, the widow of an Officer of the Galleys, and two of her sons were executed for the murder of her husband. Madame Scrignan had her hand and her head cut off, and her body cast into a fire; her sons were broken on the wheel, then their bodies, too, were burnt. A third son, who had been tried with them, was ordered to assist at the executions, for being present at the crime and not calling for help.

In Flintshire, in Wales, in 1769, a burglar named Edward Edwards was hanged by John Babington, a fellow prisoner. Flintshire had no regular hangman and, like other counties in Wales, had great difficulty finding people willing to carry out executions on a casual basis. In this case, Babington was paid £6 6s for performing the task, and his wife was paid another six guineas for persuading him to do it.

In 1924, a man was sentenced to death in the Swiss canton of Uri. The canton had no regular executioner, and a railway official was chosen from among those who volunteered to carry out the sentence. But the official's trade union expelled him and the Director of the Federal Railway forbade him to perform the task. Although the Director's right to do this was challenged, the government of the canton brought the dispute to an end by appointing somebody else.

Robert Ricketts Anderson (1816–1901), otherwise Evans, was an amateur hangman who assisted Calcraft during the last twenty years of his career and sometimes carried out executions on his own. A man of private means who had been intended for the medical profession, he lived at Fernhill, near Carmarthen, and was known locally as 'Evans the Hangman'. Newspapers sometimes called him 'the Amateur', 'the Doctor' or 'the Medical Executioner'.

The inventor of the 'long drop' method of hanging was Calcraft's successor, William Marwood (1820–83). Marwood, like Calcraft, was a shoemaker by trade; he lived in Horncastle, Lincolnshire, and carried out his first execution at Lincoln Prison in 1871. He took great pride in his work on the scaffold, and referred contemptuously to his predecessor as 'the short-drop man'. 'He *hanged* them, I *execute* them!' he would say.

George Maledon was hangman of Fort Smith, Arkansas, throughout Judge Isaac C. Parker's twenty-one-year campaign (1875–96) to bring law and order to the vast Indian country to the west of that town. He, too, was proud of his skill, remarking on one occasion that he 'never hanged a man who came back to have the job done over'. After retiring from the profession in 1896, he became a travelling showman, entertaining the public with demonstrations of hanging. He died in 1911, at the age of eighty-one.

The French executioner Louis Deibler had, in his old age, a morbid fear of blood, and was shocked in January 1897 when the blood of one of his victims spurted over him. At an execution the following year, he became hysterical, crying that he was drenched with blood when he was not. He resigned at the end of 1898, dying in 1904.

Albert Pierrepoint once hanged twenty-seven German war criminals in a day. His fastest-ever hanging, at which he was assisted by Syd Dernley, took seven seconds. After the War, Pierrepoint kept a public house in Oldham, Lancashire, ironically called 'Help The Poor Struggler'. He denied that he ever had a notice on the counter reading 'No hanging about this bar', as some newspapers claimed.

Britain's last hangman, Harry Allen, performed nearly a hundred executions and assisted at a hundred others before the death penalty was effectively brought to an end in 1965. He never relinquished his official title, and for the rest of his life held himself in readiness, hoping that he would sooner or later be asked to resume his duties. He died in August 1992, at the age of eighty.

Harry Allen's son Brian followed his father into the profession and assisted him at five executions. However, he resigned as assistant hangman in 1961, after qualifying as a state-registered mental nurse.

France's last but one executioner, André Obrecht, officiated or assisted at the execution of 387 people between

1921 and 1977, when he retired, aged seventy-eight, suffering from Parkinson's disease. He spent his last years in the south of France, refusing to visit his old haunts in Paris, as he knew that people there would recognize him and shout at him in the street. He died at the age of eighty-six in 1985.

France's last executioner of all was Obrecht's nephew by marriage, Marcel Chevalier, who took over the post on his uncle's retirement and held it until the death penalty was abolished in 1981. Chevalier was a retired printer.

Tara Masih, who was Pakistan's official executioner for twenty-five years before dying of a heart attack in 1984, was estimated to have hanged 5,000 people. In April 1979, he hanged Zulfikar Ali Bhutto, the deposed Prime Minister: a task which he said he regarded as an honour. The sum which he was paid for carrying it out was less than £2 in English money.

Fernand Meyssonnier, the retired executioner of Algeria, was among buyers at an auction of items associated with crime and punishment held in London in May 1992.

In August 1991, the Egyptian executioner, Helmi Sultan, expressed himself in favour of televised public executions as a deterrent to lawbreakers. Sultan, aged fifty-three, said that he did not enjoy his work, but had a clear conscience. 'What makes me feel psycho-logically good,' he explained, 'is when I am putting the rope around the convict's neck, I hear him muttering his last words, "Forgive me, God. Forgive me, God." These words indicate he is guilty.'

Meyssonnier, who operated the guillotine between 1948 and 1962, executing some 200 people, acquired several articles, including a hangman's rope used by Syd Dernley. He said that he would put them on show in a museum he was setting up in the south of France.

Having personally supervised the construction of the first electric chair, Edwin F. Davis, executioner of New York, lived in fear of losing his position. To guard against this danger, he patented the electrodes, but later – in return for a payment of $10,000 – he transferred the patent to the State and agreed to train two assistants. At his retirement in 1914, Davis had held his post for over twenty years.

Sources of information

1. Some Facts

THE DEATH PENALTY AROUND THE WORLD

Amnesty International: *When the State Kills* (1989).

Amnesty International: *United States of America: The Death Penalty* (1987), pp. 76–9.

Lane, Brian: *The Murder Yearbook* (Headline, 1992), pp. 403–4.

Newspapers: *The Times*, 1983, 1986–7, 1990–2. *The Sunday Times*, 1985, 1990. The *Observer*, 1984. The *Independent on Sunday*, 1992.

THE DEATH PENALTY IN BRITAIN

Laurence, John: *A History of Capital Punishment* (Sampson Low, 1932), pp. 1–27.

Bresler, Fenton: *Reprieve* (Harrap, 1965), pp. 16–38.

Cooper, David D.: *The Lesson of the Scaffold* (Allen Lane, 1974), pp. 27–53.

Goodman, Jonathan and Waddell, Bill: *The Black Museum* (Harrap, 1987), pp. 30–97.

Scott, Sir Harold (ed.): *The Concise Encyclopedia of Crime and Criminals* (Bookplan edition, 1965), p. 53.

Thompson, E.P.: *Whigs and Hunters* (Penguin edition, 1977), pp. 21–4, 270–7.

Newspapers: *The Times*, 1 February 1990; 18 June 1991.

THE DEATH PENALTY IN AMERICA

Teeters, Negley K. and Hedblom, Jack H.: *Hang by the Neck* (Charles C. Thomas, Springfield, Illinois, 1967).

Drimmer, Frederick: *Until You Are Dead* (English edition, Robert Hale, 1991).

Joyce, James Avery: *The Right to Life* (Gollancz, 1962), pp. 76, 152–3, 159.

Amnesty International: *When the State Kills*, pp. 32, 229.

Amnesty International: *United States of America* (as above), p. 13.

Lane, Brian: *The Murder Yearbook*, pp. 403–4, 439–40.

Stanford Law Review, November 1987, pp. 21–179.

Newspapers: The *New York Times*, 1990. *The Times*, 1991, 1993. The *Observer*, 1982–3. The *Independent on Sunday*, 1992.

ABOLITION OR NON-USE OF THE DEATH PENALTY

Amnesty International: *When the State Kills*.

2. Some Hangings

A SURGEON FOR JACK SHEPPARD

Bleackley, Horace and Ellis, S.M. (ed.): *Jack Sheppard* (William Hodge, 1933).

Howson, Gerald: *Thief-Taker General* (Hutchinson, 1970).

Heppenstall, Rayner: *Tales from the Newgate Calendar* (Constable, 1981), pp. 69–97.

NO MERCY FROM THE EDINBURGH MOB

Roughead, William (ed.): *Trial of Captain Porteous* (William Hodge, 1909).

Dictionary of National Biography (ref. John Porteous).

Scott, Sir Harold (ed.): *Concise Encyclopedia* (as above), p. 268.

SECOND TIME AT THE GALLOWS

Select Trials for Murders, Robberies, Rapes, Sodomy, Coining, Frauds, and other Offences at the Sessions-House in the Old-Bailey (1734–5), I, 55–9.

Bleackley, Horace: *The Hangmen of England* (Chapman and Hall, 1929), pp. 31, 35.

Howson, Gerald: *Thief-Taker General*, p. 107.

Coldham, Peter Wilson: *English Convicts in Colonial America* (Polyanthos, New Orleans, 1974–6), I, 184.

Old Bailey Sessions Papers, 1717 and 1721 (Meff); 1719 (Marvell).

Newspapers: *Original Weekly Journal*, 1717, 1719, 1721. The *Weekly Journal or Saturday's Post*, 1717, 1719, 1721. The *Weekly Journal or British Gazetteer*, 1721. The *Post Boy*, 1721. The *London Journal*, 1721.

WHEN HANGING WAS NOT THE END

(i) Anne Greene:

Newes from the Dead (1651)
Petty, Sir William: *The Petty Papers* (edited by the Marquis of Lansdowne) (Constable, 1927), II, 157–67.
Plot, Robert: *The Natural History of Oxford-shire* (1677), pp. 197–200.
Petavius, Dionisius (and others): *The History of the World* (1659), p. 502.

(ii) John Smith and Margaret Dickson:

Bland, James: *Crime Strange But True* (Futura, 1991), pp. 183–97.

(iii) William Duell:

A Journal of the Shrievalty of Richard Hoare, Esquire, in the Years 1740–41 (1815), pp. 37–8, 42–3.
Old Bailey Sessions Papers.
The London Magazine (1740), p. 560.
Coldham, Peter Wilson: *English Convicts in Colonial America*, I, 82.
Newspapers: The *Weekly Miscellany*, 1740. The *Daily Gazetteer*, 1740. The *Country Journal or The Craftsman*, 1740. The *Daily Post*, 28 January and 10 February 1741.

HANGED WITH DEFERENCE

Marks, Alfred: *Tyburn Tree: Its History and Annals* (Brown, Langham, 1908), pp. 249–52.
Heppenstall, Rayner: *Tales from the Newgate Calendar*, pp. 152–68.
Bleackley, Horace, *The Hangmen of England*, pp. 100–3.
Mencken, August (ed.): *By the Neck* (Hastings House, New York, 1942), pp. 245–51.

THE BLIND MAN

Old Bailey Sessions Papers.
The Ordinary's Account.
The Annual Register (1763), p. 96.
Newspapers: The *Gazetteer and London Daily Advertiser*. The *London Chronicle. Lloyd's Evening Post*. The *St James's Chronicle*.

THE CURSING OCTOGENARIAN
Newspapers: *Stirling Journal*. *The Times*.

HANGED IN BLACK SATIN
Borowitz, Albert: *The Bermondsey Horror* (Robson Books, 1989).
Laurence, John: *A History of Capital Punishment*, pp. 209–13.
Cooper, David D.: *The Lesson of the Scaffold*, pp. 9–11.

SHOCKING MISHAPS AT THE GALLOWS
Palm, Andrew J. : *The Death Penalty* (Putnam's, New York, 1891), pp. 103–7.
Griffiths, Arthur: *The Chronicles of Newgate* (Bracken Books edition, 1987), pp. 440–1.
Cooper, David D. : *The Lesson of the Scaffold*, pp. 22–3.
Teeters and Hedblom: *Hang by the Neck*, pp. 173–4, 176–7.
Hollon, W. Eugene: *Frontier Violence: Another Look* (Oxford University Press, New York, 1974), pp. 165–6.
Drimmer, Frederick: *Until You Are Dead*, pp. 132–3.
Bleackley, Horace: *The Hangmen of England*, pp. 139, 142–3.
The Gentleman's Magazine (1807), I, 171.
Newspapers: *The Times*, 1814, 1831, 1837, 1856. *Freeman's Journal*, 1805–6. *Cowdroy's Manchester Gazette*, 1806. The *General Evening Post*, 1785. The *Weekly Miscellany*, 1739. *Caledonian Mercury* (Edinburgh), 1818–19.

THE MEN THEY COULD NOT HANG
Bland, James: *Crime Strange But True*, pp. 200–25.
Seth, Ronald: *A Spy Has No Friends* (Andre Deutsch, 1952).
Kessel, Sim: *Hanged at Auschwitz* (English translation, Talmy Franklin, 1973).
The Times, 7 May 1807.

THE THIRTY-EIGHT INDIANS
Mencken, August (ed.): *By the Neck*, pp. 151–9.
Drimmer, Frederick: *Until You Are Dead*, pp. 106–11.
Teeters and Hedblom: *Hang by the Neck*, pp. 375–9.
The Times, 22 January 1863.

MORE OF THE ROAST
Rodell, Marie F. (ed.) *San Francisco Murders* (Duell, Sloan & Pearce, New York, 1947), pp. 73–117.

Lamott, Kenneth: *Chronicles of San Quentin* (John Long, 1963), pp. 116–20.

Mencken, August (ed.) *By the Neck*, pp. 36–48.

Teeters and Hedblom: *Hang by the Neck*, pp. 324–7.

A HANGING IN JAPAN

Ishii, Tokichi: *A Gentleman in Prison* (English translation, George H. Doran, New York, 1922).

A DOUBLE HANGING INSIDE THE ARCTIC CIRCLE

Godsell, Philip Henry: *They Got Their Man* (Robert Hale, 1941), pp. 184–207.

The *New York Times*, 21 January 1924.

3. Monstrosities and Curiosities

A HORRIBLE WAY TO AVOID THE GALLOWS

Scott, George Ryley: *The History of Capital Punishment* (Torch-stream Books, 1950), pp. 151–2.

Babington, Anthony: *The English Bastille* (Macdonald, 1971), pp. 29–30, 79.

Griffiths, Arthur: *The Chronicles of Newgate*, pp. 156–60.

Laurence, John: *A History of Capital Punishment*, pp. 228–30.

The Harleian Miscellany, VII, 9–24.

Teeters and Hedblom: *Hang by the Neck*, pp. 98–100.

WOMEN BURNT FOR THE SAKE OF DECENCY

Marks, Alfred: *Tyburn Tree: Its History and Annals*, pp. 159, 171–3, 206–7.

Laurence, John: *A History of Capital Punishment*, pp. 6, 9–12.

Scott, George Ryley: *The History of Capital Punishment*, p. 179.

Griffiths, Arthur: *The Chronicles of Newgate*, pp. 122–3.

Bleackley, Horace: *The Hangmen of England*, pp. 104, 137–9.

Rumbelow, Donald: *The Triple Tree* (Harrap, 1982), p. 188.

Blackstone, Sir William: *Commentaries on the Laws of England* (1765–9), IV, 93, 398.

EXECUTION DOCK

Wheatley, Henry B. and Cunningham, Peter: *London Past and Present* (John Murray, 1891), II, 23–5.

Timbs, John: *Curiosities of London* (Virtue & Co. edition, 1876), p. 815.

Bleackley, Horace: *The Hangmen of England*, pp. 143–5.

Laurence, John: *A History of Capital Punishment*, pp. 56, 105, 174–6.

Scott, Sir Harold (ed.): *Concise Encyclopedia*, p. 209.

Bland, James: *Crime Strange But True*, pp. 197–200.

Newspapers: *The Post Boy*, 12–14 November 1700. *The Post Man*, 12–14 November 1700. The *London Evening Post*, 18–20 January 1743.

A SHARP AND HEAVY AXE

Roberts, George: *The Life, Progresses, and Rebellion of James, Duke of Monmouth* (Longman, 1844), II, 142–53.

OTHER BUNGLED BEHEADINGS

Dictionary of National Biography (ref. Margaret Pole).

Letters and Papers, Foreign and Domestic, of the Reign of Henry VIII, XVI, 436.

Kershaw, Alister: *A History of the Guillotine* (Tandem edition, 1965), pp. 46n, 79.

Schmidt, Franz: *A Hangman's Diary* (English translation, Philip Allan, 1928), pp. 95–6.

Hampe, Theodor: *Crime and Punishment in Germany* (English translation, Routledge & Sons, 1929), p. 136.

PARDONED ON CONDITION OF LOSING A LEG

Old Bailey Sessions Papers, 1763 and 1767.

The Ordinary's Account, 4 May 1763.

Calendar of Home Office Papers of the Reign of George III, II, 175–6.

The Gentleman's Magazine (1811), I, 388.

Newspapers: *The Loyal Protestant*, 19–26 March 1681. The *London Chronicle*, 11–13 August 1785. *The London Journal*, 19 August 1721. The *Weekly Journal or British Gazetteer*, 2 September 1721.

A LONG DELAY AT TYBURN

Old Bailey Sessions Papers.

Newspapers: The *London Chronicle*. *Lloyd's Evening Post*. The *Gazetteer and New Daily Advertiser*.

FORERUNNERS OF THE GUILLOTINE

Andrews, William: *Old-Time Punishments* (Andrews & Co., 1890), pp. 231–45.

Kershaw, Alister: *A History of the Guillotine*, pp. 30–40.

Laurence, John: *A History of Capital Punishment*, pp. 69–71.

HANGMEN WHO WERE HANGED

Bland, James: *The Common Hangman* (Ian Henry, 1984).

THE EXECUTION OF ANIMALS

Evans, E. P.: *The Criminal Prosecution and Capital Punishment of Animals* (Faber & Faber edition, 1987).

HOW FIVE REVOLUTIONARIES DIED

Laurence, John: *A History of Capital Punishment*, pp. 198–209.

The Gentleman's Magazine (1820), II, 268–9.

Newspapers: The *Morning Chronicle*, 2 May 1820. *Glasgow Courier* 12 September 1820.

THE GUILLOTINE'S MOST SHOCKING FAILURE

Hugo, Victor: *The Last Days of a Condemned* (English translation, Smith, Elder & Co., 1840).

Newspapers: *The Times*, 24 September 1831. The *York Courant*, 4 March 1841.

STABBED TO DEATH – AND THEN GUILLOTINED

Hadfield, R. L.: *Picturesque Rogues* (H. F. & G. Witherby, 1931), pp. 107–19.

Heppenstall, Rayner: *French Crime in the Romantic Age* (Hamish Hamilton, 1970), pp. 265–8.

Newspapers: *The Times*, 1 April 1847; 21–22 January 1870. The *Illustrated Police News*, 17 September 1904.

LIFE AFTER DECAPITATION

Morain, Alfred: *The Underworld of Paris* (English translation, Jarrolds, 1930), pp. 300–2.

Kershaw, Alister: *A History of the Guillotine*, pp. 100–3.

REPRIEVED MURDERER LIVED TO BE 101

(i) Anton Nilsson:
The Times, 19 August 1989.

(ii) Constance Kent:
Taylor, Bernard: *Cruelly Murdered* (Souvenir Press, 1979).

HE SURVIVED THE FIRING SQUAD
Newspapers: *The Times-Picayune*, 2 September 1945. The *Observer* 4 July 1982.

BURIED ALIVE AT SEA
Rickards, Colin: *The Man from Devil's Island* (Belmont Tower edition, New York, 1974), pp. 64–6, 99n, 111–12.

THREE WARTIME EXECUTIONS
Drimmer, Frederick: *Until You Are Dead*, pp. 104–12.
Master Detective, August 1992.
Kershaw, Alister: *A History of the Guillotine*, p. 148.

THIRTY-TWO YEARS ON DEATH ROW

(i) Sadamichi Hirasawa:
Newspapers: *The Times*, 1984–5, 1987. The *Observer*, 1984–5. The *New York Times*, 1985, 1987. *San Francisco Chronicle*, 1987.

(ii) Other cases:
Newspapers: *The Times*, 1984, 1986–7, 1989–90. *The Daily Star*, 1983. *Chicago Tribune* 1983–4, 1989.

CHINESE EXECUTIONS CONVENIENT FOR TRANSPLANT SURGERY
Newspapers: *The Sunday Times*, 24 June 1990. *The People*, 27 January 1991.

DEATH FOR ADULTERY – AND AN EXECUTIONER WITH
TWENTY-FOUR WIVES
Foot, Paul: *The Helen Smith Story* (Fontana, 1983), pp. 105–10.
Newspapers: The *Guardian*, 23 January 1978. *Daily Express*, 26 January 1978. *Daily Star*, 19 June 1989. *The Sunday Times*, 3 August 1986. *The Times*, 25 November 1986, 1 February 1988, 6 February 1988, 1 March 1988, 4 May 1989.

4. Some American Cases

CELEBRITIES OF DEATH ROW

Drimmer, Frederick: *Until You Are Dead*.
Brian, Denis: *Murderers Die* (St Martin's Press, New York, 1986).
Joyce, James Avery: *The Right to Life*, pp. 19–51, 170–5.

HANGINGS NO BAR TO THE PRESIDENCY

Mencken, August (ed.), *By the Neck*, pp. 109–13.
Teeters and Hedblom: *Hang by the Neck*, pp. 52–3.
New York Times, 15 February 1873.

PANIC IN THE EXECUTION CHAMBER

Drimmer, Frederick: *Until You Are Dead*, pp. 1–17.
Elliott, Robert G. with Beatty, Albert R.: *Agent of Death* (E. P. Dutton, New York, 1940), pp. 26–7, 29, 30–1, 56–8.
Squire, Amos O.: *Sing Sing Doctor* (Garden City Publishing Co., New York, 1937), p. 15.
Laurence, John: *A History of Capital Punishment*, p. 65.
Newspapers: The *New York Times*, 6–10 May 1947, 23 April 1983, 25 July 1990. *The Times*, 25 April 1983. *Sunday Telegraph*, 24 April 1983. The *Observer*, 24 April 1983. *San Francisco Chronicle*, 5 May 1990.

FOUR EXECUTED WITHOUT KNOWING WHY

Squire, Amos O.: *Sing Sing Doctor*, pp. 132–47.

THE SCOTTSBORO BOYS

Scott, Sir Harold (ed.): *Concise Encyclopedia*, pp. 307–8.
Patterson, Haywood and Conrad, Earl: *Scottsboro Boy* (Gollancz, 1950).
The Times, 27 January 1989.

NO ONE TO TAKE HIS PICTURE

Donovan, Robert J.: *The Assassins* (Elek Books, 1956), pp. 148–68.
Drimmer, Frederick: *Until You Are Dead*, p. 245.

LAST PUBLIC HANGINGS

Teeters and Hedblom: *Hang by the Neck*, pp. 6–7.
Newspapers: The *New York Times*, 15 August 1936, 30 May 1937.
The Times-Picayune (New Orleans), 22 May 1937.

EXECUTED FOR 'MESSIN' AROUND'

McGehee, Edward G. and Hildebrand, William H. (ed.): *The Death Penalty* (D.C. Heath & Co., Boston, 1964), pp. 85–91.
Stanford Law Review (as above), pp. 91–2, 106–7, 145–6.
The *New York Times*, 8, 9 and 13 May 1951.

HANGING ON HIS MIND

The Saturday Evening Post, 8 April 1950.
San Rafael Independent, 8 September 1939.

MUSIC IN THE DEATH HOUSE

Duffy, Clinton T. with Hirshberg, Al: *88 Men and 2 Women* (Gollancz, 1962), pp. 121–9.
San Francisco Examiner, 29 January 1944.

A BOY OF FOURTEEN

Newspapers: The *New York Times*, 16 June 1984. *Chicago Daily Tribune*, 17 June 1944. *The Times*, 9 October 1991.

THE MAN WHO BLAMED GOD

Brian, Denis: *Murderers Die*, pp. 52–4.
Drimmer, Frederick: *Until You Are Dead*, pp. 53–4.
Newspapers: *San Francisco Examiner*, 7 April 1956, 10 March 1990. *San Rafael Independent Journal*, 25 March 1990. *The New York Times*, 27 November 1943.

CARYL CHESSMAN'S FINAL ORDEAL

Singer, Kurt: *Crime Omnibus* (W.H. Allen, 1961), pp. 1–41.
Drimmer, Frederick: *Until You Are Dead*, pp. 64–70.
Joyce, James Avery: *The Right to Life*, pp. 19–51.
Wolf, Marvin J. and Mader, Katherine: *Fallen Angels* (Ballantine Books, New York, 1988), pp. 213–23.
Chessman, Caryl: *Cell 2455 Death Row* (Prentice-Hall, Englewood Cliffs, New Jersey, 1954).

TOO MUCH HASTE AT HUNTSVILLE

Drimmer, Frederick: *Until You Are Dead*, pp. 79–83, 84, 260.
Newspapers: The *New York Times*, 1983–5, 1987. *Los Angeles Times*, 1987. The *Washington Post*, 13–14 December 1988. *Chicago Tribune*, 13–14 December 1988. *The Times*, 1983–4, 1987.

DEATH ROW'S BIGGEST BREAKOUT
Newspapers: The *New York Times*, 2, 4 and 20 June 1984, 7 July 1984, 13 October 1984, 19 April 1985. *The Times*, 24 August 1991.

MURDER ON DEATH ROW
Lane, Brian, *The Murder Yearbook*, pp. 419–22.
Newspapers: The *New York Times*, 29 May 1976, 13 September 1982, 7 October 1982, 6–7 September 1991. *Chicago Tribune*, 6 October 1982, 23 June 1983.

EXECUTION VIDEOTAPED BY JUDICIAL ORDER

(i) Robert Alton Harris:
Newspapers: *The Times*, 1990–92. *Sunday Telegraph*, 31 March 1991. The *Guardian*, 22 April 1992. The *Independent*, 22 April 1992. The *Independent on Sunday*, 26 April 1992.

(ii) Other cases:
Amnesty International: *When the State Kills*, p. 60.
Newspapers: *The Times*, 18 June 1991, 31 July 1992. The *Independent on Sunday*, 26 April 1992. *The Standard*, 19 September 1991.

5. Some Executioners

HOW THE HANGMAN GOT HIS NAME
Bland, James: *The Common Hangman*, pp. 19–25.

A GERMAN HANGMAN'S CHRONICLE OF BLOOD
Schmidt, Franz: *A Hangman's Diary*.

A FAMILY OF EXECUTIONERS
Levy, Barbara: *Legacy of Death* (Prentice-Hall, 1973).
Lenotre, G.: *The Guillotine and Its Servants* (English translation, Hutchinson & Co., 1929).

MUTTON CURRY – THE SHEEP THIEF WHO BECAME A HANGMAN
Bland, James: *The Common Hangman*, pp. 95–9, 148–51.

ALEXANDER GREEN – THE MONSTER OF NEW SOUTH WALES
Beckett, Ray and Richard: *Hangman* (Nelson, Melbourne, 1980).

THE HANGMAN WHO COULD NOT KILL CHICKENS
Laurence, John: *A History of Capital Punishment*, pp. 128–36.
Bailey, Brian: *Hangmen of England* (W.H. Allen, 1989), pp. 129–56.
Newspapers: *Thomson's Weekly News*, 22 March 1924, 12 April
    1924, 24 September 1932. The *Illustrated Police News*, 29
    September 1932. The *Rochdale Observer*, 30 August 1924, 24
    September 1932.

EXECUTIONER AGAINST THE DEATH PENALTY
Elliott, Robert G. with Beatty, Albert R.: *Agent of Death*.
Drimmer, Frederick: *Until You Are Dead*, pp. 27–41.
Bailey, Brian: *Hangmen of England*, pp. 89–110.
Pierrepoint, Albert: *Executioner: Pierrepoint* (Harrap, 1974).
Newspapers: *The Times*, 13 July 1992. The *Daily Telegraph*, 13 July
    1992.

JIMMY THOMPSON – EXECUTIONER AND HYPNOTIST
Life, 7 October 1940.
The *American Mercury*, January 1942, pp. 93–7.
Newspapers: *Jackson Daily News*, 18 December 1946, 13 October
    1952. *Magee Courier* (Mississippi), 26 April 1984.

SOME OTHER EXECUTIONERS
Bland, James: *The Common Hangman*.
Schmidt, Franz: *A Hangman's Diary*, p. 43.
Lenotre, G.: *The Guillotine and Its Servants*, pp. 24, 81, 213–14.
Kershaw, Alister: *A History of the Guillotine*, pp. 112–13, 117, 122–3,
    145.
Levy, Barbara: *Legacy of Death*, pp. 244–5.
Teeters and Hedblom: *Hang by the Neck*, pp. 71–2, 398–404.
Bleackley, Horace: *The Hangmen of England*, pp. 232–4.
Drimmer, Frederick: *Until You Are Dead*, pp. 150–3.
Pierrepoint, Albert: *Executioner: Pierrepoint*, p. 166.
Elliott, Robert G. with Beatty, Albert R.: *Agent of Death*, pp. 51–2,
    83.
Calvert, E. Roy: *Capital Punishment in the Twentieth Century*
    (Putnam's, 1927), pp. 75–6.
Newspapers: The *Times Literary Supplement*, ('Hangmen's Dia-

ries'), 24 June 1926. *The Post Boy*, 17–20 April 1714. The *Guardian*, 13 July 1992. *The Times*, 3 August 1985, 29 August 1991, 30 May 1992, 17 August 1992. The *Daily Telegraph*, 11 July 1979, 17 August 1992. *The Sunday Times*, 14 June 1981. The *New York Times*, 8 July 1984.

Index

318 Index